More Praise for
the invisible gorilla

"**Should be required reading** by every judge and jury member in our criminal justice system, along with every battlefield commander, corporate CEO, member of Congress, and, well, you and me . . . because the **mental illusions so wonderfully explicated in this book can fool every one of us.**"

—Michael Shermer, publisher of *Skeptic* magazine, monthly columnist for *Scientific American,* and author of *Why People Believe Weird Things*

"**A breathtaking and insightful journey through the illusions that influence every moment of our lives.**"

—Richard Wiseman, author of *Quirkology: How We Discover the Big Truths in Small Things*

"**Not just witty and engaging but also insightful. . . .** Reading this book won't cure you of all these limitations, but it will at least help you recognize and compensate for them."

—Thomas W. Malone, author of *The Future of Work* and founder of the MIT Center for Collective Intelligence

"Everyday illusions trick us into thinking that we see—and know—more than we really do, and that we can predict the future when we can't. *The Invisible Gorilla* teaches us exactly why, and it does so in an **incredibly engaging** way. **Chabris and Simons provide terrific tips on how to cast off our illusions and get things right.** Whether you're a driver wanting to steer clear of oncoming motorcycles, a radiologist hoping to spot every tumor, or just an average person curious about how your mind *really* works, **this is a must-read.**"

—Elizabeth Loftus, PhD, Distinguished Professor, University of California–Irvine, and author of *Memory* and *Eyewitness Testimony*

"**An eye-opening book.** After reading *The Invisible Gorilla* you will look at yourself and the world around you differently. **Like its authors, the book is both funny and smart, filled with insights into the everyday illusions that we all walk around with.** No matter what your job is or what you do in life, you will learn something from this book."

—Joseph T. Hallinan, Pulitzer Prize–winning
author of *Why We Make Mistakes*

"Cognitive scientists Chris Chabris and Dan Simons deliver an entertaining tour of the many ways our brains mislead us every day. ***The Invisible Gorilla* is engaging, accurate, and packed with real-world examples—some of which made me laugh out loud.** Read it to find out why weathermen might make good money managers, and what Homer Simpson can teach you about thinking clearly."

—Sandra Aamodt, PhD, coauthor of *Welcome to Your Brain*
and former editor, *Nature Neuroscience*

"**Wonderfully refreshing . . . *The Invisible Gorilla* makes us smarter by reminding us how little we know.** Through a lively tour of the brain's blind spots, this book will change the way you drive your car, hire your employees, and invest your money."

—Amanda Ripley, senior writer, *Time* magazine,
and author of *The Unthinkable*

the invisible gorilla

the invisible gorilla

And Other Ways Our Intuitions Deceive Us

Christopher Chabris

and Daniel Simons

CROWN

New York

Published in the United States by Crown Publishers, an imprint of the Crown Publishing Group, a division of Random House, Inc., New York.
www.crownpublishing.com

CROWN and the Crown colophon are registered trademarks of Random House, Inc.

Library of Congress Cataloging-in-Publication Data

Chabris, Christopher F.
   The invisible gorilla : and other ways our intuitions deceive us / Christopher F. Chabris and Daniel J. Simons.
      p. cm.
   Includes bibliographical references and index.
   1. Perception. 2. Memory. 3. Thought and thinking. I. Simons, Daniel J. II. Title.

   BF321.C43 2010
   153.7'4—dc22

                                                                2009045325

ISBN 978-0-307-45965-7

Printed in the United States of America

Design by Ralph Fowler / rlf design

10 9 8 7 6 5 4

CONTENTS

everyday illusions

*"There are three things extremely hard: steel,
a diamond, and to know one's self."*

—Benjamin Franklin, *Poor Richard's Almanack* (1750)

ABOUT TWELVE YEARS AGO, we conducted a simple experiment with the students in a psychology course we were teaching at Harvard University. To our surprise, it has become one of the best-known experiments in psychology. It appears in textbooks and is taught in introductory psychology courses throughout the world. It has been featured in magazines such as *Newsweek* and *The New Yorker* and on television programs, including *Dateline NBC*. It has even been exhibited in the Exploratorium in San Francisco and in other museums. The experiment is popular because it reveals, in a humorous way, something unexpected and deep about how we see our world—and about what we don't see.

You'll read about our experiment in the first chapter of this book. As we've thought about it over the years, we've realized that it illustrates a broader principle about how the mind works. We all believe that we are capable of seeing what's in front of us, of accurately remembering important events from our past, of understanding the limits of our knowledge, of properly determining cause and effect. But these intuitive beliefs are often mistaken ones that mask critically important limitations on our cognitive abilities.

We must be reminded not to judge a book by its cover because we take outward appearances to be accurate advertisements of inner, unseen qualities. We need to be told that a penny saved is a penny earned because we think about cash coming in differently from money we already have. Aphorisms like these exist largely to help us avoid the mistakes that intuition can cause. Likewise, Benjamin Franklin's observation about extremely hard things suggests that we should question the intuitive belief that we understand ourselves well. As we go through life, we act as though we know how our minds work and why we behave the way we do. It is surprising how often we really have no clue.

The Invisible Gorilla is a book about six everyday illusions that profoundly influence our lives: the illusions of attention, memory, confidence, knowledge, cause, and potential. These are distorted beliefs we hold about our minds that are not just wrong, but wrong in dangerous ways. We will explore when and why these illusions affect us, the consequences they have for human affairs, and how we can overcome or minimize their impact.

We use the word "illusions" as a deliberate analogy to visual illusions like M. C. Escher's famous never-ending staircase: Even after you realize that something about the picture as a whole is not right, you still can't stop yourself from seeing each individual segment as a proper staircase. Everyday illusions are similarly persistent: Even after we know how our beliefs and intuitions are flawed, they remain stubbornly resistant to change. We call them *everyday* illusions because they affect our behavior literally every day. Every time we talk on a cell phone while driving, believing we're still paying enough attention to the road, we've been affected by one of these illusions. Every time we assume that someone who misremembers their past must be lying, we've succumbed to an illusion. Every time we pick a leader for a team because that person expresses the most confidence, we've been influenced by an illusion. Every time we start a new project convinced that we know how long it will take to complete, we are under an illusion. Indeed, virtually no realm of human behavior is untouched by everyday illusions.

As professors who design and run psychology experiments for a living, we've found that the more we study the nature of the mind, the more we see the impact of these illusions in our own lives. You can develop the same sort of x-ray vision into the workings of your own mind. When you finish this book, you will be able to glimpse the man behind the curtain and some of the tiny gears and pulleys that govern your thoughts and beliefs. Once you know about everyday illusions, you will view the world differently and think about it more clearly. You will see how illusions affect your own thoughts and actions, as well as the behavior of everyone around you. And you will recognize when journalists, managers, advertisers, and politicians—intentionally or accidentally—take advantage of illusions in an attempt to obfuscate or persuade. Understanding everyday illusions will lead you to recalibrate the way you approach your life to account for the limitations—and the true strengths—of your mind. You might even come up with ways to exploit these insights for fun and profit. Ultimately, seeing through the veils that distort how we perceive ourselves and the world will connect you—for perhaps the first time—with reality.

the invisible gorilla

CHAPTER

1

"i think i would have seen that"

Around two o'clock on the cold, overcast morning of January 25, 1995, a group of four black men left the scene of a shooting at a hamburger restaurant in the Grove Hall section of Boston.[1] As they drove away in a gold Lexus, the police radio erroneously announced that the victim was a cop, leading officers from several districts to join in a ten-mile high-speed chase. In the fifteen to twenty minutes of mayhem that ensued, one police car veered off the road and crashed into a parked van. Eventually the Lexus skidded to a stop in a cul-de-sac on Woodruff Way in the Mattapan neighborhood. The suspects fled the car and ran in different directions.

One suspect, Robert "Smut" Brown III, age twenty-four, wearing a dark leather jacket, exited the back passenger side of the car and sprinted toward a chain-link fence on the side of the cul-de-sac. The first car in pursuit, an unmarked police vehicle, stopped to the left of the Lexus. Michael Cox, a decorated officer from the police antigang unit who'd grown up in the nearby Roxbury area, got out of the passenger seat and took off after Brown. Cox, who also is black, was in plainclothes that night; he wore jeans, a black hoodie, and a parka.[2]

Cox got to the fence just after Smut Brown. As Brown scrambled over the top, his jacket got stuck on the metal. Cox reached for Brown and tried to pull him back, but Brown managed to fall to the other side. Cox prepared to scale the fence in pursuit, but just as he was starting to climb, his head was struck from behind by a blunt object, perhaps a baton or a flashlight. He fell to the ground. Another police officer had mistaken him for a suspect, and several officers then beat up Cox, kicking him in the head, back, face, and mouth. After a few moments, someone yelled, "Stop, stop, he's a cop, he's a cop." At that point, the officers fled, leaving Cox lying unconscious on the ground with facial wounds, a concussion, and kidney damage.[3]

Meanwhile, the pursuit of the suspects continued as more cops arrived. Early on the scene was Kenny Conley, a large, athletic man from South Boston who had joined the police force four years earlier, not long after graduating from high school. Conley's cruiser came to a stop about forty feet away from the gold Lexus. Conley saw Smut Brown scale the fence, drop to the other side, and run. Conley followed Brown over the fence, chased him on foot for about a mile, and eventually captured him at gunpoint and handcuffed him in a parking lot on River Street. Conley wasn't involved in the assault on Officer Cox, but he began his pursuit of Brown right as Cox was being pulled from the fence, and he scaled the fence right next to where the beating was happening.

Although the other murder suspects were caught and that case was considered solved, the assault on Officer Cox remained wide open. For the next two years, internal police investigators and a grand jury sought answers about what happened at the cul-de-sac. Which cops beat Cox? Why did they beat him? Did they simply mistake their black colleague for one of the black suspects? If so, why did they flee rather than seek medical help? Little headway was made, and in 1997, the local prosecutors handed the matter over to federal authorities so they could investigate possible civil rights violations.

Cox named three officers whom he said had attacked him that night, but all of them denied knowing anything about the assault. Initial police reports said that Cox sustained his injuries when he slipped on a patch of ice and fell against the back of one of the police cars. Although many of the nearly sixty cops who were on the scene must have known what happened to Cox, none admitted knowing anything about the beating. Here, for example, is what Kenny Conley, who apprehended Smut Brown, said under oath:

Q: So your testimony is that you went over the fence within seconds of seeing him go over the fence?

A: Yeah.

Q: And in that time, you did not see any black plainclothes police officer chasing him?

A: No, I did not.

Q: In fact, no black plainclothes officer was chasing him, according to your testimony?

A: I did not see any black plainclothes officer chasing him.

Q: And if he was chasing him, you would have seen it?

A: I should have.

Q: And if he was holding the suspect as the suspect was at the top of the fence, he was lunging at him, you would have seen that, too?

A: I should have.

When asked directly if he would have seen Cox trying to pull Smut Brown from the fence, he responded, "I think I would have seen that." Conley's terse replies suggested a reluctant witness who had been advised by lawyers to stick to yes or no answers and not volunteer information. Since he was the cop who had taken up the chase, he was in an ideal position to know what happened. His persistent refusal to admit to having seen Cox effectively blocked the federal prosecutors' attempt to indict the officers involved in the attack, and no one was ever charged with the assault.

The only person ever charged with a crime in the case was Kenny Conley himself. He was indicted in 1997 for perjury and obstruction of justice. The prosecutors were convinced that Conley was "testilying"—outlandishly claiming, under oath, not to have seen what was going on right before his eyes. According to this theory, just like the officers who filed reports denying any knowledge of the beating, Conley wouldn't rat out his fellow cops. Indeed, shortly after Conley's indictment, prominent Boston-area investigative journalist Dick Lehr wrote that "the Cox scandal shows a Boston police code of silence . . . a tight inner circle of officers protecting themselves with false stories."[4]

Kenny Conley stuck with his story, and his case went to trial. Smut Brown testified that Conley was the cop who arrested him. He also said that after he dropped over the fence, he looked back and saw a tall white cop standing near the beating. Another police officer also testified that Conley was there. The jurors were incredulous at the notion that Conley could have run to the fence in pursuit of Brown without noticing the beating, or even seeing Officer Cox. After the trial, one juror explained, "It was hard for me to believe that, even with all the chaos, he didn't see something." Juror Burgess Nichols said that another juror had told him that his father and uncle had been police officers, and officers are taught "to observe everything" because they are "trained professionals."[5]

Unable to reconcile their own expectations—and Conley's—with Conley's testimony that he didn't see Cox, the jury convicted him. Kenny Conley was found guilty of one count each of perjury and obstruction of justice, and he was sentenced to thirty-four months in jail.[6] In 2000, after the U.S. Supreme Court declined to hear his case, he was fired from the Boston police force. While his lawyers kept him out of jail with new appeals, Conley took up a new career as a carpenter.[7]

Dick Lehr, the journalist who reported on the Cox case and the "blue wall of silence," never actually met with Kenny Conley until the summer of 2001. After this interview, Lehr began to wonder whether Conley might actually be telling the truth about what he saw and experienced during his pursuit of Smut Brown. That's when Lehr brought the former cop to visit Dan's laboratory at Harvard.

Gorillas in Our Midst

The two of us met over a decade ago when Chris was a graduate student in the Harvard University psychology department and Dan had just arrived as a new assistant professor. Chris's office was down the hall from Dan's lab, and we soon discovered our mutual interest in how we perceive, remember, and think about our visual world. The Kenny Conley case was in full swing when Dan taught an undergraduate course in research methods with Chris as his teaching assistant. As part of their classwork, the students assisted us in conducting some experiments, one of which has become famous. It was based on an ingenious series of studies of visual attention and awareness conducted by the pioneering cognitive psychologist Ulric Neisser in the 1970s. Neisser had moved to Cornell University when Dan was in his final year of graduate school there, and their many conversations inspired Dan to build on Neisser's earlier, groundbreaking research.

With our students as actors and a temporarily vacant floor of the psychology building as a set, we made a short film of two teams of people moving around and passing basketballs. One team wore white shirts and the other wore black. Dan manned the camera and directed. Chris coordinated the action and kept track of which scenes we needed to shoot. We then digitally edited the film and copied it to videotapes, and our students fanned out across the Harvard campus to run the experiment.[8]

They asked volunteers to silently count the number of passes made by the players wearing white while ignoring any passes by the players wearing black. The video lasted less than a minute. If you want to try the task yourself, stop reading now and go to the website for our book, www.theinvisiblegorilla.com, where we provide links to many of the experiments we discuss, including a short version of the basketball-passing video. Watch the video carefully, and be sure to include both aerial passes and bounce passes in your count.

Immediately after the video ended, our students asked the subjects to report how many passes they'd counted. In the full-length version, the correct answer was thirty-four—or maybe thirty-five. To be honest, it doesn't matter. The pass-counting task was intended to keep people engaged in doing something that demanded attention to the action on the screen, but we weren't really interested in pass-counting ability. We were actually testing something else: Halfway through the video, a female student wearing a full-body gorilla suit walked into the scene, stopped in the middle of the players, faced the camera, thumped her chest, and then walked off, spending about nine seconds onscreen. After asking subjects about the passes, we asked the more important questions:

Q: Did you notice anything unusual while you were doing the counting task?

A: No.

Q: Did you notice anything other than the players?

A: Well, there were some elevators, and S's painted on the wall. I don't know what the S's were there for.

Q: Did you notice *anyone* other than the players?

A: No.

Q: Did you notice a gorilla?

A: A what?!?

Amazingly, roughly half of the subjects in our study did not notice the gorilla! Since then the experiment has been repeated many times, under different conditions, with diverse audiences, and in multiple countries, but the results are always the same: About half the people fail to see the gorilla. How could people not see a gorilla walk directly in front of them, turn to face them, beat its chest, and walk away? What made the gorilla invisible? This error of perception results from a lack of attention to an unexpected object, so it goes by the scientific name "inattentional blindness." This name distinguishes it from forms of blindness resulting from a damaged visual system; here, people don't see the gorilla, but not because of a problem with their eyes. When people devote their attention to a particular area or aspect of their visual world, they tend not to notice unexpected objects, even when those unexpected objects are salient, potentially important, and appear right where they are looking.[9] In other words, the subjects were concentrating so hard on counting the passes that they were "blind" to the gorilla right in front of their eyes.

What prompted us to write this book, however, was not inattentional blindness in general or the gorilla study in particular. The fact that people miss things is important, but what impressed us even more was the *surprise* people showed when they realized what they had missed. When they watched the video again, this time without counting passes, they all saw the gorilla easily, and they were shocked. Some spontaneously said, "I missed that?!" or "No way!" A man who was tested later by the producers of *Dateline NBC* for their report on this research said, "I know that gorilla didn't come through there the first time." Other subjects accused us of switching the tape while they weren't looking.

The gorilla study illustrates, perhaps more dramatically than any other, the powerful and pervasive influence of the *illusion of attention:* We experience far less of our visual world than we think we do. If we were fully aware of the limits to attention, the illusion would vanish. While writing this book we hired the polling firm SurveyUSA to contact a representative sample of American adults and ask them a series of questions about how they think the mind works. We found that more than 75 percent of people agreed that they would notice such unexpected events, even when they were focused on something else.[10] (We'll talk about other findings of this survey throughout the book.)

It's true that we vividly experience some aspects of our world, particularly those that are the focus of our attention. But this rich experience inevitably leads to the erroneous belief that we process *all* of the detailed information around us. In essence, we know how vividly we see some aspects of our world, but we are completely unaware of those aspects of our world that fall outside of that current focus of attention. Our vivid visual experience masks a striking mental blindness—we assume that visually distinctive or unusual objects will draw our attention, but in reality they often go completely unnoticed.[11]

Since our experiment was published in the journal *Perception* in 1999, under the title "Gorillas in Our Midst,"[12] it has become one of the most widely demonstrated and discussed studies in all of psychology. It earned us an Ig Nobel Prize in 2004 (awarded for "achievements that first make people laugh, and then make them think") and was even discussed by characters in an episode of the television drama *CSI*.[13] And we've lost count of the number of times people have asked us whether we have seen the video with the basketball players and the gorilla.

Kenny Conley's Invisible Gorilla

Dick Lehr brought Kenny Conley to Dan's laboratory because he had heard about our gorilla experiment, and he wanted to see how Conley would do in it. Conley was physically imposing, but stoic and taciturn; Lehr did most of the talking that day. Dan led them to a small, window-less room in his laboratory and showed Conley the gorilla video, asking him to count the passes by the players wearing white. In advance, there was no way to know whether or not Conley would notice the unex-pected gorilla—about half of the people who watch the video see the gorilla. Moreover, Conley's success or failure in noticing the gorilla would not tell us whether or not he saw Michael Cox being beaten on Woodruff Way six years earlier. (These are both important points, and we will return to them shortly.) But Dan was still curious about how Conley would react when he heard about the science.

Conley counted the passes accurately and saw the gorilla. As is usual for people who do see the gorilla, he seemed genuinely surprised that anyone else could possibly miss it. Even when Dan explained that people often miss unexpected events when their attention is otherwise en-gaged, Conley still had trouble accepting that anyone else could miss what seemed so obvious to him.

The illusion of attention is so ingrained and pervasive that everyone involved in the case of Kenny Conley was operating under a false no-tion of how the mind works: the mistaken belief that we pay attention to—and therefore should notice and remember—much more of the world around us than we actually do. Conley himself testified that he should have seen the brutal beating of Michael Cox had he actually run right past it. In their appeal of his conviction, Conley's lawyers tried to show that he hadn't run past the beating, that the testimony about his presence near the beating was wrong, and that descriptions of the incident from other police officers were inaccurate. All of these arguments were founded on the assumption that Conley could only be telling the truth if he didn't have the opportunity to see the beating. But what if, instead, in the cul-de-sac on Woodruff Way, Conley found himself in a real-life version of our gorilla experiment? He could have been right next to the beating of Cox, and even focused his eyes on it, without ever actually seeing it.

Conley was worried about Smut Brown scaling the fence and escaping, and he pursued his suspect with a single-minded focus that he described as "tunnel vision." Conley's prosecutor ridiculed this idea, saying that what prevented Conley from seeing the beating was not tunnel vision but video editing—"a deliberate cropping of Cox out of the picture."[14]

But if Conley was sufficiently focused on Brown, in the way our subjects were focused on counting the basketball passes, it is entirely possible that he ran right past the assault and still failed to see it. If so, the only inaccurate part of Conley's testimony was his stated belief that he *should have* seen Cox. What is most striking about this case is that Conley's own testimony was the primary evidence that put him near the beating, and that evidence, combined with a misunderstanding of how the mind works, and the blue wall of silence erected by the other cops, led prosecutors to charge him with perjury and obstruction of justice. They, and the jury that convicted him, assumed that he too was protecting his comrades.

Kenny Conley's conviction was eventually overturned on appeal and set aside in July 2005. But Conley prevailed not because the prosecutors or a judge were convinced that he actually was telling the truth. Instead, the appeals court in Boston ruled that he had been denied a fair trial because the prosecution didn't tell his defense attorneys about an FBI memo that cast doubt on the credibility of one of the government's witnesses.[15] When the government decided not to retry him in September 2005,

Conley's legal troubles were finally over. On May 19, 2006, more than eleven years after the original incident on Woodruff Way that changed his life, Conley was reinstated as a Boston police officer—but only after being forced to redo, at age thirty-seven, the same police academy training a new recruit has to endure.[16] He was granted $647,000 in back pay for the years he was off the force,[17] and in 2007 he was promoted to detective.[18]

Throughout this book, we will present many examples and anecdotes, like the story of Kenny Conley, that show how everyday illusions can have tremendous influence on our lives. However, two important caveats are in order. First, as Robert Pirsig writes in *Zen and the Art of Motorcycle Maintenance,* "The real purpose of scientific method is to make sure Nature hasn't misled you into thinking you know something that you actually don't."[19] But science can only go so far, and although it can tell us *in general* how galaxies form, how DNA is transcribed into proteins, and how our minds perceive and remember our world, it is nearly impotent to explain a single event or individual case. The nature of everyday illusions almost never allows for *proof* that any particular incident was caused entirely by a specific mental mistake. There is no certainty that Conley missed the beating because of inattentional blindness, nor is there even certainty that he missed it at all (he could have seen it and then consistently lied). Without doing a study of attention under the same conditions Conley faced (at night, running after someone climbing a fence, the danger in chasing a murder suspect, the unfamiliar surroundings, and a gang of men attacking someone), we cannot estimate the probability that Conley missed what he said he missed.

We can, however, say that the intuitions of the people who condemned and convicted him were way off the mark. What *is* certain is that the police investigators, the prosecutors, and the jurors, and to some extent Kenny Conley himself, were all operating under the illusion of attention and failed to consider the possibility—which we argue is a strong possibility—that Conley could have been telling the truth about both where he was *and* what he didn't see on that January night in Boston.

The second important point to keep in mind is this: We use stories and anecdotes to convey our arguments because narratives are compelling, memorable, and easily understood. But people tend to believe convincing, retrospective stories about why something happened even when there is no conclusive evidence of the event's true causes. For that reason, we try to back up all of our examples with scientific research of the highest quality, using endnotes to document our sources and provide additional information along the way.

Our goals are to show you how everyday illusions influence our thoughts, decisions, and actions, and to convince you that they have large effects on our lives. We believe that once you have considered our arguments and evidence, you will agree, and that you will think about your own mind and your own behavior much differently. We hope that you will then act accordingly. So as you read on, read critically, keeping your mind open to the possibility that it doesn't work the way you think it does.

The Nuclear Submarine and the Fishing Boat

Do you remember the first major international incident of George W. Bush's presidency? It happened less than a month after he took office, on February 9, 2001.[20] At approximately 1:40 p.m., Commander Scott Waddle, captaining the nuclear submarine USS *Greeneville* near Hawaii, ordered a surprise maneuver known as an "emergency deep," in which the submarine suddenly dives. He followed this with an "emergency main ballast tank blow," in which high-pressure air forces water from the main ballasts, causing the submarine to surface as fast as it can. In this kind of maneuver, shown in movies like *The Hunt for Red October,* the bow of the submarine actually heaves out of the water. As the *Greeneville* zoomed toward the surface, the crew and passengers heard a loud noise, and the entire ship shook. "Jesus!" said Waddle. "What the hell was that?"

His ship had surfaced, at high speed, directly under a Japanese fishing vessel, the *Ehime Maru.* The *Greeneville*'s rudder, which had been specially reinforced for penetrating ice packs in the Arctic, sliced the fishing boat's hull from one side to the other. Diesel fuel began to leak and the *Ehime Maru* took on water. Within minutes, it tipped up and sank by its stern as the people onboard scrambled forward toward the bow. Many of them reached the three lifeboats and were rescued, but three crew members and six passengers died. The *Greeneville* received only minor damage, and no one onboard was injured.

What went wrong? How could a modern, technologically advanced submarine, equipped with state-of-the-art sonar and manned by an experienced crew, not detect a nearly two-hundred-foot-long fishing boat so close by? In attempting to explain this accident, the National Transportation Safety Board's fifty-nine-page report exhaustively documents all of the ways in which the officers failed to follow procedure, all of the distractions they faced in accommodating a delegation of civilian visitors, all of the errors they made along the way, and all of the miscommunication that contributed to poor tracking of the *Ehime Maru*'s actual position. It contains no evidence of alcohol, drugs, mental illness, fatigue, or personality conflicts influencing the crew's actions. The report is most interesting, however, for the crucial issue it does not even attempt to resolve: why Commander Waddle and the officer of the deck failed to see the *Ehime Maru* when they looked through the periscope.

Before a submarine performs an emergency deep maneuver, it returns to periscope depth so the commander can make sure no other ships are in the vicinity. The *Ehime Maru* should have been visible through the periscope, and Commander Waddle looked right toward it, but he still missed it. Why? The NTSB report emphasized the brevity of the periscope scan, as did *Dateline NBC* correspondent Stone Phillips: ". . . had Waddle stayed on the periscope longer, or raised it higher, he might have seen the *Ehime Maru*. He says there is no doubt he was looking in the right direction." None of these reports consider any other reasons why Waddle could have failed to see the nearby vessel—a failure that surprised Waddle himself. But the results of our gorilla experiment tell us that the USS *Greeneville*'s commanding officer, with all his experience and expertise, could indeed have looked right at another ship and just not have seen it. The key lies in what he *thought* he would see when he looked: As he said later, "I wasn't looking for it, nor did I expect it."[21]

Submarines rarely surface into other ships, so don't lose sleep over the prospect on your next boat trip. But this kind of "looked but failed to see" accident is quite common on land. Perhaps you have had the experience of starting to turn out of a parking lot or a side road and then having to stop suddenly to avoid hitting a car you hadn't seen before that moment. After accidents, drivers regularly claim, "I was looking right there and they came out of nowhere . . . I never saw them."[22] These situations are especially troubling because they run counter to our intuitions about the mental processes involved in attention and perception. We think we should see anything in front of us, but in fact we are aware of only a small portion of our visual world at any moment. The idea that we can look but not see is flatly incompatible with how we understand our own minds, and this mistaken understanding can lead to incautious or overconfident decisions.

In this chapter, when we talk about looking, as in "looking without seeing," we don't mean anything abstract or vague or metaphorical. We literally mean looking right at something. We truly are arguing that directing our eyes at something does not guarantee that we will consciously see it. A skeptic might question whether a subject in the gorilla experiment or an officer chasing a suspect or a submarine commander bringing his ship to the surface actually looked right at the unexpected object or event. To perform these tasks, though (to count the passes, pursue a suspect, or sweep the area for ships), they needed to look right where the unexpected object appeared. It turns out that there is a way, in a laboratory situation at least, to measure exactly where on a screen a person fixates their eyes (a technical way of saying "where they are looking") at any moment. This technique, which uses a device called an "eye tracker," can provide a continuous trace showing where and for how long a subject is looking during any period of time—such as the time of watching the gorilla video. Sports scientist Daniel Memmert of Heidelberg University ran our gorilla experiment using his eye tracker and found that the subjects who failed to notice the gorilla had spent, on average, a full second looking right at it—the same amount of time as those who did see it![23]

Ben Roethlisberger's Worst Interception

In February 2006, at the age of twenty-three and in just his second season as a professional football player, Ben Roethlisberger became the youngest quarterback in NFL history to win a Super Bowl. During the off-season, on June 12 of that same year, he was riding his black 2005 Suzuki motorcycle heading outbound from downtown Pittsburgh on Second Avenue.[24] As he neared the intersection at Tenth Street, a Chrysler New Yorker driven by Martha Fleishman approached in the opposite direction on Second Avenue. Both vehicles had green lights when Fleishman then turned left onto Tenth Street, cutting off Roethlisberger's motorcycle. According to witnesses, Roethlisberger was thrown from his motorcycle, hit the Chrysler's windshield, tumbled over the roof and off the trunk, and finally landed on the street. His jaw and nose were broken, many of his teeth were knocked out, and he received a large laceration on the back of his head, as well as a number of other minor injuries. He required seven hours of emergency surgery, but considering that he wasn't wearing a helmet, he was lucky to survive the crash at all. Fleishman had a nearly perfect driving record—the only mark against her was a speeding ticket nine years earlier. Roethlisberger was cited for not wearing a helmet and for driving without the right type of license; Fleishman was cited and fined for failing to yield. Roethlisberger eventually made a full recovery from the accident and was ready to resume his role as the starting quarterback by the season opener in September.

Accidents like this one are unfortunately common. More than half of all motorcycle accidents are collisions with another vehicle. Nearly 65 percent of those happen much like Roethlisberger's—a car violates the motorcycle's right-of-way, turning left in front of the motorcyclist (or turning right in countries where cars drive on the left side of the road).[25] In some cases, the car turns across oncoming traffic onto a side street. In others, the car turns across a lane of traffic onto the main street. In the typical accident of this sort, the driver of the car often says something like, "I signaled to turn left, and started out when it was clear. Then something hit my car and I later saw the motorcycle and the guy lying in the street. I never saw him!" The motorcyclist in such accidents says, "All of a sudden this car pulled out in front of me. The driver was looking right at me." This experience leads some motorcyclists to assume that car drivers violate their right-of-way intentionally—that they see the motorcyclist and turn anyway.

Why do drivers turn in front of motorcyclists? We favor, at least for some cases, an explanation that appeals to the illusion of attention. People don't see the motorcyclists because they aren't looking for motorcyclists. If you are trying to make a difficult left turn across traffic, most of the vehicles blocking your path are cars, not motorcycles (or bicycles, or horses, or rickshaws . . .). To some extent, then, motorcycles are unexpected. Much like the subjects in our gorilla experiment, drivers often fail to notice unexpected events, even ones that are important. Critically, though, they assume they will notice—that as long as they are looking in the right direction, unexpected objects and events will grab their attention.

How can we remedy this situation? Motorcycle safety advocates propose a number of solutions, most of which we think are doomed to fail. Posting signs that implore people to "look for motorcycles" might lead drivers to adjust their expectations and become more likely to notice a motorcycle appearing shortly after the sign. Yet, after a few minutes of not seeing any motorcycles, their visual expectations will reset, leading them to again expect what they see most commonly—cars. Such advertising campaigns assume that the mechanisms of attention are permeable, subject to influence from our intentions and thoughts. Yet, the wiring of our visual expectations is almost entirely insulated from our conscious control. As we will discuss extensively in Chapter 4, our brains are built to detect patterns automatically, and the pattern we experience when driving features a preponderance of cars and a dearth of motorcycles. In other words, the ad campaign itself falls prey to the illusion of attention.

Suppose that one morning, we told you to watch for gorillas. Then, at some point a week later, you participated in our gorilla experiment.

Do you think our warning would have any effect? Most likely not; in the time between the warning and the experiment, your expectations would have been reset by your daily experience of seeing no gorillas. The warning would only be useful if we gave it shortly before showing you the video.

Only when people regularly look for and expect motorcycles will they be more likely to notice. In fact, a detailed analysis of sixty-two accident reports involving cars and motorcycles found that none of the car drivers had any experience riding motorcycles themselves.[26] Perhaps the experience of riding a motorcycle can mitigate the effects of inattentional blindness for motorcycles. Or, put another way, the experience of being unexpected yourself might make you better able to notice similar unexpected events.

Another common recommendation to improve the safety of motorcycles is for riders to wear bright clothing rather than the typical attire of leather jacket, dark pants, and boots. The intuition seems right: A yellow jumpsuit should make the rider more visually distinctive and easier to notice. But as we've noted, looking is not the same as seeing. You can look right at the gorilla—or at a motorcycle—without seeing it. If the gorilla or motorcycle were physically imperceptible, that would be trivially true—nobody would be surprised if you failed to see a gorilla that was perfectly camouflaged in a scene. What makes the evidence for inattentional blindness important and counterintuitive is that the gorilla is so obvious once you know it is there. So looking is necessary for seeing—if you don't look at it, you can't possibly see it. But looking is not sufficient for seeing—looking at something doesn't guarantee that you will notice it. Wearing conspicuous clothing and riding a brightly colored motorcycle will increase your visibility, making it easier *for people who are looking for you* to see you. Such bright clothing doesn't guarantee that you will be noticed, though.

We did not always realize this ourselves. When we first designed the gorilla experiment, we assumed that making the "gorilla" more distinctive would lead to greater detection—of course people would notice a bright red gorilla. Given the rarity of red gorilla suits, we and our colleagues Steve Most (then a graduate student in Dan's lab and now a professor at the University of Delaware) and Brian Scholl (then a postdoctoral fellow in the psychology department and now a professor at Yale) created a computerized version of the "gorilla" video in which the players were replaced by letters and the gorilla was replaced by a red cross (+) that unexpectedly traversed the display.[27] Subjects counted how many times the white letters touched the sides of the display window while ignoring the black letters.

Even jaded researchers like us were surprised by the result: 30 percent of viewers missed the bright red cross, even though it was the only cross, the only colored object, and the only object that moved in a straight path through the display. We thought the gorilla had gone unnoticed, at least in part, because it didn't really stand out: It was dark-colored, like the players wearing black. Our belief that a distinctive object should "pop out" overrode our knowledge of the phenomenon of inattentional blindness. This "red gorilla" experiment shows that when something is unexpected, distinctiveness does not at all guarantee that we will notice it.

Reflective clothing helps increase visibility for motorcyclists, but it doesn't override our expectations. Motorcyclists are analogous to the cross in this experiment. People fail to see them, but not just because they are smaller or less distinctive than the other vehicles on the road. They fail to see the motorcycles precisely *because* they stand out. Wearing highly visible clothing is better than wearing invisible clothing (and less of a technological challenge), but increasing the visual distinctiveness of the rider might be of limited use in helping drivers notice motorcyclists. Ironically, what likely would work to increase detection of motorcycles is to make them look more like cars. For example, giving motorcycles two headlights separated as much as possible, to resemble the visual pattern of a car's headlights, could well increase their detectability.

There is one proven way to eliminate inattentional blindness, though: Make the unexpected object or event less unexpected. Accidents with bicyclists and pedestrians are much like motorcycle accidents in that car drivers often hit the bikers or walkers without ever seeing them.

Peter Jacobsen, a public health consultant in California, examined the rates of accidents involving cars and either pedestrians or bicyclists across a range of cities in California and in a number of European countries.[28] For each city, he collected data on the number of injuries or fatalities per million kilometers people traveled by biking and by walking in the year 2000. The pattern was clear, and surprising: Walking and biking were the *least* dangerous in the cities where they were done the *most,* and the most dangerous where they were done the least.

Why are motorists less likely to hit pedestrians or bicyclists where there are more people bicycling or walking? Because they are more used to seeing pedestrians. Think of it this way: Would you be safer crossing the pedestrian-clogged streets of London, where drivers are used to seeing people swarm around cars, or the wide, almost suburban boulevards of Los Angeles, where drivers are less accustomed to people popping up right in front of their cars without warning? Jacobsen's data show that if you were to move to a town with twice as many pedestrians, you would reduce your chance of being hit by a car while walking by one-third.

In one of the most striking demonstrations of the power of expectations,[29] Steve Most, who led the "red gorilla" study, and his colleague Robert Astur of the Olin Neuropsychiatry Research Center in Hartford, Connecticut, conducted an experiment using a driving simulator. Just before arriving at each intersection, subjects looked for a blue arrow that indicated which way they should turn, and they ignored yellow arrows. Just as subjects entered one of the intersections, a motorcycle unexpectedly drove right into their path and stopped. When the motorcycle was blue, the same color as the attended direction arrows, almost all of the drivers noticed it. When it was yellow, matching the ignored direction arrows, 36 percent of them hit the motorcycle, and two of them failed to apply their brakes at all! Your moment-to-moment expectations, more than the visual distinctiveness of the object, determine what you see—and what you miss.

Of course, not every automobile-versus-motorcycle collision is entirely the fault of the person driving the car. In the Ben Roethlisberger accident, the driver and the rider both had green lights, but Roethlisberger was going straight and had the right-of-way. A witness at the scene quoted Martha Fleishman, the driver of the car, as saying, "I was watching him approach but he was not looking at me."[30] Roethlisberger might never have seen Fleishman's car, even though it was right in front of him. Had he seen it, he might have been able to avoid the accident.

A Hard Landing

NASA research scientist Richard Haines spent much of his career at Ames Research Center, a space and aeronautics think tank in northern California. He is best known publicly for his attempts to document UFO experiences. But in the late 1970s and early 1980s, he and his colleagues Edith Fischer and Toni Price conducted a pioneering study on pilots and information display technologies using a flight simulator.[31] Their experiment is important because it is one of the most dramatic demonstrations of looking without seeing. They tested commercial airline pilots who were rated to fly the Boeing 727, one of the most common planes of the time. Commercial airline pilots tend to be among the most experienced and expert pilots—many flew in the military for years, and only the top pilots get to fly the larger commercial planes, where they have responsibility for hundreds of passengers on every flight. The subjects in this study were either first officers or captains who had flown 727s commercially for over one thousand hours.

During the experiment, the pilots underwent extensive training on the use of a "head-up display." This technology, which was relatively new at the time, displayed much of the critical instrumentation needed to fly and land the simulated 727—altitude, bearing, speed, fuel status, and so on—in video form directly on the windshield in front of the pilots, rather than below or around it as in an ordinary cockpit. Over the course of multiple sessions, the pilots flew a number of simulated landings under a wide range of weather conditions, either with or without the head-up display. Once they were practiced with the simulator, Haines inserted a surprise into one of the landing trials. As the pilots broke through the cloud ceiling and the runway came into view, they prepared for landing as they had on all of the previous trials, monitoring their instruments and the weather conditions to decide whether or not to abort. In this case, however, some of them never saw the large jet on the ground turning onto the runway right in front of them.

Such "runway incursions"—which happen when planes enter runways when they shouldn't—are among the more common causes of airplane accidents. More than half of the incursions result from pilot error—a pilot taxis into the path of another aircraft. Just as the USS *Greeneville* was exceptionally unlikely to surface into another ship, most runway incursions present little or no risk of a collision. In fiscal year 2007, the Federal Aviation Administration recorded a total of 370 runway incursions at American airports. In only 24 of them was there a significant potential for a collision, and only 8 of those involved commercial flights. Over the four years from 2004 through 2007, there were a total of 1,353 runway incursions in the United States, 112 of which were classified as serious, and only 1 of which resulted in a collision. That said, the single worst accident in aviation history involved a runway incursion. In 1977, in the Canary Islands, KLM flight 4805 took off down the runway and collided at full speed with Pan Am flight 1736, which was taxiing in the other direction on the same runway. The collision of these two Boeing 747s resulted in 583 deaths.

Although runway incursions are relatively common compared with other aviation accidents, airplane collisions of every sort are exceptionally rare. With only eight runway incursions out of more than 25 million flights in 2007, you would need to take an average of one commercial round-trip flight every day for about three thousand years to have a more than even chance of encountering a serious runway incursion. These incidents are relatively common, with the key word being "relatively." They are still exceedingly rare—and consequently, they are unexpected.[32]

What's surprising about Haines's flight simulator experiment is that the head-up display should—or at least our intuition suggests that it should—have kept the pilots' attention on the place where the parked plane was going to appear. They never had to look away from the run-way to see their instruments. But two of the pilots using the head-up display would have plowed right through the plane on the runway had the experimenter not aborted the trial. The plane was clearly visible just seconds after the pilots cleared the clouds, and they had about seven more seconds to safely abort their landing. The pilots using the head-up display were also slower to respond, and when they tried to execute a "missed approach" (by pulling up to go around and make a new land-ing attempt), they were late in doing so. The two who didn't manage to abort their landings in time were both rated either good or excellent in their simulator flying performance. When the trial was over, Haines asked them whether they saw anything, and both said no. After the experiment, Haines showed the pilots a videotape of the landing with the airplane stationed in their path, and both expressed surprise and concern that they had missed something so obvious. One said, "If I didn't see [the tape], I wouldn't believe it. I honestly didn't see anything on that runway."[33] The plane on the runway was their invisible gorilla—they didn't expect it to be there, so they never saw it.

Now that we understand that looking is not seeing, we can see that the intuition that a head-up display will enhance our ability to detect unexpected events is wrong. Head-up displays can help in some re-spects: Pilots get faster access to relevant information from their instru-ments and need to spend less time searching for that information. In fact, flight performance can be somewhat better with a well-designed head-up display than without one. Using a so-called conformational display, which superimposes a graphical indication of the runway on top of the physical runway visible through the windshield, pilots can fly more precisely.[34] Although the head-up display helps pilots perform the task they are trying to accomplish (like landing a plane), it doesn't help them see what they are not expecting to see, and it might even im-pair their ability to notice important events in the world around them.

How is it possible that spending more time with the world in view actually reduces our ability to see what is right in front of us? The answer, it seems, stems from our mistaken beliefs about how attention works. Although the plane on the runway was right in front of the pilots, fully in view, the pilots were focusing their *attention* on the task of landing the plane and not on the possibility of objects on the runway. Unless pilots inspect the runway to see if there are any obstructions, they are unlikely to see something unexpected, such as a plane taxiing onto their landing strip. Air traffic controllers are, after all, supposed to control the traffic to make sure that this doesn't happen. If a failure to inspect the runway were the only factor in play, though, a head-up display would be no worse than looking away at your instruments and then back to the windshield. After all, in both cases, you could spend the same amount of time ignoring the runway. You either focus attention on the readings on the windshield or focus attention on the instruments surrounding the windshield. But as Haines's study showed, pilots are slower to notice unexpected events when they are using a head-up display. The problem has to do not as much with the limits on attention—which are in effect regardless of whether the readings are displayed on the windshield or around it—as with our mistaken beliefs about attention.

Hold All Calls, Please

Imagine that you are driving home from work, thinking about what you will do when you get there and everything you left unfinished at the office. Just as you begin to make a left turn across a lane of oncoming traffic, a boy chases a ball into the road in front of you. Would you notice him? Maybe not, you should now be thinking. What if, rather than being lost in thought while you were driving, you were talking on a cell phone? Would you notice then? Most people believe that as long as their eyes are on the road and their hands are on the wheel, they will see and react appropriately to any contingency. Yet extensive research has documented the dangers of driving while talking on a phone. Both experimental and epidemiological studies show that the driving impairments caused by talking on a cell phone are comparable to the effects of driving while legally intoxicated.[35] When talking on a cell phone, drivers react more slowly to stoplights, take longer to initiate evasive maneuvers, and suffer from generally reduced awareness of their surroundings. In most cases, neither drunk driving nor driving while talking on a cell phone lead to accidents. In part, that is because most driving is predictable and lawful, and even if you aren't driving perfectly, the other drivers are trying not to hit you. The situations in which such impairments are catastrophic, though, are those that require an emergency reaction to an unexpected event. A slight delay in braking might make the difference between stopping short of the boy in the street and running him over.

For the most part, people are at least familiar with the dangers of talking on a cell phone while driving. We've all seen distracted drivers run a stop sign, obliviously veer into another lane, or drive at 30 mph in a 45 mph zone. As columnist Ellen Goodman wrote, "The very same people who use cell phones . . . are convinced that they should be taken out of the hands of (other) idiots who use them."[36]

The realization that (other) people are unable to drive safely while talking on the phone led to a movement to regulate the use of handheld cell phones while driving. New York was one of the first states to pass such legislation. The law banned the use of handheld phones while driving, based on the intuition that taking our hands off the wheel to use the phone is the main danger posed by talking while driving. In fact, the New York legislation provided for tickets to be waived if drivers could prove that they subsequently purchased a hands-free headset. Not surprisingly, the telecommunications industry supported the New York bill and regularly promotes the safety and advantages of hands-free headsets. A flier from AT&T Wireless proclaims, "If you use your wireless phone while driving, you can keep both hands on the wheel," and a similar brochure from Nokia ranks using a hands-free device whenever possible as second on their list of ten safety recommendations. In our survey, 77 percent of Americans agreed with the statement, "While driving, it's safer to talk on a hands-free phone than a handheld phone." The assumption underlying these beliefs and claims as well as most laws on distracted driving—that as long as you are looking at the road, you will notice unexpected events—is precisely the illusion of attention. Given what you now know about the gorilla experiment, you can probably guess what we will say next.

The problem isn't with our eyes or our hands. We can drive just fine with one hand on the wheel, and we can look at the road while holding a phone. Indeed, the acts of holding a phone and turning a steering wheel place little demand on our cognitive capacities. These motor-control processes are almost entirely automatic and unconscious; as an experienced driver, you don't have to think about how to move your arms to make the car turn left or to keep the phone up to your ear. The problem is not with limitations on motor control, but with limitations on attentional resources and awareness. In fact, there are few if any differences between the distracting effects of handheld phones and hands-free phones. Both distract in the same way, and to the same extent.[37] Driving a car and having a conversation on a cell phone, despite being well-practiced and seemingly effortless tasks, both draw upon the mind's limited stock of attention resources. They require multitasking, and despite what you may have heard or may think, the more attention-demanding tasks your brain does, the worse it does each one.

In a second part of our original gorilla experiment, we tested the limits of attention by making the task of the subjects (counting basketball passes) more difficult. Rather than just a single count of the total number of passes made by the white team, we asked people to keep two separate mental counts, one of aerial passes and one of bounce passes (but still focusing on the white team). As we predicted, this increased by 20 percent the number of people missing an unexpected event.[38] Making the counting task harder requires people to devote more attention to it, leaving fewer mental resources available to see the gorilla. As we use more of our limited attention, we are that much less likely to notice the unexpected. The problem is with consuming a limited cognitive resource, not with holding the phone. And most important, as the incredulous reactions of our study participants demonstrate, most of us are utterly unaware of this limit on our awareness. Experiment after experiment has shown no benefit whatsoever for hands-free phones over handheld ones. In fact, legislation banning the use of handheld phones might even have the ironic effect of making people more confident that they can safely use a hands-free phone while driving.

One could argue that our gorilla experiment isn't really comparable to the scenario of driving while talking on a cell phone. That is, increasing the difficulty of the counting task as we did might increase the burden on attention more than a cell phone conversation would. There's an easy way to account for this possibility, though: Do an experiment! To explore the effects of cell phone conversations on inattention directly, Brian Scholl and his students at Yale used a variant of the "red gorilla" computerized task described earlier and compared a group who performed the task as usual with one that performed it while simultaneously carrying on a cell phone conversation.[39] In their particular variant of the task, about 30 percent of the participants missed the unexpected object when they were just doing the tracking task. However, participants who performed the task while talking on a phone missed the unexpected object 90 percent of the time! Simply having a conversation on a phone tripled the chances that they would fail to see something unexpected.

This sobering finding shows that cell phone conversations dramatically impair visual perception and awareness. These impairments are due to the limits of attention and not due to the nature of the phone; even though both tasks seem effortless, both demand our attention. Intriguingly, the cell phone conversation didn't impair the subjects' ability to do the tracking task—it just decreased their chances of noticing something unexpected. This finding may explain why people falsely think that cell phones have no effect on their driving: People are lulled into thinking that they drive just fine because they can still perform the primary task (staying on the road) properly. The problem is that they're much less likely to notice rare, unexpected, potentially catastrophic events, and our daily experience gives us little feedback about such events.

If you're like many people who have heard us speak about inattention, cell phones, and driving, you may wonder why talking to someone on a phone should be any more dangerous than talking to the person in the passenger seat, which doesn't seem objectionable. (Or, if you have responded enthusiastically to our arguments—and thank you for doing so—you may be getting ready for a campaign to make "driving while talking" illegal, no matter whom you are talking to.) It may come as a surprise, then, to learn that talking to a passenger in your car is not nearly as disruptive as talking on a cell phone. In fact, most of the evidence suggests that talking to a passenger has little or no effect on driving ability.[40]

Talking to a passenger could be less problematic for several reasons. First, it's simply easier to hear and understand someone right next to you than someone on a phone, so you don't need to exert as much effort just to keep up with the conversation. Second, the person sitting next to you provides another set of eyes—a passenger might notice something unexpected on the road and alert you, a service your cell-phone conversation partner can't provide. The most interesting reason for this difference between cell-phone conversation partners and passengers has to do with the social demands of conversations. When you converse with the other people in your car, they are aware of the environment you are in. Consequently, if you enter a challenging driving situation and stop speaking, your passengers will quickly deduce the reason for your silence. There's no social demand for you to keep speaking because the driving context adjusts the expectations of everyone in the car about social interaction. When talking on a cell phone, though, you feel a strong social demand to continue the conversation despite difficult driving conditions because your conversation partner has no reason to expect you to suddenly stop and start speaking. These three factors, in combination, help to explain why talking on a cell phone is particularly dangerous when driving, more so than many other forms of distraction.

For Whom Does Bell Toil?

All of the examples we have discussed so far show how we can fail to see what is right in front of us: A submarine captain fails to see a fishing vessel, a driver fails to notice a motorcyclist, a pilot fails to see a runway obstruction, and a Boston cop fails to see a beating. Such failures of awareness and the illusion of attention aren't limited to the visual sense, though. People can experience inattentional *deafness* as well.[41]

In 2008, the Pulitzer Prize for Feature Writing went to Gene Weingarten for his *Washington Post* cover story describing a social "experiment" he conducted with the help of virtuoso violinist Joshua Bell.[42] As a four-year-old in Indiana, Bell impressed his parents, both psychologists, by using rubber bands to pluck out songs he had heard. They engaged a series of music teachers and by age seventeen Bell had played Carnegie Hall. He was on his way to repeatedly topping the classical music charts, receiving numerous awards for his performances, and appearing on *Sesame Street.* The official biography on his website begins with these words: "Joshua Bell has captured the public's attention like no other classical violinist of his time."

On a Friday morning at rush hour, Bell took his Stradivarius violin, for which he'd paid more than $3 million, to the L'Enfant Plaza subway stop in Washington, D.C. He set up shop between an entrance and an escalator, opened his violin case to take donations, seeded it with some cash of his own, and began to perform several complex classical pieces. Over the course of his forty-three-minute performance, more than one thousand people passed within a few feet of him, but only seven stopped to listen. And not counting a donation of $20 from a passerby who recognized him, Bell made only $32.17 for his work.

Weingarten's article bemoaned the lack of appreciation for beauty and art in modern society. Reading it, you can sense the pain and disappointment he must have felt while watching the people go past Bell:

It was all videotaped by a hidden camera. You can play the recording once or 15 times, and it never gets any easier to watch. Try speeding it up, and it becomes one of those herky-jerky World War I–era silent newsreels. The people scurry by in comical little hops and starts, cups of coffee in their hands, cellphones at their ears, ID tags slapping at their bellies, a grim *danse maca- bre* to indifference, inertia and the dingy, gray rush of modernity.

Fellow staffers at the *Washington Post* magazine apparently expected a different result. According to Weingarten's story, they had been worried that the performance might cause a riot:

> In a demographic as sophisticated as Washington, the thinking went, several people would surely recognize Bell. Nervous "what-if" scenarios abounded. As people gathered, what if others stopped just to see what the attraction was? Word would spread through the crowd. Cameras would flash. More people flock to the scene; rush-hour pedestrian traffic backs up; tempers flare; the National Guard is called; tear gas, rubber bullets, etc.

After the stunt was over, Weingarten asked famous conductor Leonard Slatkin, who directs the National Symphony Orchestra, to predict how a professional performer would do as a subway artist. Slatkin was convinced a crowd would gather: "Maybe 75 to 100 will stop and spend some time listening." During the actual performance, less than one-tenth that number stopped, and the National Guard did not mobilize.

Weingarten, his editors, Slatkin, and perhaps the Pulitzer committee members fell prey to the illusion of attention. Even Bell, when he saw the video of his performance, was "surprised at the number of people who don't pay attention at all, as if I'm invisible. Because, you know what? I'm makin' a lot of noise!"[43] Now that you've read about invisible gorillas, neglected fishing vessels, and unseen motorcycles, you can likely guess one reason why Bell went unrecognized for the great musician he is. People weren't looking (or listening) for a virtuoso violinist. They were trying to get to work. The one person interviewed for the story who correctly understood the minimal response to Bell was Edna Souza, who shines shoes in the area and finds buskers distracting. She wasn't surprised that people would rush by without listening: "People walk up the escalator, they look straight ahead. Mind your own business, eyes forward."

Under the conditions Weingarten established, commuters were already engaged in the distracting task of rushing to get to work, making them unlikely to notice Bell at all, let alone focus enough attention on his playing to distinguish him from a run-of-the-mill street musician. And that is the key. Weingarten's choice of time and location for the stunt nearly guaranteed that nobody would devote much attention to the quality of Bell's music. Weingarten is concerned that "if we can't take the time out of our lives to stay a moment and listen to one of the best musicians on Earth play some of the best music ever written; if the surge of modern life so overpowers us that we are deaf and blind to something like that—then what else are we missing?" Probably a lot, but this stunt provides no evidence for a lack of aesthetic appreciation. A more plausible explanation is that when people are focusing attention (visual and auditory) on one task—getting to work—they are unlikely to notice something unexpected—a brilliant violinist along the way.

If we were designing an experiment to test whether or not Washingtonians are willing to stop and appreciate beauty, we would first pick a time and location where an average street performer would attract an average number of listeners. We would then randomly place either a typical street performer or Joshua Bell there on several different days to see who earned more money. In other words, to show that people don't appreciate beautiful music, you first have to show that at least some people are listening to it and then show that they reward it no more than they do average music. Weingarten wouldn't have won a Pulitzer had he stationed Bell next to a jackhammer. Under those conditions, nobody would be surprised by the lack of attention to the musician— the deafening sound would have drowned out the violin. Placing Bell next to a subway station escalator during rush hour had the same effect, but for a different reason. People physically could have heard Bell playing, but because their attention was diverted by their morning commute, they suffered from inattentional deafness.

Other factors worked against Bell as well—he was performing

relatively unfamiliar classical pieces rather than music that most commuters would know. If Bell had played *The Four Seasons* or other better-known classical pieces, he might have done better. By doing so, a far less talented musician could have taken in more money than Bell did. When Dan lived in Boston, he occasionally walked from downtown to the North End to get Italian food. At least half a dozen times, he walked past an accordion player who stationed himself at one end of an enclosed walkway that ran past a highway—a perfect place to attract listeners with time on their hands, walking to restaurants that they'd probably have to wait to get into anyhow. For street artists, like for real estate, location is everything. The accordionist played with gusto, showing an emotional attachment to his instrument and his art. Yet, Dan only ever heard him play one song: the theme from *The Godfather*. He played it when Dan walked to dinner and when Dan walked back from dinner, every time Dan made that trip. Either he spotted Dan before he was within earshot and instantly started playing the *Godfather* theme as some odd sort of joke or warning (Dan has yet to wake up with a bloody horse's head at his feet), or he simply recognized the appeal to his audience of playing what may be the most familiar accordion piece. Our bet is that he did quite well. Had Bell performed on a Saturday afternoon, he likely would have attracted more listeners. Had he played shorter pieces on a subway platform rather than extended pieces next to the exit escalator, he might have attracted more listeners who had to wait for trains. And had he played the theme from *The Godfather* on his three-hundred-year-old violin, who knows.

Who Notices the Unexpected?

Chris once demonstrated the gorilla experiment to students in a seminar he was teaching. One of them told him the next week that she'd shown the video to her family, and that her parents had both missed the gorilla but her older sister had seen it. The sister then proceeded to crow about her triumph in this gorilla-noticing competition, claiming that it showed how smart she was. Dan regularly receives e-mails from people he's never met asking why they missed the gorilla but their children saw it, or whether girls always notice but boys never do. A hedge fund manager found out about our study and had the people in her office do it. She tracked Chris down through a chain of acquaintances and interrogated him about the differences between people who notice the gorilla and people who don't.

Many people who have experienced the gorilla experiment see it as a sort of intelligence or ability test. The effect is so striking—and the balance so even between the number who notice and the number who don't—that people often assume that some important aspect of your personality determines whether or not you notice the gorilla. When Dan was working with *Dateline NBC* to create demonstrations, the show's producers speculated that employees in detail-oriented occupations would be more likely to notice the gorilla, and they asked most of their "subjects" what their jobs were. They assumed that how you perform on the task depends on what kind of person you are: a "noticer" or a "misser." This is the question of *individual differences*. If we could figure out whether some people consistently notice the gorilla and other unexpected events in laboratory tasks, then we could figure out whether they are immune to inattentional blindness more generally, and potentially train the missers to become noticers.

Despite the intuitive appeal of the gorilla video as a Rosetta stone for personality types, there is almost no evidence that individual differences in attention or other abilities affect inattentional blindness. In theory, people could differ in the total attentional resources they have available, and those with more resources (perhaps those with higher IQs) might have enough "left over" after allocating some to the primary task to be better at detecting unexpected objects. One argument against this possibility, though, is the consistency in the pattern of results we obtain with the gorilla demonstration. We conducted the original experiment on Harvard undergraduates—a fairly elite group—but the experiment works just as well at less prestigious institutions and with subjects who aren't students. In all cases, about half of the subjects see the gorilla and half don't. According to an online survey by Nokia,

60 percent of women *and* men think that women are better at multi-tasking. If you agree, you might also think that women would be more likely to notice the gorilla. Unfortunately, there is little experimental evidence to support the popular belief about multitasking, and we haven't found any evidence that men are more prone than women to miss the gorilla. <u>In fact, the main conclusion from studies of multitasking is that virtually nobody does it well</u>: <u>As a rule, it is more efficient to do tasks one at a time rather than simultaneously.</u>[44]

It's still possible—even reasonable—to suspect that people differ in their ability to focus attention on a primary task, but that this ability isn't related to general intelligence or educational achievement. If individual differences in the ability to focus attention lead to differences in noticing unexpected objects, then people for whom the counting task is easier should be more likely to notice the gorilla—they are devoting fewer resources to the counting task and have more left over.

Dan and his graduate student Melinda Jensen recently conducted an experiment to test exactly this hypothesis. They first measured how well people could do a computer-based tracking task like the one we used in the "red gorilla" experiment and then looked to see whether those who performed the task well were more likely to notice an unexpected object. They weren't. Apparently, whether you detect unexpected objects and events doesn't depend on your capacity for attention. Consistent with this conclusion, Dan and sports scientist Daniel Memmert, the researcher who tracked children's eye movements while they watched the gorilla video, found that who noticed and who missed an unexpected object was unrelated to several basic measures of attention capacity. These findings have an important practical implication: Training people to improve their attention abilities may do nothing to help them detect unexpected objects. If an object is truly unexpected, people are unlikely to notice it no matter how good (or bad) they are at focusing attention.

As far as we can tell, there are no such people as "noticers" and "missers"—at least, no people who consistently notice or consistently miss unexpected events in a variety of contexts and situations. There is one way, however, to predict how likely a person is to see the unexpected. But it is not a simple trait of the individual or a quality of the event; it is the combination of a fact about the individual and a fact about the situation in which the unexpected event occurs. Only seven people out of more than one thousand stopped to listen to Joshua Bell playing in the L'Enfant Plaza subway station. One had been to a concert Bell had given just three weeks earlier. Two of the remaining six were musicians themselves. Their expertise helped them recognize his skill—and the pieces he was playing—through the din. One, George Tindley, worked in a nearby Au Bon Pain restaurant. "You could tell in one second that this guy was good, that he was clearly a professional," he told Weingarten. The other, John Picarello, said, "This was a superb violinist. I've never heard anyone of that caliber. He was technically proficient, with very good phrasing. He had a good fiddle, too, with a big, lush sound."

Experiments support this observation. Experienced basketball players are more likely to notice the gorilla in the original basketball-passing video than are novice basketball players. In contrast, team handball players are no more likely to notice unexpected objects even though they are experts in a team sport that places demands on attention comparable to those of basketball.[45] Expertise helps you notice unexpected events, but only when the event happens in the context of your expertise. Put experts in a situation where they have no special skill, and they are ordinary novices, taxing their attention just to keep up with the primary task. And no matter what the situation, experts are not immune to the illusory belief that people notice far more than they do. Gene Weingarten described John Picarello's behavior as he watched Bell play: "On the video, you can see Picarello look around him now and then, almost bewildered. 'Yeah, other people just were not getting it. It just wasn't registering. That was baffling to me.'"

How Many Doctors Does It Take . . .

Even within their field of specialty, experts are not immune to inattentional blindness or the illusion of attention. Radiologists are medical specialists responsible for reading x-rays, CT scans, MRIs, and other images in order to detect and diagnose tumors and other abnormalities. Radiologists perform this visual detection task under controlled conditions every day of their careers. In the United States, their training involves four years of medical school, followed by up to five years in residency at a teaching hospital. Those who specialize in specific body systems spend another year or two in fellowship training. In total, they often have more than ten years of post-undergraduate training, followed by on-the-job experience in studying dozens of films each day. Despite their extensive training, radiologists can still miss subtle problems when they "read" medical images.

Consider a recent case described by Frank Zwemer and his colleagues at the University of Rochester School of Medicine.[46] An ambulance brought a woman in her forties to the emergency room with severe vaginal bleeding. Doctors attempted to insert an intravenous line in a peripheral vein, but failed, so they instead inserted a central line via a catheter in the femoral vein, the largest vein in the groin. Getting the line in correctly requires also inserting a guidewire, which is removed once the line is in place.

The line was introduced successfully, but due to an oversight, the physician neglected to remove the guidewire.[47] To address her blood loss, the patient was given transfusions, but she then developed difficulty breathing due to pulmonary edema (a swelling or fluid buildup in the lungs). She was intubated for respiratory support, and a chest x-ray was taken to confirm the diagnosis and make sure that the breathing tube was placed correctly. The ER doctor and the attending radiologist agreed on the diagnosis, but neither of them noticed the guidewire. The patient went next to the intensive care unit for several days of treatment, and after she improved she went to a standard unit. There she developed shortness of breath, which was caused by pulmonary embolism—a blood clot in her lung. During this time she received two more x-rays, as well as an echocardiogram and a CT scan. Only on the fifth day of her stay in the hospital did a physician happen to notice and remove the guidewire while performing a procedure to correct the pulmonary embolism. The patient then made a full recovery. (It was determined later that the guidewire probably didn't cause the embolism because it was constructed of so-called nonthrombogenic material specifically intended not to promote blood clotting.)

When the various medical images were examined afterward, the guidewire was clearly visible on all three x-rays and on the CT, but none of the many doctors on the case noticed it. Their failure to see the anomalous guidewire illustrates yet again the dangers of inattentional blindness. The radiologists and other physicians who reviewed the chest images looked at them carefully, but they did not see the guidewire because they did not expect to see it.

Radiologists have a tremendously difficult task. They often review a large number of images at a time, typically looking for a specific problem—a broken bone, a tumor, and so on. They can't take in everything in the image, so they focus their attention on the critical aspects of the image, just as the subjects in the gorilla study focused on counting the passes of one team of players. Due to the limits of attention, radiologists are unlikely to notice aspects of the image that are unexpected, like the presence of a guidewire. But people assume that radiologists should notice any problem in a medical image regardless of whether it is expected; any failure to do so must therefore be the result of the doctor's negligence. Radiologists are regularly sued for missing small tumors or other problems.[48] These lawsuits are often based on the illusion of attention—people assume that radiologists will notice anything anomalous in an image, when in reality they, like the rest of us, tend to see best what they are looking for in the image. If you tell radiologists to find the guidewire in a chest x-ray, they will expect to see one and will notice it. But if you tell them to find a pulmonary embolism, they may not notice the guidewire. (It's also possible that when searching for the guidewire, they will miss more pulmonary embolisms.) An unexpected tumor that was missed during the original reading might seem obvious in hindsight.

Unfortunately, people often confuse what is easily noticed when it is expected with what should be noticed when it is unexpected. Moreover, the procedures frequently used in hospitals when reviewing radiographs are affected by the illusion of attention; doctors themselves also assume that they will notice unexpected problems in an image, even when they are looking for something else. To reduce the effects of inattentional blindness, one can deliberately reexamine the same images with an eye toward the unexpected. When participants in our studies know that something unexpected might happen, they consistently see the gorilla—the unexpected has become the target of focused attention. Devoting attention to the unexpected is not a cure-all, however. We have limited attention resources, and devoting some attention to unexpected events means that we have less attention available for our primary task. It would be imprudent to ask radiologists to take time and resources away from detecting the expected problem in an x-ray ("Doctor, can you confirm that this patient has a pulmonary embolism so that we can begin treatment?") to focus instead on things that are unlikely to be there ("Doctor, can you tell us whether we left anything behind in this patient's body?"). A more effective strategy would be for a second radiologist, unfamiliar with the case and the tentative diagnosis, to examine the images and to look for secondary problems that might not have been noticed the first time through.

So it turns out that even experts with a decade of training in their medical specialty can miss unexpected objects in their domain of expertise. Although radiologists are better able than laypeople to detect unusual aspects of radiographs, they suffer from the same limits on attention as everyone else. Their expertise lies not in greater attention, but in more precise expectations formed by their experience and training in perceiving the important features of the images. Experience guides them to look for common problems rather than rare anomalies, and in most cases, that strategy is wise.

What Can We Do About the Illusion of Attention?

If this illusion of attention is so pervasive, how has our species survived to write about it? Why weren't our would-be ancestors all eaten by un-

noticed predators? In part, inattentional blindness and the accompanying illusion of attention are a consequence of modern society. Although
our ancestors must have had similar limitations on awareness, in a less
complex world there was less to be aware of. And few objects or events
needed immediate attention. In contrast, the advance of technology has
given us devices that require greater amounts of attention, more and
more often, with shorter and shorter lead times. Our neurological cir-
cuits for vision and attention are built for pedestrian speeds, not for
driving speeds. When you are walking, a delay of a few seconds in noticing an unexpected event is likely inconsequential. When you are
driving, though, a delay of even one-tenth of a second in noticing an
unexpected event can kill you (or someone else). The effects of inattention are amplified at high speeds, since any delay in noticing happens at
the highest speed.

The effects of inattention are further amplified by any device or activity that takes attention away from what we are trying to do. Such
devices and activities were rare in the BlackBerryless, iPhone-free, pre-
GPS past, but they're common today. Fortunately, accidents are still
rare, because most of the time, nothing unexpected happens. But it is
those rare unexpected events that matter. People are confident that they
can drive and talk on the phone simultaneously precisely because they
almost never encounter evidence that they cannot. And by "evidence"
we don't mean a news story about accident rates or a safety institute's
latest report, or even a story of a friend who zoned out while driving
and almost hit something. We mean a personal experience, like a collision or a near miss, that was unambiguously caused by a depletion of
attention and that cannot be explained away as the other person's fault
(a rationalization we are as good at making as we are at overestimating
our own levels of attention). We will almost never be aware of the more
subtle evidence of our distraction. Drivers who make mistakes usually
don't notice them; after all, they're distracted.

The problem is that we lack positive evidence for our lack of attention.
That is the basis of the illusion of attention. We are aware only of the unexpected objects we do notice, not the ones we have missed. Consequently,

all the evidence we have is for good perception of our world. It takes an experience like missing the chest-thumping gorilla, which is hard to explain away (and which we have little incentive to explain away), to show us how much of the world around us we must be missing.

If the mechanisms of attention are opaque to us, how can we eliminate inattentional blindness so that we can be sure to spot the gorilla? The answer isn't simple. In order to eliminate inattentional blindness, we would effectively have to eliminate focused attention. We would have to watch the gorilla video without bothering to focus on counting passes or even to focus on what we found interesting in the display. We would have to watch the display without expectations and without goals. But for the human mind, expectations and goals are inextricably intertwined with the most basic processes of perception and are not readily extinguished. Expectations are based on our prior experiences of the world, and perception builds on that experience. Our experience and expectations help us to make sense of what we see, and without them, the visual world would just be an unstructured array of light, a "blooming, buzzing confusion" in the classic words of William James.[49]

For the human brain, attention is essentially a zero-sum game: If we pay more attention to one place, object, or event, we necessarily pay less attention to others. Inattentional blindness is thus a necessary, if unfortunate, by-product of the normal operation of attention and perception. If we are right that inattentional blindness results from inherent limits on the capacity of visual attention, it might be impossible to reduce or eliminate it in general. In essence, trying to eliminate inattentional blindness would be equivalent to asking people to try flying by flapping their arms really rapidly. The structure of the human body doesn't permit us to fly, just as the structure of the mind doesn't permit us to consciously perceive everything around us.

The issue of how best to allocate our limited attention relates to a larger principle of attention. For the most part, inattentional blindness isn't a problem. In fact, it is a consequence of the way attention works; it is the cost of our exceptional—and exceptionally useful—ability to focus our minds. Focused attention allows us to avoid distraction and use our limited resources more effectively; we don't want to be distracted by everything else around us. Most drivers follow the rules of the road, most doctors don't leave guidewires in patients, most fishing vessels aren't floating right above submarines, most planes aren't guided in to land right on top of other planes, most cops don't viciously beat suspects, and most world-class violinists don't play in the subway. And gorillas rarely saunter through basketball games. Unexpected events are unexpected for a good reason: They are rare. More important, in most cases, failing to spot the unexpected has little consequence.

Attention Writ Large

The illusion of attention affects us all in both mundane and potentially life-threatening ways—it truly is an everyday illusion. It contributes to everything from traffic accidents and airplane cockpit displays to cell phones, medicine, and even subway busking. As the gorilla experiment has become more widely known, it has been used to explain countless failures of awareness, from the concrete to the abstract, in diverse domains. It's not just limited to visual attention, but applies equally well to all of our senses and even to broader patterns in the world around us. The gorilla experiment is powerful because it forces people to confront the illusion of attention. It provides an effective metaphor precisely because the illusion of attention has such broad reach. Here are some examples:[50]

- A trainer uses it to show people how they can miss safety infractions that are right in front of them.

- A Harvard professor uses it to explain how discriminatory practices in the workplace can go unnoticed even by intelligent, fair-minded individuals.

- Antiterrorism experts cited it to explain how Australian intelligence officials could have missed the presence in their own country of the Jemaah Islamiyah group, which was responsible for the 2002 Bali bombings that killed 202 people.

- A weight-loss website compares the unseen gorilla to an unplanned snack that can ruin your diet.

- Promoter of the paranormal Dean Radin likens the inattentional blindness of our subjects to the failure of scientists to see the "reality" of ESP and other extrasensory phenomena.

- A high school principal uses inattentional blindness to explain how teachers and administrators often fail to notice bullying.

- An Episcopal priest used it in a sermon to explain how easily people can miss evidence of God all around them.

- A British ad campaign encouraged drivers to watch for bicyclists by creating a television and viral Web advertisement based on our video, with the chest-thumping gorilla replaced by a moonwalking bear.

Within the realm of visual perception, noticing suffers from even more limitations than the ones we have discussed so far. For example, it is hard to look for multiple things at once, to distinguish similar-looking objects, and to remain vigilant over long periods of time performing the same task. Our underappreciation of these constraints can have dire consequences for our safety and security. We expect airport baggage scanners to spot weapons in luggage, but they regularly fail to notice contraband items planted by authorities during tests of security procedures. The task of security scanners is much like the task of radiologists (though the training is, shall we say, much less extensive), and it is difficult if not impossible to see everything in a briefly viewed image. That's especially true given that the things being searched for are rare.[51]

Similarly, we expect lifeguards at swimming pools to notice anyone in danger of drowning, but this is a false sense of safety brought on by the illusion of attention. Lifeguards have the nearly impossible task of scanning a large expanse of water and detecting the rare event of someone drowning.[52] The difficulty of their task is exacerbated because swimmers regularly do things that look like drowning but aren't, such as swimming under water, lying on the bottom of the pool, splashing frantically, and so on. Lifeguards take regular breaks, change their viewing stations repeatedly during shifts, and take many other steps to maintain their vigilance, but vigilance, besides being subject to its own limitations, cannot eliminate inattentional blindness. The lifeguards simply cannot see everything, but the illusion of attention makes us believe they will.

Only becoming aware of the illusion of attention can help us to take steps to avoid missing what we need to see. In some cases, like lifeguarding, technological innovations such as automated scanning could help. Without awareness of our limitations, though, technological intervention can hurt. Head-up displays might improve our ability to navigate and to keep our eyes on the road, but they might impair our ability to detect unexpected events. Similarly, in-car GPS navigation systems might help us find our way, but when trusted implicitly, they can lead us to drive without noticing where we are going.[53] A driver in Germany followed his navigation instructions despite several "closed for construction" signs and barricades, eventually barreling his Mercedes into a pile of sand. Twice in 2008, drivers in New York State blindly followed their GPS instructions and turned onto a set of train tracks in front of an oncoming train (neither was injured, fortunately). A driver in Britain caused a train crash after unwittingly driving onto the Newcastle-Carlisle rail line tracks.

A more common problem in Britain occurs when truck drivers follow their GPS commands onto streets that are too small for their trucks. In one case, a driver wedged his truck so firmly into a country lane that he couldn't move backward, move forward, or even open his door. He had to sleep in his cab for three days before being towed out by a tractor. The problem, of course, is that the navigation system doesn't know or take account of the size of the vehicle—and some of us don't know that it doesn't know. Our favorite example of GPS-induced blindness comes from the British town of Luckington. In April 2006, rising waters made a ford through the start of the Avon River temporarily impassable, so it was closed and markers were put on both sides. Every day during the two weeks following the closure, one or two cars drove right past the warning signs and into the river. These drivers apparently were so focused on their navigation displays that they didn't see what was right in front of them.

Technology can help us to overcome the limits on our abilities, but only if we recognize that any technological aid will have limits too. If we misunderstand the limits of the technology, these aids can actually make us *less* likely to notice what is around us. In a sense, we tend to generalize our illusion of attention to the aids we use to overcome the limits on our attention. In the next chapter, we will consider this question: If we successfully pay attention to something and notice it, will it then be remembered? Most people think yes, but we will argue that this too is an illusion—the illusion of memory.

the coach who choked

B EFORE RETIRING FROM COACHING COLLEGE basketball in 2008, Bobby Knight led his teams to victory in more than nine hundred college games, more than any other Division I coach. He was a four-time national coach of the year, led the 1984 Olympic gold medal basketball team that featured future NBA stars Michael Jordan and Patrick Ewing, and won three national collegiate titles as the coach of the Indiana University Hoosiers. He was famous for running a "clean" basketball operation: His organizations were never accused of the sorts of recruiting violations that plague many top-tier basketball programs, and the majority of his players completed their college degrees. He was a coaching innovator whom many of his former players credit for their personal and professional successes. Despite this unparalleled record of achievement, Bobby Knight was fired from Indiana University in September 2000 after an undergraduate yelled "Hey, Knight, what's up?" and Knight responded by grabbing the student's arm and lecturing him on being respectful.

That Knight's dismissal was triggered by a lecture on respect is ironic. Throughout his coaching career, Knight had a national reputation for a volatile temper, crass behavior, and a disdainful attitude toward the press and others. He regularly berated referees and journalists, and on occasion, he even threw chairs onto the court. He was the subject of a *Saturday Night Live* parody in which Jim Belushi played a high school chess coach who knocked over an opponent's pieces and yelled at his own player, "Move it! Move it! Move the bishop!" Compared with other events in his career, the "what's up" incident was actually small beer. It was considered a firing offense only because of a report published earlier that year that had led the university to adopt a zero-tolerance policy for his future indiscretions.

In March 2000, CNN and *Sports Illustrated* ran a story about why several top recruits had left the Indiana program. It focused on an incident described by Neil Reed, one of Knight's former players. Reed was a star recruit, a high school All-American who scored an average of about ten points per game during his three years at Indiana. During a practice in 1997, Knight confronted Reed for failing to call out a teammate's name when making a pass, but Reed stood his ground against Knight, claiming he had in fact yelled the name. According to Reed, Knight then physically attacked him:

> At that point coach thrust right at me, just came right at me, wasn't far away enough to where I couldn't see it coming, was close enough to come at me and reach and put his hand around my throat. He came at me with two hands but grabbed me with one hand. People came in and separated us like we were in a school yard to fight. . . . He had me by the throat for I would probably say that little situation lasted about 5 seconds. I grabbed his wrist and started walking back and by this time people, coaches Dan Dakich, Felling grabbed coach Knight and pulled him away.

The national reporting of this incident caused a sensation and led Indiana officials to shorten their coach's leash. Reed's account vividly confirmed Knight's stormy reputation and put it in an even darker light. But shortly after the *Sports Illustrated* report, other people present at the time told a different story. Knight's former assistant Dan Dakich said, "His allegation that I had to separate him from coach Knight is totally false." Another player who had been on the team at the time said, "The statement that he was choked by coach Knight is totally ridiculous." Christopher Simpson, a vice president of the university who attended many practices, was quoted as saying about Reed's statements, ". . . I question anything Neil Reed says." The team's trainer at the time, Tim Garl, stated baldly, "The choking thing never happened . . . give me a lie detector." Bobby Knight himself said, "I might have grabbed him by the back of the neck. I might have grabbed the guy and moved him over. I mean, if you choke a guy, I would think he would need hospitalization." Everyone involved believed that their memories had accurately recorded what had happened, but their recollections were contradictory.[1]

How We Think About Memory

This chapter is about this *illusion of memory:* the disconnect between how we think memory works and how it actually works. But how, exactly, do we think it works? Before answering this question, we'd like you to try a brief memory test. Read through the following list of words: *bed, rest, awake, tired, dream, wake, snooze, blanket, doze, slumber, snore, nap, peace, yawn, drowsy.* We'll get back to them in a few paragraphs.

Most of us cannot remember a fifteen-digit number, and we know that we cannot, so we do not even try. We all sometimes forget where we put our car keys (or our car), we fail to recall a friend's name, or we neglect to pick up the dry cleaning on the way home from work. And we know that we often make these mistakes—our intuitive beliefs about such everyday memory failures are reasonably accurate. Our intuitions about the persistence and detail of memory are a different story.

In the national survey of fifteen hundred people we commissioned in 2009, we included several questions designed to probe how people think memory works. Nearly half (47%) of the respondents believed that "once you have experienced an event and formed a memory of it, that memory doesn't change." An even greater percentage (63%) believed that "human memory works like a video camera, accurately recording the events we see and hear so that we can review and inspect them later." People who agreed with both statements apparently think that memories of all our experiences are stored permanently in our brains in an immutable form, even if we can't access them. It is impossible to disprove this belief—the memories *could* in principle be stored somewhere—but most experts on human memory find it implausible that the brain would devote energy and space to storing every detail of our lives (especially if that information could never be accessed).[2]

Just as the illusion of attention leads us to think that important and distinctive events capture our attention when they don't, the illusion of memory reflects a basic contrast between what we think we remember and what we actually remember. Why do people easily grasp the limitations of short-term memory, but misunderstand the nature of long-term memory? This chapter is about how our memories can mislead us and how our beliefs about the workings of memory are mistaken. The illusion of attention happens when what we notice is different from what we think we notice. The illusion of memory happens when what we remember is different from what we think we remember.

Now we'd like you to try to recall all of the words from the list you read. Do your best to recall as many as you can. Write them down on a piece of paper before you continue reading.

What could be simpler than recalling a list of words that you read only moments ago? Not much, but even a task as simple as this reveals systematic distortions in memory. Look at the list you wrote down. How do you think you did? Most likely, you didn't recall all fifteen words. When we use this task as a classroom demonstration, most students recall a few words from the beginning of the list and a few from the end of the list.[3] They often recall fewer than half of the words from the middle of the list, though, and on average, they tend to recall only about seven or eight of the fifteen words correctly. Stop to think about this for a moment. Those words were all utterly common and familiar, you were not under any special stress (we hope) when you read them, and there was no time pressure when you had to recall them. Computers built in the 1950s were able to perfectly store fifteen words in memory, but despite our magnificent cognitive abilities, we cannot remember with precision what we read just minutes ago.

If you ask a small child to remember a short list of words for a few minutes, you will notice that as late as age four kids still don't appear to realize that they need to exert special effort to keep the words in memory. As adults, though, we have learned that there are limits to how much we can maintain in memory for a short time. When we have to remember a phone number long enough to dial it, we repeat it to ourselves, either silently or out loud, as long as necessary. Once an arbitrary list is longer than the "magic number" of about seven items, most people have trouble holding it in their short-term memories.[4] That is why license plates have only about seven letters and numbers and why phone numbers historically only required seven numbers (and why the three-digit prefix often began with the first two letters of the town or neighborhood's name; where Chris grew up, in Armonk, New York, some old signs and advertisements still listed the numbers of local businesses as starting with AR-3 instead of 273). When we have to remember anything more than this, we use memory crutches (notepads, voice recorders, and so on) to help.

The reason your difficulty recalling all fifteen words in our list illustrates the illusion of memory is not that it reveals limits on how much we can remember. People generally understand those limits. It reflects the illusion of memory because it highlights *how* we remember what we do. Take a look at the list of words you recalled. Does it contain the word "sleep"? About 40 percent of the people reading this book will recall having seen the word "sleep." If you are one of those people, you are probably as confident about having seen "sleep" as you are about any of the other words you remembered. You might even have a distinct recollection of seeing it on the list—but it wasn't there. You fabricated it.

Memory depends both on what actually happened and on how we made sense of what happened. The list you read was designed to produce just this type of false memory. All of the words are closely associated with the missing word "sleep." As you read the words on the list, your mind made sense of them, automatically processing the connections among them. At some level, you knew that they were all related to sleep, but you didn't take special note of the fact that "sleep" was not on the list. Then, when you recalled the words, your mind *reconstructed* the list as best it could, based on both your specific memory for the words you saw and on your knowledge of how the words were generally related.

When we perceive something, we extract the meaning from what we see (or hear, or smell . . .) rather than encode everything in perfect detail. It would be an uncharacteristic waste of energy and other resources for evolution to have designed a brain that took in every possible stimulus with equal fidelity when there is little for an organism to gain from such a strategy. Likewise, memory doesn't store everything we perceive, but instead takes what we have seen or heard and associates it with what we already know. These associations help us to discern what is important and to recall details about what we've seen. They provide "retrieval cues" that make our memories more fluent. In most cases, such cues are helpful. But these associations can also lead us astray, precisely because they lead to an inflated sense of the precision of memory. We cannot easily distinguish between what we recall verbatim and what we construct based on associations and knowledge. The word-list example, originally devised in the 1950s by psychologist James Deese and then studied extensively by Henry Roediger and Kathleen McDermott in the 1990s,[5] is a simple way to demonstrate this principle, but memory distortions and the illusion of memory extend well beyond arbitrary lists of words.

Just as the gorilla experiment showed that people see what they expect to see, people often remember what they expect to remember. They make sense of a scene, and that interpretation colors—or even determines—what they remember about it. In a dramatic demonstration of this principle, psychologists William Brewer and James Treyens conducted a clever experiment using a simple ruse.[6] Subjects in their study were led to a graduate student office and asked to wait there for a minute while the experimenter made sure the previous subject was finished. About thirty seconds later, the experimenter returned and led the subjects to another room, where they unexpectedly were asked to write down a list of everything that they had seen in the waiting room. In most respects, the waiting room was a typical graduate student office, with a desk, chairs, shelves, and so on. Almost all of the subjects recalled such common objects. Thirty percent of them also recalled seeing books, and 10 percent recalled seeing a file cabinet. But this office was unusual—it contained no books or file cabinets.

In the same way that people tended to recall having seen the word "sleep" when remembering a list of words associated with sleep, their memory reconstructed the contents of the room based both on what actually was there and on what *should have* been there. (If you look at a picture of the office, it will probably seem perfectly normal until someone points out what's missing, and then it will suddenly start to look strange.) What is stored in memory is not an exact replica of reality, but a re-creation of it. We cannot play back our memories like a DVD—each time we recall a memory, we integrate whatever details we do remember with our expectations for what we should remember.

Memories in Conflict

Neil Reed recalled Coach Knight choking him during a practice. He remembered Assistant Coach Dan Dakich having to pull Knight off him, but Dakich claimed it never happened. One of them had a distorted memory for the event, but which one? In most cases of disputed memory like this, there's no definitive way to determine who was right and who was wrong. What makes this example particularly interesting is that well after Reed, Dakich, and others went public with their accusations and memories, a videotape of the practice surfaced. It showed Knight approach Reed, grab him by the front of the neck with one hand for several seconds, and push him backward. Other coaches and players stopped what they were doing and watched. Nobody came to rescue Reed. No assistant coaches separated them. Reed correctly recalled that Knight had grabbed him by the throat, at least momentarily, but over time, in his mind, the memory was elaborated and distorted. It was made consistent with what plausibly might have happened rather than what did happen. And, to Reed, his totally false memory of being forcibly separated from Coach Knight was just as real as his more accurate memory of being choked. *After* viewing the video for a follow-up CNN/*Sports Illustrated* report, Reed said:

> I know what happened and that [tape] proves what happened. I think the moment after something like that, especially a 20-year-old kid being in that situation, I don't think you can find fault in a little bit of . . . I mean . . . I'm not lying. That's how I remember the thing happening and [former assistant coach Ron] Felling's five feet from me. As far as people coming in between, I remember people coming between us.[7]

Why did Reed remember an embellished event while Knight remembered nothing at all? Before the tape surfaced, Knight told HBO's Frank Deford that he didn't remember choking Reed, and added, "There isn't anything that I have done with one kid that I haven't done with a lot of other kids."[8] For Knight, this was an unremarkable event—it was business as usual. His memory for the event was distorted to become consistent with his broader beliefs and expectations for what happens at practices: Coaches grab kids and move them around, showing them where to stand and what to do. Physical contact, for Knight, is a regular part of coaching. He misremembered the event as being less consequential than it was, distorting it to be more consistent with his own beliefs about typical coaching situations. For Reed, this event likely was far more consequential. As he noted, he was a "twenty-year-old kid" at the time and he probably hadn't been grabbed by the neck often in practice. To him, it was a jarring and unusual event, one that he stored in his memory as "coach choked me." He remembered the event based on the ways that it was salient to him, and as a result, it was distorted in the opposite direction from Knight's version, becoming traumatic rather than trivial. For Knight, the incident was just like another arbitrary word in a list. For Reed, the incident had a powerful meaning, and the details were filled in accordingly.

People involved in the case of Neil Reed and Bobby Knight had sharply different recollections of what happened, but by the time they told their stories to the media in 2000, several years had already passed since the incident. It's not unreasonable to think that memories can fade and morph over the years, and that they can be influenced by the motives and goals of the rememberer. But what if two people witness the exact same incident, and the delay before they have to describe it is no more than the length of time spent on hold waiting for a 911 operator?[9]

Leslie Meltzer and Tyce Palmaffy, a young couple who had met as undergraduates at the University of Virginia, were on their way home from dinner on a summer night in 2002 in Washington, D.C. They drove their Camry north on Fourteenth Street and stopped at a traffic light at the intersection of Rhode Island Avenue.[10] Today, it costs upward of $300,000 to buy a small apartment near the Whole Foods supermarket in this area, but then, the neighborhood was still recovering from the effects of race riots and arson that took place in the 1960s. Tyce, a writer on education policy, was driving. His wife, Leslie, who had recently earned a law degree at Yale, was in the passenger seat. To her right, Leslie saw a man riding a bicycle down the sidewalk in their direction. Suddenly, seemingly out of nowhere, another man approached the cyclist, pulled him off the bicycle, and began stabbing him repeatedly. Leslie heard the victim scream. She grabbed her cell phone and dialed 911, only to be greeted by a voice saying, "You have reached the emergency 911 service, all lines are busy, please hold."

By the time the 911 operator got on the line, less than a minute had passed, but the assault was over and the light had turned green. Leslie described what she saw as they continued driving with the traffic down Fourteenth Street. The victim was a man in his twenties or thirties riding a bicycle. What about the assailant? He was dressed in jeans, she said. Overhearing her, Tyce interrupted to say that he was wearing sweatpants. They also disagreed about the kind of shirt he was wearing, how tall he was, and even whether he was black or Hispanic. They soon realized that they could agree only on the attacker's age (twenties), on his weapon (a knife), and on the fact that they were not painting the clearest picture for the operator.

It is rare to witness exactly the same event, from the same vantage point as someone else, and then try to recall it in the presence of the other witness so soon afterward. Normally, when we observe an event, we store some memory of it. When we later recall the event, we do our best to retrieve our memory and report its contents. The memory seems vivid to us, and we typically lack any specific reason to doubt its accuracy. Had Tyce not been there to hear and correct—or at least contradict—Leslie's report to the 911 operator, neither would have discovered the stark contradictions between their separate memories. Both were surprised by the extent of the differences. Tyce later recalled realizing right after the unnerving experience "how unbelievably untrustworthy witnesses must be," an issue we'll return to later in this book.

Didn't They Just Shoot Up His Windshield?

In a famous scene in the movie *Pretty Woman*, Julia Roberts is having breakfast with Richard Gere in his hotel room. She picks up a croissant but then takes a bite out of a pancake. In *Jagged Edge*, Glenn Close's outfit changes three times during a single courtroom scene. In *The Godfather*, Sonny's car is riddled with bullets at a tollbooth, but seconds later its windshield is miraculously repaired. Did you know about these mistakes or others like them? These inadvertent changes, known as continuity errors, are common in movies, in part because of how movies are created. Rarely are movies shot in sequence and in real time from start to finish. They are completed piecemeal, with scenes filmed in an order determined by the actors' schedules, the availability of physical locations for filming, the cost of hiring the crew at different times, the weather conditions, and many other factors. Each scene is filmed from many different angles, and the final movie is spliced together and put in order in the editing room.

Just one person on the set is responsible for making sure that everything in each scene matches from one shot to the next.[11] That person, known as the script supervisor, is charged with remembering all of the details: what people were wearing, where they were standing, which foot was forward, whether a hand was on a waist or in a pocket, whether an actress was eating a croissant or a pancake, and whether the windshield should be intact or bullet-ridden. If the script supervisor makes a mistake during filming, it's often impossible to go back and reshoot the scene. And the editor may decide to ignore the error because other aspects of the shot are more important. As a result, some mistakes almost inevitably make it into the final product. That's why some of the slaves in *Spartacus*, set during the Roman Empire, can occasionally be seen wearing wristwatches.

Dozens of books and websites are devoted to cataloging such errors for the curious and obsessed.[12] For *The Godfather*, one site lists forty-two separate continuity errors (plus dozens of other mistakes and anomalies). In part, such lists appeal because of the irony involved: Hollywood, despite spending tens of millions of dollars on a movie, makes clear mistakes that anyone can see. Finding such errors gives the amateur continuity sleuth a feeling of superiority—the filmmakers must have been sloppy not to notice what I can see clearly. And indeed, when you see an error in a movie, it suddenly seems obvious.

Several years ago, *Dateline NBC* ran a story on film flubs in movies like *Shakespeare in Love* and *Saving Private Ryan*, which had both won Academy Awards and been acclaimed for their editing. Correspondent Josh Mankiewicz revealed an error in *Saving Private Ryan* in which eight soldiers walked across a field in the distance, even though one had been killed a few minutes earlier in the film, so by then there should have been only seven soldiers. In a disbelieving voice, he said, "This is Steven Spielberg, one of the most talented and most careful moviemakers out there. You've got to figure he watched the film several times before it actually got to the theaters. And he didn't see it?" Later, Mankiewicz asked, "What is it about filmmakers that they can shoot so carefully, many takes, and still miss something so obvious, something the audience can see clearly?" The questions are nearly perfect illustrations of how the illusion of memory operates. Mankiewicz (and his producers) assumed that people have an accurate memory of everything that has happened and that they will automatically notice any discrepancies.[13]

When they were in graduate school together at Cornell, Dan and his friend Daniel Levin (now a professor at Vanderbilt University) decided to explore experimentally how well people actually notice such errors in movies.[14] With this project "the two Dans" began a long, productive, and ongoing collaboration. For their first study, they made a brief movie of a conversation between two friends, Sabina and Andrea, about a surprise party for their mutual friend Jerome. Sabina sat at a table when Andrea entered the scene. As they talked about the party, the camera cut back and forth between them, sometimes showing a close-up of one of them, and other times showing both of them. After about a minute, the conversation ended and the screen faded to black.

Imagine being a subject in their experiment. You come to a laboratory room and are told that before you do another task, the experimenters would like you to watch a brief movie and then to answer some detailed questions about it. They advise you to pay close attention and they start the movie. As soon as the movie ends, they hand you a piece of paper that asks, "Did you notice any unusual differences from one shot to the next where objects, body positions, or clothing suddenly changed?" If you are like almost all of the subjects in this experiment, you would answer no—you would not have noticed any of the nine editing mistakes the two Dans intentionally made![15]

These "errors," which were of the same type that end up in books and websites on film flubs, included plates on the table changing color and a scarf disappearing and reappearing. They were much more obvious than the ones Josh Mankiewicz disparaged in his *Dateline* report. Yet even when subjects watched the film a second time, now looking for changes, they still noticed, on average, just two of the deliberate errors. This phenomenon, the surprising failure to notice seemingly obvious changes from one moment to the next, is now known as *change blindness*—people are "blind" to the changes between what was in view moments before and what is in view now.[16] This phenomenon is related to the inattentional blindness we discussed in the last chapter, but it is not the same. Inattentional blindness usually happens when we fail to notice the appearance of something we weren't expecting to see. The thing we miss, such as a gorilla, is fully visible, right in front of us the entire time. For change blindness, unless we remember that Julia Roberts was eating a croissant, the fact that she is now eating a pancake is unremarkable. Change blindness occurs when we fail to compare what's there now with what was there before. Of course, in the real world, objects don't abruptly change into other objects, so checking all the visual details from moment to moment to make sure they haven't changed would be a spectacular waste of brainpower.

What is in some ways even more important than a failure to notice changes is the mistaken belief that we *should* notice them. Daniel Levin cheekily named this misbelief *change blindness blindness,* because people are blind to the extent of their own change blindness. In one experiment, Levin showed photographs from the Sabina/Andrea conversation to a group of undergraduates, described the film, and pointed out that the plates were red in one shot and white in another. That is, rather than run the change blindness experiment, he explained everything about it, including the intentional "flub." He then asked these subjects to decide whether or not they would have noticed the change if they had just watched the film without being alerted to its presence. More than 70 percent confidently said that they would have spotted the change, even though in the original study no one actually did! For the disappearing scarf, more than 90 percent said they would have noticed, when again, in the original experiment, no one actually did.[17] This is the illusion of memory at work: Most people firmly believe that they will notice unexpected changes, when in fact almost nobody does.

Now imagine you are in another experiment conducted by the two Dans. You come to the lab and again you are asked to watch a brief silent movie. You are warned that it is really short and that you should pay close attention. The movie shows a person sitting at a desk who gets up and walks toward the camera. The shot then cuts to the hallway and shows a person exiting the door and answering a phone on the wall. He stands still, holding the phone to his ear and facing the camera for about five seconds before the scene fades to black. As soon as the movie ends, you are asked to write a detailed description of what you saw.

Having just read about the Sabina/Andrea film, you've probably guessed that there's more to this one than just the simple action of answering a phone. When the camera cut from a view of the actor walking toward the doorway to a shot of the actor entering the hall and answering the phone, the original actor was replaced by a different person! Wouldn't you notice the only actor in a scene being replaced by a different person wearing different clothes, parting his hair the opposite way, and wearing different glasses?

If you answered yes, you're still under the illusion of memory. Here is what two subjects wrote after seeing the film:

> Subject 1: A young man with slightly long blond hair and large glasses turned around from the chair at a desk, got up, walked past the camera to a phone in the hallway, spoke into the phone and listened and looked at the camera.

> Subject 2: There was a blond guy with glasses sitting at a desk . . . not too cluttered but not exactly neat. He looked at the camera, rose, and walked out to the front right of the screen, his blue shirt billowing out a bit on his right over his white with light pattern tee-shirt . . . went into hallway, picked up phone, said something that didn't seem to be "hello," and then stood there looking kind of foolish for a bit.[18]

Not a single subject who viewed this video spontaneously reported anything different before and after the change. Even when prompted more specifically with the question, "Did you notice anything unusual about the video?" no subjects reported the change in the actor's identity or even his clothes from the first shot to the second. In a separate experiment, subjects watched the same video, but with the person-change pointed out to them. They were then asked whether they would have noticed the change had they viewed the video without the warning; 70 percent said they would have, compared with 0 percent who actually did. In this case, when people know about the change in advance, it becomes obvious and they all see it.[19] But when they don't expect the change, they completely miss it.

Professional Change Detectors

In most cases, we have almost no feedback about the limits on our ability to spot changes. We are aware only of the changes we do detect, and, by definition, changes we don't notice cannot modify our beliefs about our change-detection acumen. One group, though, has extensive experience looking for changes to scenes: script supervisors, the professionals responsible for detecting continuity errors when making movies.[20] Are they immune to change blindness? If not, do they at least have above-average awareness of the limits on their ability to retain and compare visual information from one moment to the next?

Trudy Ramirez has been a Hollywood script supervisor for nearly thirty years. She got her start working on commercials and quickly moved up to feature films. She has been the script supervisor on dozens of major movies and television programs, including *Total Recall, Basic Instinct, Terminator 2,* and *Spider-Man 3.* Dan spoke with Trudy Ramirez while she was working on the set of *Iron Man 2.*[21] "I have a very good visual memory, but I also take copious notes," she said. "I know that writing something down that I want to remember will often cement it into my memory." The key, according to Ramirez, is that script supervisors realize they don't need to remember everything. They focus on those details and aspects of a scene that matter, and ignore the rest.

"Most of the time, I will remember what is important to the scene," she continued. "We know what to look for. We know how to look." Everyone on a film set has their own area of focus when watching a scene, but script supervisors are trained to look for those aspects of the scene that are central to facilitating the editing of the film. Ramirez noted, "There are points in the action of a scene where you know the editor will most likely cut: when someone sits or stands up, when someone turns around, or when someone comes into or goes out of a room. . . . You start to develop a sense of how things will cut together, and therefore what is important to notice." Script supervisors also learn what is important from experience, often painfully: "Over time, we all make tragic continuity errors which train us what to look for—whatever you didn't notice that you later wished you had trains you to notice that thing or action next time."[22]

So script supervisors are not immune to change blindness. The difference between them and everyone else is that script supervisors get direct feedback that they can and do miss changes. Through their experience of searching for errors and learning about their mistakes, they become less prone to the illusion that they can notice and retain everything around them. Ramirez said, "The one thing this has taught me is that my memory is very fallible. It's shockingly fallible. You wouldn't necessarily have any reason to think about how your memory was working unless you were doing something such as script supervising where it's such an important part of it." Critically, though, she knows that other people have similar limits. "When I am watching a movie, the more into the story I am, the less I notice things that are out of continuity. If I'm being swept along by the story and I'm involved with the characters, I am much less apt to notice something out of visual continuity. If you're really into the story, huge continuity errors will go right by you—you're not looking for those kinds of details. . . . You can get away with a lot."

What does that say about people who make a habit of searching for continuity errors? If people spot continuity errors when watching a film, then the movie may have a bigger problem: It doesn't engage viewers' attention enough to keep them from searching for minor changes! Of course, some people will watch a movie multiple times just to look for errors. And if they do that, they are likely to find some. The impossibility of noticing everything is what guarantees the business prospects for books and websites on film flubs.

Do You Have Any Idea Who You're Talking To?

Professor Ulric Neisser, whose research inspired our gorilla experiment, watched the change blindness demonstration in which an actor changed into another person while answering a phone, and he pointed out a possible limitation of all of these studies: They all used videos. He commented that watching video is an inherently passive activity: The action unfolds in front of us, but we do not actively engage with it the way we do when we interact socially with other people. Neisser argued that change blindness might not occur if a person were changed in the middle of a real-world encounter rather than across a cut in a passively viewed motion picture. The two Dans thought Neisser probably was right, that people would notice such a change in the real world, but they decided to run an experiment to test Neisser's prediction anyway.

Imagine you are strolling across a college campus and up ahead of you, you see a man holding a map and looking lost. The man approaches you and asks directions to the library. You start giving him directions, and as you're pointing to the map, a couple of people behind you abruptly say "Excuse me, coming through," and they rudely carry a big wooden door right between you and the lost pedestrian. Once they pass, you finish giving directions. Would you notice if the original lost pedestrian were replaced by a different person as the workers carried the door through? What if the two people wore different clothes, differed in height by about three inches, had different builds, and had noticeably different voices? You would have to be pretty oblivious to miss the change. After all, you were in the middle of a conversation with the man, and you had plenty of time to look at him. That's certainly what the two Dans and Ulric Neisser thought.

That's also what more than 95 percent of undergraduates thought when asked whether they would notice.[23] And they were all wrong. All of us, undergraduates as well as scientists familiar with all of the research leading up to these experiments, fell prey to the illusion of memory. All were convinced that only the rare, unusually oblivious person could possibly miss the change. Yet nearly 50 percent of the people in the original experiment did not notice that they were talking to different people before and after the interruption![24]

Serendipitously, one day several years later when we were conducting a followup experiment at Harvard, many of the undergraduate psychology students were attending a lecture in the basement of the building. During the lecture, Professor Stephen Kosslyn (Chris's graduate school mentor and longtime collaborator) happened to describe the "door" study in detail as an example of research being conducted by other faculty members in the department. When they left the lecture, several students were overheard making comments like, "There's no way I would have missed that change." Our recruiter asked them if they would like to be in an experiment and sent them to the eighth floor. As they stood at a counter after filling out a form, the experimenter who had been talking to them ducked down behind the counter—ostensibly to file away some papers—and a different person stood up. All of the students missed the change![25]

Change blindness is a surprisingly pervasive phenomenon considering that it has only been studied intensely since the 1990s. It occurs for simple shapes on a computer display, for photographs of scenes, and for people in the middle of a real-world interaction.[26] And the illusion of memory leads people to believe that they're great at change detection even though they're lousy. This illusion is so powerful that even change blindness researchers regularly experience it. We only came to recognize the limits of our intuitions about memories when our own data repeatedly showed us how wrong we could be. Similarly, filmmakers learn about the illusion of memory the hard way, by seeing evidence of their own mistakes on the big screen. Trudy Ramirez, the Hollywood script supervisor, has experienced this many times: "The way you remember something, how your memory shapes what you think you saw, as sure as you think you are . . . often it's different if you can actually look back at it. There were times when I would have staked my life on something and later on realized I was wrong."

There are limits to change blindness, of course. When we spoke publicly about the early person-change studies, we were often asked whether people would notice if a man changed into a woman. "Of course they would," we thought, but of course our certainty was another reflection of the illusion of memory. The only way to find out was to try it. Later experiments in Dan's lab showed that people do in fact notice when you change a man into a woman or when you change the race of an actor in a movie. And people are more likely to notice a change to the identity of a person who is a member of their own social group.[27] But most other changes often go undetected.

Even when subjects notice the person swap in these real-world experiments, they're far from perfect in picking the original experimenter from a photographic lineup. And people who miss the change do no better with the lineup than they would have done by just guessing randomly.[28] In a brief encounter, we appear to store so little information about another person that we not only fail to see changes, but we also can't even identify the person we saw just minutes earlier. When you interact briefly with a stranger, there are only a few pieces of general information you can be certain of retaining: sex, race, and social group (student, blue-collar worker, businessperson, and so on). Most of the rest of what you perceive about the person probably won't make it into memory at all.

Recall Leslie Meltzer and Tyce Palmaffy, who witnessed a knife attack from their car but recalled it differently just moments later. In light of the evidence that people sometimes fail to notice that a person has almost instantaneously been replaced by someone completely different, Leslie and Tyce's discrepant eyewitness memories are unsurprising. After all, they were just observing the person from a distance, not standing face-to-face with him and giving him directions.

"I Sat Next to Captain Picard"

About ten years ago at a party Dan hosted, a colleague of ours named Ken Norman told us a funny story about sitting next to the actor Patrick Stewart (best known for his roles as Captain Jean-Luc Picard of *Star Trek* and Charles Xavier in the *X-Men* films) at a Legal Sea Food restaurant in Cambridge, Massachusetts. The story was prompted when Chris noticed that Dan had a small figurine of Captain Picard perched next to his television screen. "Can I buy your Captain Picard?" asked Chris. Dan said that it was not for sale. Chris offered five, then ten dollars. Dan refused. Chris eventually raised his bid to fifty dollars—for reasons that escape him now—but Dan still refused. (Neither of us remembers why Dan refused, but to this day, Picard has not left his place amid Dan's electronics.)

At this point Ken told us that at Legal Sea Food, Patrick Stewart had been dining with an attractive younger woman who, based on snippets of overheard conversation, appeared to be a publicist or agent. For dessert Stewart ordered Baked Alaska—a choice that stood out in memory because it appears rarely on restaurant menus. Toward the end of his meal, another distinctive event happened: Two members of the kitchen staff came out to Stewart's table and asked for his autograph, which he readily granted. Moments later, a manager appeared and apologized, explaining that the "Trekkie" cooks' action was against restaurant policy. Stewart shrugged off the supposed offense, and he and his companion were soon on their way.

The only problem with the story was that it had actually happened not to Ken, but to Chris. Ken had heard Chris tell the story some time before and had incorporated it into his own memory. In fact, Ken felt so strongly that the memory was his, and had so completely forgotten that Chris was the original raconteur, that even Chris's presence when Ken retold the story did not jog his memory of the way in which he had actually "encountered" Captain Picard. But when Chris pointed out the error, Ken quickly realized that this memory was not his own. This anecdote illustrates another aspect of the illusion of memory: When we retrieve a memory, we can falsely believe that we are fetching a record of something that happened to us rather than someone else.

Although we believe that our memories contain precise accounts of what we see and hear, in reality these records can be remarkably scanty. What we retrieve often is filled in based on gist, inference, and other influences; it is more like an improvised riff on a familiar melody than a digital recording of an original performance. We mistakenly believe that our memories are accurate and precise, and we cannot readily separate those aspects of our memory that accurately reflect what happened from those that were introduced later. That's how Ken appropriated Chris's story—he had a vivid memory for the event, but mistakenly attributed it to his own experience. In the scientific literature, this type of distortion is known as a *failure of source memory*. He forgot the source of his memory, but because it was so vivid, he assumed that it came from his own experience.

Source memory failures contribute to many cases of unintentional plagiarism. In the classes we teach, we occasionally encounter intentional plagiarism (or a gross misunderstanding of the right way to do research) when a student copies sections of a paper from Wikipedia or other sources. Unintentional plagiarism refers to cases in which people are convinced that an idea was their own when they actually learned about it from someone else. Recently, bestselling spiritual author Neale Donald Walsch was caught plagiarizing a story originally written by Candy Chand that had circulated on spirituality websites and blogs for more than a decade.[29] The story describes a group of students who were using placards to spell out "Christmas Love" in a winter pageant rehearsal. One student accidentally held her letter "m" upside down, resulting in the phrase "Christ was Love." Walsch posted the story to Beliefnet.com in December 2008 as if it had happened to his son Nicholas. But it actually happened to Chand's son, who also is named Nicholas, twenty years earlier—before Walsch's son was even born. In this case, it is clear that Walsch appropriated someone else's story. The question, though, is whether he was plagiarizing intentionally or whether he merely misappropriated the memory. In acknowledging a "serious error," Walsch stated:

> I am truly mystified and taken aback by this. . . . Someone must
> have sent it to me over the internet ten years or so ago. . . .
> Finding it utterly charming and its message indelible, I must
> have clipped and pasted it into my file of "stories to tell that have
> a message I want to share." I have told the story verbally so many

times over the years that I had it memorized . . . and then, somewhere along the way, internalized it as my own experience.

This case bears all the hallmarks of a failure of source memory.
Walsch remembered the story, having read and retold it many times.
The fact that the child in the story had the same name as his son made
it easier for him to come to believe that the memory was his. (Our friend
Ken Norman probably picked up Chris's story more readily because he
had dined at the same Legal Sea Food restaurant.) Walsch kept a record
of the story in his file and came to believe that he had written it. In his
interview with the *New York Times,* Walsch said, "I am chagrined and
astonished that my mind could play such a trick on me." Chand, however, thinks the theft was intentional: "If he knew this was wrong, he
should have known it was wrong before he got caught . . . quite frankly,
I'm not buying it." Both Chand's indignation and Walsch's astonish-
ment are entirely consistent with the illusion of memory. Walsch doesn't
understand how he could have mistakenly appropriated another person's
memory, and Chand doesn't believe that he could have done so innocently. They both think that memory must be more faithful to experience than it really is.

Just as we cannot be certain that Kenny Conley suffered from inattentional blindness when he reported not seeing Michael Cox being
beaten, we cannot say for certain whether Walsch's plagiarism was intentional or accidental. What we can say, though, is that it is possible that
Walsch internalized someone else's memory and lost track of the source
of the story. Such source memory failures are common, and they even can
be created in the laboratory. In a clever study, psychologists Kimberly
Wade, Maryanne Garry, Don Read, and Stephen Lindsay asked subjects
to view a doctored photograph showing the subject enjoying a hot air
balloon ride as a child.[30] The subjects were each interviewed several times,
and were asked each time to recall the event, or if they could not recall it,
to imagine that it *had* happened to themselves. Although none of the
subjects had ever taken a hot air balloon ride, the photograph and attempts to recall it led some of them to incorporate information about the

image into their personal narrative memories. Half the subjects created a false memory about the balloon ride, some embellishing their memories substantially beyond what was shown in the photograph.

The ability to change memories using doctored photographs has Orwellian ramifications. If we can induce false memories simply by editing images, it might be possible to literally revise history, changing the past by doctoring it. Using a similar approach, Dario Sacchi, Franca Agnoli, and Elizabeth Loftus showed subjects an edited version of the famous photograph of a single person standing in front of a column of tanks during the 1989 protests at Tiananmen Square in Beijing.[31] In the original version of the photograph, only the lone protester was visible on the wide road. The doctored version shows crowds of people lining a narrower road on both sides of the tanks. When they were quizzed about the historical facts of Tiananmen Square only moments later, those who viewed the doctored photograph believed that far more people had been at the protest.

Forgetting a Life-and-Death Matter

Memory distortions are not limited to irrelevant details like whether or not books were in an office or particular words were part of a list. In fact, they can apply to life-and-death decisions, even those that you yourself have made. Australian psychologist Stefanie Sharman and her colleagues conducted an experiment that calls to mind the classic *Seinfeld* episode in which Kramer asks Elaine to help him and his lawyer work through a long list to decide the medical circumstances under which he would be willing to carry on living. (Lawyer: "OK. One lung, blind and you're eating through a tube." Kramer: "Naw, that's not my style." Elaine: "Borrrr-ing.") The researchers interviewed adults and asked them to make (more realistic) decisions about which life-sustaining treatments they'd want if they were seriously ill.[32] For example, would they want only CPR performed, or would they also want to be fed artificially if necessary? They interviewed the same people twelve months later using the same questions.

Overall, 23 percent of all their decisions changed between the initial interview and the follow-up, meaning that people who said during the first interview that they would want a life-extending treatment said during the second interview that they wouldn't want it (or vice versa). That people would change their preferences is not terribly surprising. Perhaps they had discussed the possibilities with friends, relatives, or doctors in the interim; maybe they encountered news stories about end-of-life issues. What is striking is that 75 percent of the people who changed their minds were unaware that they had done so! They thought that the decision they reported in the second interview was the same as their decision in the first interview. Their memory for what they had said earlier was rewritten to match their current beliefs.

The illusion of memory leads us to assume—unless we receive direct evidence to the contrary—that our memories, beliefs, and actions are mutually consistent and stable over time. Amid the national grief after President Kennedy was assassinated, a poll showed that two-thirds of people claimed they had voted for him in the 50/50 squeaker election of 1960.[33] At least some of them must have revised their memories of how they voted three years earlier, probably to make them consistent with the positive feelings they had about their fallen leader. More broadly, we tend to assume that everything in our world is stable and unchanging unless something draws our attention to a discrepancy. When our beliefs change, though, our memories can change along with them. A living will you produced a few years ago may not reflect your current preferences—but you are likely to misremember its contents and assume that it expresses what you want today. If you become seriously ill and are unable to communicate, doctors will rely on this document and may inadvertently take actions that contradict your wishes.

Where Were You on 9/11?

Try to recall exactly where you were when you first heard about the attacks of September 11, 2001. If you're like us, you have a vivid memory of how you learned about the attacks, where you were, who else was with you, what you were doing immediately beforehand, and what you did immediately afterward. Chris recalls waking up late that morning, after the first plane had hit the World Trade Center. He listened to the *Howard Stern Show* on the radio until it ended around noon, at which point he turned on the TV. He got in touch with an Israeli colleague, who told him it was already obvious who the perpetrators must be, and he received an e-mail update from a friend who was living in Brooklyn, watching the events safely from her rooftop. He received another e-mail from the manager of his office building at Harvard, William James Hall, recommending evacuation.

Dan recalls working in his office that morning when his graduate student Stephen Mitroff came in to tell him that a plane hit the first tower. He spent the next few minutes seeking information online, and when the second plane hit, he turned on the television in his lab and he and his three graduate students watched the towers collapse. He then spent a few frantic minutes on the phone trying to reach his brother David's girlfriend because David was traveling back from New York to Boston that morning (he was sitting on a plane waiting to take off from LaGuardia Airport when the attacks happened). Dan remembers becoming concerned that the fifteen-story building he was in might also be a target. He left before noon to pick up his wife in downtown Boston and they went home together and watched the television coverage for the rest of the day.

Neither of us has any idea what we were doing or whom we talked to the day before 9/11. We suspect that the same is true for you. Your memories of 9/11 are more vivid, detailed, and emotional than your memories of more ordinary events from that time period. Memories of dramatic events of personal or national importance often are recalled in greater detail. Some significant events appear to be imprinted in our minds in a way that lets us play them back in video-like detail, perfectly preserved despite the passage of time. This intuition is powerful and pervasive. It is also wrong.

Such detailed memories for a significant event were first studied systematically in 1899 by Frederick Colgrove as part of his doctoral research at Clark University. Colgrove asked 179 middle-aged and older adults where they were when they heard about the assassination of Abraham Lincoln.[34] Even though he asked people to recall events that happened more than thirty years earlier, 70 percent remembered where they were and how they heard about it, and some provided exceptional amounts of detail.

Nearly eighty years later, social psychologists Roger Brown and James Kulik coined the term *flashbulb memories* to characterize these vivid, detailed memories for surprising and important events.[35] The name, by analogy to photography, reflects the idea that the details surrounding surprising and emotionally significant events are preserved in the instant they occur: Events meriting permanent storage are imprinted in the brain just as a scene is imprinted onto film. According to Brown and Kulik, the memory is "very like a photograph that indiscriminately preserves the scene in which each of us found himself when the flashbulb was fired."

In their study, Brown and Kulik surveyed eighty Americans (forty black and forty white) about a variety of events, most of which involved assassinations or attempted assassinations in the United States during the 1960s and 1970s. Much as Colgrove did before them, Brown and Kulik documented that all but one of their subjects had a flashbulb memory for the Kennedy assassination. Majorities had flashbulb memories for the assassinations of Bobby Kennedy and Martin Luther King, and many had flashbulb memories for other similar events.

In their research papers, Colgrove and Brown and Kulik provided vivid examples from their own memories to go along with the detailed, emotionally charged recollections their subjects had for these political assassinations. We all have such flashbulb experiences, and we can retrieve them with ease and fluency. Recounting or asking about a flashbulb memory can start a conversation that goes on for hours; try it the next time you're at a boring dinner party. It is the richness of these particular recollected experiences that leads us to believe so strongly in their accuracy. Ironically, the conclusions drawn from the initial research on flashbulb memories were based entirely on the illusion of

THE COACH WHO CHOKED 69

memory. The recollections of their subjects were so vivid and detailed that the researchers assumed they must be accurate.

After writing down his personal recollection of 9/11 for this book, Dan e-mailed his former students and asked them to send him their own for comparison. The first to respond was Stephen Mitroff, now a professor at Duke University:

> I got an email from my girlfriend saying a plane hit the World Trade Center. I did a quick look at CNN and then went into your office where you and Michael Silverman were chatting. I told you. We went back to my office and we were looking at the images on Steve Franconeri's computer. You surmised it must have been a small plane and the pilot lost control. We saw a picture of a huge commercial plane right next to the tower and you thought it must be a Photoshopped pic. We looked at various websites, including airline sites to look at the status updates of the flights that were being reported as hijacked. After more web searching, you hooked up the TV in our testing room and lots of people watched more in there. I *think* we witnessed one of the towers collapse, but I am not confident in that. We definitely were watching during one of the key events. We all started to feel an unwarranted uneasiness over being in the tallest building in town and left before lunch time. Michael and I walked back to Boston . . .

Dan's other two graduate students at the time both reported being away from the lab that morning, so they could not have followed the news reports with Dan. Mitroff remembered Michael Silverman— Dan's postdoctoral fellow at the time, now a professor at Mount Sinai School of Medicine—being in Dan's office but Dan did not. Dan e-mailed Silverman the same question he had asked the three Steves. The following report came back:

> I was standing in your office discussing something with you. The radio on your bookshelf was on. Mitroff yelled from his office

something to the extent that CNN was reporting that a plane just flew into the World Trade Center. I went to his office to see but the page was loading very slowly. I mentioned that little planes fly the Hudson corridor regularly, so I guessed it was possible. The page loaded and it showed a large plane flying toward the WTC. I said something to the extent that putting up a Photoshopped image like that was disgusting—I was still convinced that only a small plane had crashed. The next information we received came from your radio (CNN was slow and not loading anything additional). We heard that not one but two planes had hit. I then went to my office and tried to call my wife. She was also trying to call me. Neither of us could get through. . . . When I left my office, someone had turned on a television in the testing room. The picture was noisy. It showed that one tower had already dropped and we watched the second one fall. (I'm not sure if the second tower falling was live, but I suspect it wasn't.) You made the decision for us to leave and go home around 11:00. Mitroff and I walked to his apartment and then I walked home.

There are interesting similarities and differences among these accounts. First the similarities: Everyone agrees that Dan heard about the attack from Steve Mitroff, they spent some time searching online for information, and then Dan turned on the television in the lab where he and Mitroff watched footage of a tower collapsing. Now for the differences: Dan did not recall Michael Silverman being present and he mistakenly remembered his other graduate students being there. All three remember Mitroff coming into Dan's office, but Silverman remembers Mitroff yelling from his office first. Dan recalled nothing about a discussion of the image of a plane next to the tower; Mitroff recalled Dan commenting that the plane was small and that the image of a larger plane was edited; and Silverman recalls making those comments himself.

Three cognitive psychologists had vivid memories for what they experienced on 9/11, but their memories conflicted in several ways. If memory worked like a video recording, all three reports about 9/11 would be identical. In fact, there is no way to verify which of the accounts is most accurate. The best we can do is to assume that two independent and mutually consistent recollections are more likely to be correct than one recollection that conflicts with both. Many cases of memory failure are just like this, in that there is no documentary evidence to establish the ground truth of what actually happened.

In some cases, like Neil Reed's confrontation with Bobby Knight, it is possible to compare people's recollections to documentary evidence of what actually happened. President George W. Bush experienced a similar distortion to his memory of how he first learned about the attacks on the morning of 9/11. You might recall the video footage of Bush reading the story "The Pet Goat" to an elementary school class in Florida when his chief of staff, Andrew Card, walked in and whispered in his ear. His stunned reaction provided fodder for comics and commentators alike. That moment, caught on video, was how he heard about the plane hitting the *second* tower. It was his moment of realization that the United States was under attack. He'd already heard about the first plane before entering the classroom, but like many in the media, he believed that crash to have been a small aircraft accidentally veering into the tower.

On at least two occasions, Bush publicly recalled having seen the first plane hit the tower on television *before* entering the classroom. For example, on December 4, 2001, in response to a question from a young boy, he recalled, "I was sitting outside the classroom waiting to go in, and I saw an airplane hit the tower—the TV was obviously on, and I use[d] to fly myself, and I said, 'There's one terrible pilot.' And I said, 'It must have been a horrible accident.'" The problem is that the only video footage broadcast the day of the attacks was of the second plane. There was no video footage of the first plane's impact available until long afterward.[36] Bush's memory, although plausible, could not have been right. He correctly recalled Andrew Card entering the classroom following the crash of the second plane and telling him that America was under attack, but his memory of how and when he first heard about the attacks mixed up these details in a plausible but inaccurate way.

There was nothing necessarily malicious in Bush's false memory—details sometimes shift in memory from one time to another or from one event to another. Yet conspiracy theorists, suffering from the illusion of memory (among other things), decided that Bush's false recollections were not false at all, but Freudian slips that revealed a hidden truth. He said that he saw the first plane crash on television, so he must have seen it. And if he saw it, whoever shot that secret footage must have known where to point a camera in advance, so Bush must have known the attack was going to happen before it did. The illusion of memory made some people jump to the conclusion that the government deliberately permitted or possibly even planned the attacks, skipping right over the more plausible (but less intuitive) explanation that Bush simply conflated some aspects of his memory for the first and second plane impacts in the attack.[37]

Experiments building on Brown and Kulik's article on flashbulb memories have sought ways to verify the accuracy of these memories, often by obtaining recollections immediately after some tragic event and then testing the same people months or even years later. These studies consistently find that flashbulb memories, although richer and more vivid, are subject to the same sorts of distortions as regular memories. On the morning of January 28, 1986, the space shuttle *Challenger* exploded shortly after takeoff. The very next morning, psychologists Ulric Neisser and Nicole Harsch asked a class of Emory University undergraduates to write a description of how they heard about the explosion, and then to answer a set of detailed questions about the disaster: what time they heard about it, what they were doing, who told them, who else was there, how they felt about it, and so on.[38] Reports like these, written as soon as practicable after the event, provide the best possible documentation of what actually happened, just as the video of Bobby Knight and Neil Reed recorded the reality of the choking incident.

Two and a half years later, Neisser and Harsch asked the same students to fill out a similar questionnaire about the *Challenger* explosion. The memories the students reported had changed dramatically over time, incorporating elements that plausibly fit with how they could have learned about the events, but that never actually happened. For example, one subject reported returning to his dormitory after class and hearing a commotion in the hall. Someone named X told him what happened and he turned on the television to watch replays of the explosion. He recalled the time as 11:30 a.m., the place as his dorm, the activity as returning to his room, and that nobody else was present. Yet the morning after the event, he reported having been told by an acquaintance from Switzerland named Y to turn on his TV. He reported that he heard about it at 1:10 p.m., that he worried about how he was going to start his car, and that his friend Z was present. That is, years after the event, some of them remembered hearing about it from different people, at a different time, and in different company.

Despite all these errors, subjects were strikingly confident in the accuracy of their memories years after the event, because their memories were so vivid—the illusion of memory at work again. During a final interview conducted after the subjects completed the questionnaire the second time, Neisser and Harsch showed the subjects their own handwritten answers to the questionnaire from the day after the *Challenger* explosion. Many were shocked at the discrepancy between their original reports and their memories of what happened. In fact, when confronted with their original reports, rather than suddenly realizing that they had misremembered, they often persisted in believing their current "memory."

Those rich details you remember are quite often wrong—but they *feel* right. As Neil Reed said about his memory of being choked by Bobby Knight, *after* seeing the videotape of what really happened: "As far as people coming in between, I remember people coming between us."[39] A memory can be so strong that even documentary evidence that it never happened doesn't change what we remember.

Memories That Are Too Good to Be True

At a Thanksgiving dinner during the time we were writing this book, Chris's father, who served in the U.S. Army during World War II, recounted some of his memories of famous events. These included how he learned of Germany's invasion of Poland in 1939 (he was in summer camp at the time) and of the Japanese attack on Pearl Harbor in 1941 (he and a friend were listening to a football game on the radio when the broadcast was interrupted by a news bulletin). Chris asked his father what he remembered of 9/11. He said that he was trying to travel from Connecticut to New York City that morning, and that he left home before hearing any of the news. He had to change trains at New Haven, but he was turned back with the news of the plane crashes and a statement that no trains were being permitted to enter the city. He decided to take a taxi home, for which he negotiated a fixed rate rather than the metered charge. The driver was listening to a call-in show on the radio, but none of the calls were about the morning's news. He was wearing something like a turban on his head and appeared to be an Arab.[40]

This detail, that his taxi driver on the morning of 9/11 was of the same ethnicity or religion as the terrorists who attacked his destination, is a striking coincidence. We tend to put more trust in memories that include this sort of detail than we do in vague or generic recollections, especially when the detail has such a neat relationship to the rest of the story. Had Chris not been present, Ken Norman would have gotten away with his Captain Picard story in part because of the distinctiveness of the Baked Alaska, autograph-seeking cooks, and embarrassed manager. But as we have seen, these deceptively vivid details can be telltale traces of the processes of distortion and reconstruction that operate on memories *after* they are formed. Could the detail about the taxi driver be accurate? Certainly. Might Chris's father have fabricated the Arab driver out of whole cloth? Possibly. Could he have inadvertently combined two separate memories, one of going home by taxi on 9/11 and another of having an Arab taxi driver (a common experience for someone living in the New York area)? Absolutely. The ironic final twist does make for a more compelling story—which is exactly what our memory systems are constantly, unbeknownst to us, striving to do.

Let's revisit the story of Leslie and Tyce, the couple who witnessed a stabbing and were put on hold by 911. Within a minute of the event, they realized that they already disagreed about what they had seen. Despite recounting this story many times over the six years between the incident itself and their interviews with Chris, their memories have only diverged further: Leslie reported honking their horn to draw attention to the crime scene; when told of this, Tyce said "Really?" Leslie remembered being several lanes away from the sidewalk; Tyce recalled just a row of parked cars between them and the assault. Leslie thinks the attack happened in front of a dark, boarded-up building; Tyce recalls "a convenience store or takeout chicken store, a place with big neon lights in front." Leslie says the attacker was bigger than the victim; Tyce says the opposite. Leslie thinks it took about thirty seconds for 911 to pick up, and that the conversation lasted three or four minutes; Tyce remembers a five-minute wait followed by a one-minute conversation. And while we told you that Leslie placed the call from the passenger seat while Tyce was driving, Tyce remembers himself calling 911 while Leslie was driving. It seems that our memory systems do like to place us in the center of the action.[41]

Think back one last time to your own memory of how you learned about the attacks of September 11, 2001. Now that you know about the illusion of memory, you know that you should doubt the veracity of your own recollections. But if you still have trouble overcoming the convincing impression that your memory is right, you aren't alone. In a more recent flashbulb memory study, psychologists Jennifer Talarico and David Rubin examined people's accounts of how they heard about the 9/11 attacks.[42] Unlike all previous studies of flashbulb memories, theirs compared how well people remembered the flashbulb event with how well they remembered another event from about the same time. Thinking creatively and quickly at an emotional time, on September 12, 2001, Talarico and Rubin had a group of Duke University undergraduates come into the lab and complete a detailed questionnaire about how they first heard about the attacks. They also had the undergraduates recall another personal memory of their choosing that was still fresh in their minds from the few days just prior to the attacks. Then either 1, 6, or 32 weeks later, they asked their subjects to recall each event again. *All of the memories,* whether of 9/11 or of the more ordinary event, became more inaccurate as more time passed. The longer the gap between the original recollection and the later test, the less consistent the memories, and the more false details they included.

Talarico and Rubin did one more clever thing. They asked the students to rate how strongly they believed in the accuracy of their own memories. For the everyday memory, people had a good sense of how accurate they were: As their memories got worse, they were less confident in them. That is, they did *not* suffer from the illusion of memory for everyday events. Just as people know that memory for arbitrary facts is fallible, they know that they forget otherwise trivial details about their experiences. When they cannot recollect the details well, they become less trusting of their memories.

The flashbulb memories showed an entirely different pattern, though. Subjects continued to believe strongly in the accuracy of their memories even though their memories became less accurate over time. The illusion of memory—the difference between how accurate our memories are and how accurate we think they are—operates at maximum strength for flashbulb memories. Early writing on flashbulb memories suggested that they were created by the activation of a special "print now" mechanism in the brain. In light of Talarico and Rubin's findings, it may be better to think of this mechanism as saying instead "believe now."

Can We Ever Trust Our Memories?

In many cases, memory distortions and embellishments are minor matters, but in some contexts they have tremendous consequences, precisely because of the illusion of memory. When people are subject to the illusion of memory, they impugn the intentions and motivations of those who are innocently misremembering. The power of this illusion was revealed in a crucial incident in the 2008 presidential campaign. Running against Barack Obama for the Democratic nomination, Hillary Clinton repeatedly emphasized her greater experience in international affairs. In a speech at George Washington University, she described a particularly harrowing March 1996 mission to Tuzla, Bosnia: "I remember landing under sniper fire. There was supposed to be some kind of a greeting ceremony at the airport, but instead we just ran with our heads down to get into the vehicles to get to our base." Unfortunately for Clinton, the *Washington Post* looked into her story and published a photograph showing not a dash for cover but . . . a greeting ceremony, featuring the then First Lady kissing a Bosnian child who had just read a welcoming poem. Out of one hundred contemporary news reports of the event, none even mentioned a security threat. Several news videos also surfaced, all showing a calm stroll from the plane to an uneventful ceremony on the tarmac.

A commenter on the *Post*'s website responded to the fact-checking article: "There are only three ways to explain Clinton's story here: (a) she is a bald-faced liar; (b) her perception of reality is utterly skewed; or (c) her memory is utterly demented." Political commentator Peggy Noonan wrote in the *Wall Street Journal* that "we have to hope they were lies, because if they weren't, if she thought what she was saying was true, we are in worse trouble than we thought. . . . It was as if she'd watched the movie *Wag the Dog,* with its fake footage of a terrified refugee woman running frantically from mortar fire, and found it not a cautionary tale about manipulation and politics, but an inspiration." A cover of the *New Republic* depicted a bug-eyed Clinton hearing "voices in her head" and ranting that she offered to sacrifice her own life to protect her traveling companions in Bosnia ("And I said to Sinbad, 'Leave me, save yourself!'"). This is the typical response of the human mind to another person's false memory, especially an arguably self-serving memory like Clinton's grace-under-fire brush with death. Even Bill Clinton later proffered commonsense excuses for his wife's memory lapse, claiming (incorrectly) that she made the comments late at night and pointing out (correctly but perhaps unhelpfully) that she was sixty years old.

An entirely plausible alternative explanation for Clinton's fictitious snipers is that, like all fallible human minds, hers automatically and unconsciously reconstructed the landing in Tuzla to be consistent with the image of herself that she was convinced was accurate. Like Neil

Reed's memory of being reprimanded by Bobby Knight, Clinton's memory of arriving in Bosnia was systematically distorted to become consistent with her internalized, personal narrative. Like Reed, and the students whose flashbulb memories of the *Challenger* explosion proved inaccurate, Clinton could easily have had full confidence in the accuracy of her memory. And, as in Reed's case, videos revealed the truth. Hillary Clinton's distorted memory contributed to her loss of the presidential nomination by helping to revivify the popular impression, fair or not, that she would say anything to get elected (an impression that was compounded by her initial refusal to acknowledge the error after the videos surfaced).[43]

Is it possible to distinguish calculated deception from accidental distortion? We noted earlier that the illusion of memory does not apply equally to all memories. We are more aware of the limits on our ability to remember arbitrary facts and details, and we do not expect others to remember such details. We do not expect people to be able to remember random fifteen-digit numbers, although even for digit memory, people do overestimate their own ability to remember. It turns out that more than 40 percent of respondents to a survey thought they could remember ten random digits, even though less than 1 percent of people can actually do this when they are tested.[44] However, the illusion of memory is more powerful when we remember personally relevant information or experiences. The critical factor driving the illusion seems to be the extent to which a memory triggers a strong recollective experience. In other words, if you recall *how* you experienced and learned something rather than merely *what* you experienced and learned, you are far more likely to trust the veracity of your memory. Just as the vividness of our visual perception makes us think we are paying attention to more than we are, our experience of fluent, vivid recollection fuels the illusion of memory. When we recall a set of arbitrary digits or facts, we do not have a strong recollective experience. When we recall how we learned about the 9/11 attacks, we do. That is why Hillary Clinton and Neil Reed held firm to what they remembered—they had distinct and powerful recollections of what happened, and the vividness of their memories led them to believe them more strongly.[45]

The vividness of our recollections is tied to how they affect us emotionally. For most people, lists of numbers do not inspire fear or sadness, but thoughts of 9/11 do. And these emotions affect how we *think* we remember, even if they do not affect how much we *actually* remember. Subjects in an experiment were asked to view either emotionally neutral photographs, such as a farm scene, or strongly arousing and negative images, such as a gun pointed right at the camera.[46] Later, when asked to decide whether they had seen these images before, they had stronger recollective experiences for the emotional pictures than the neutral ones. Emotional memories, like the ones we have for 9/11, are more likely to induce strong, vivid recall—regardless of whether they are accurate. Beware of memories accompanied by strong emotions and vivid details—they are just as likely to be wrong as mundane memories, but you're far less likely to realize it.

Unfortunately, people regularly use vividness and emotionality as an indicator of accuracy; they use these cues to assess how confident they are in a memory. Critically, people also judge the accuracy of *another person's* memory based on how much confidence that person expresses in the memory. As we will see in the next chapter, the tendency to assume that confidently recalled memories are accurate ones illustrates another cognitive illusion: the illusion of confidence.

what smart chess players and stupid criminals have in common

ONE SUMMER DAY when he was in graduate school, Chris woke up with a headache. This wasn't unusual—he has always been prone to headaches. Later that day the aches spread to the rest of his body, and he began to feel exhausted and apathetic. It was a chore to get up from bed, walk into the living room of his apartment, sit down, and turn on the TV. His whole body hurt when he tried to stand up. Simple tasks like taking a shower left him breathless. The symptoms suggested a bad flu, but strangely he had no respiratory symptoms, and July is not exactly the height of flu season. After feeling awful for a few days, Chris went to Harvard's health service. The nurse who saw him concluded that it probably was a virus and told him to rest and stay hydrated.

The next day, a Sunday, his symptoms unchanged, Chris took one of those enervating showers. Moving slowly to conserve energy, he turned to let the water hit the back of his legs, and just when it did he felt a sharp pain. Twisting his neck and looking down, he saw a huge red rash that looked like a sunburst, right in the middle of his left calf. It was much larger than any mosquito bite he'd ever seen. Armed with a new symptom, he went into the after-hours care department and proudly displayed the rash. The doctor on duty asked Chris whether he'd been bitten by a tick recently. At first Chris was inclined to say no, since he'd never even seen a tick in the city of Cambridge, Massachusetts. But then he remembered that he'd visited his parents in Armonk, a suburb of New York City, a couple of weeks earlier, and had spent time with his mother in her vegetable garden. There were plenty of ticks there. The doctor showed Chris a picture from a medical book that illustrated the characteristic skin rash produced from infection by *Borrelia burgdorferi,* the tick-borne bacteria that cause Lyme disease. It looked exactly like Chris's calf.[1]

If Lyme disease isn't diagnosed early, it becomes more difficult to treat and has the potential to cause chronic disability. After the doctor explained the diagnosis, she excused herself from the room. She returned moments later with another book, in which she looked up the treatment for acute Lyme disease. She wrote a prescription for twenty-one days of the antibiotic doxycycline and handed it to Chris.

Chris was a little unnerved by this experience. First, the diagnosis itself seemed ominous. But more unsettling was the doctor's open consultation of reference books during the session. Chris had never seen a doctor do this before, and this one did it twice. Did she know what she was doing? In the northeastern United States, where Lyme disease is prevalent, how could an urgent-care doctor not be familiar with its diagnosis and treatment? Chris went straight to the drugstore to fill the prescription, but he couldn't help feeling uneasy about the doctor's uncertainty.

If you encountered a doctor who had to look up the diagnostic criteria and recommended treatment for your condition, wouldn't you wonder too? To do so would only be natural: We all tend to think of a confident doctor as a competent one and an uncertain doctor as a potential malpractice suit. We treat confidence as an honest signal of a person's professional skill, accurate memory, or expert knowledge. But as you'll see in this chapter, the confidence that people project, whether they are diagnosing a patient, making decisions about foreign policy, or testifying in court, is all too often an illusion.

Where Everyone Thinks They Are Underrated

To understand this illusion of confidence, we will begin in an unlikely place: the ballroom of the Adams Mark Hotel in Philadelphia, longtime site of the aptly named World Open, one of the largest annual open chess tournaments in the world. Anyone who pays the entry fee, from novice to grandmaster, can play. In 2008, more than fourteen hundred players competed for over $300,000 in prize money. The scene is not necessarily what you'd expect. For one thing, silence does not reign; there is a constant patter of chess pieces clicking against other pieces and buttons on chess clocks being slapped as players make their moves. Outside the playing rooms, it's even noisier. Players chatter about the games they just finished, the games they're about to play, and even about the games they're playing at that moment. (The rules permit general conversation about your game, as long as you don't solicit or receive advice from anyone.) The players themselves aren't all like the geeky, dateless high school chess team members you remember. Nor are they all bearded, pensive old men. Some could definitely use a shower or a makeover, but most are normal-looking children, parents, lawyers, doctors, engineers; there are also professional chess players, many from foreign countries. One stereotype does hold true, though: There is a distinct absence of women. Fewer than 5 percent of tournament chess players are female.

The strangest thing about the players in this tournament—indeed, about the players in every chess tournament—is that they know precisely how good they are at chess compared with the other players. This is not true of most activities in life, or even of most competitive endeavors. There is no master ranking scale to tell you how you compare in skill with other drivers, business managers, teachers, or parents. Even professions like law and medicine have no clear way of determining who is best. This lack of a clear measure of ability makes it easy to get an inflated sense of your own skill. But chess has a mathematically objective, public rating system that provides up-to-date, accurate, and precise numerical information about a player's "strength" (chess jargon for ability) relative to other players. All tournament players know that if you win a tournament game, your rating goes up, and if you lose a game, your rating goes down. Battling a higher-rated player to a draw also raises your rating, while drawing with a lower-rated player reduces it. Ratings are public knowledge and are printed next to each player's name on tournament scoreboards; many players ask their opponent "What's your rating?" before beginning a game. Ratings are valued so highly that chess players will remember their opponents better by their ratings than by their names or faces. "I beat a 1726" or "I lost to a 1455" are not uncommon things to hear in the hallway outside the playing room.

In July 1998, the average U.S. Chess Federation rating of the 27,562 people who'd played at least twenty tournament games was 1337. Masters are players rated 2200 or higher. Chris achieved this milestone when he was in college. Dan had a rating just under 1800 in high school but hasn't played competitively since then. Comparing two players' ratings gives the odds that one will defeat the other. Ratings are set and adjusted so that over a long series of games, a player rated two hundred points higher than his opponent should score about 75 percent of the points (wins count as one point, draws count as half a point). A player rated four hundred points higher than his or her opponent is expected to win almost every game.

Despite playing hundreds of tournament games in high school and being well above average for a tournament player, Dan never beat a master-level player, and he would stand effectively no chance of beating Chris in a tournament game. Similarly, Chris has defeated only one grandmaster in tournament play, despite once being ranked among the top 2 percent of players nationally. The differences in skill between these levels are just too large. If you consistently beat a player with the same rating as yours, then your rating will go up and theirs will go down so that the forecasts predict that you will beat them in the future. Unlike the rankings published for most sports, the chess rating system is extremely accurate; for practical purposes, your rating is a nearly perfect indicator of your ability. Armed with knowledge of their own ratings, and the workings of the rating system, players ought to be exquisitely aware of how competent they are. But what do they actually think about their own abilities?

Together with our friend Dan Benjamin, who was then an undergraduate student at Harvard and is now an economics professor at Cornell University, we ran an experiment at the World Open in Philadelphia and at another tournament, the U.S. Amateur Team Championship in Parsippany, New Jersey. As players walked by on their way to or from their games we asked them to fill out a short questionnaire. We posed two simple questions: "What is your most recent official chess rating?" and "What do you think your rating should be to reflect your true current strength?"[2]

As expected, the players knew their ratings: Half reported their ratings exactly, and most of the rest were off by only a few points. Since the players know what they are rated, they ought to be able to correctly answer the second question about what they *should* be rated. The correct answer *is* their current rating, because the rating system's design ensures that ratings are an accurate measure of skill. But only 21 percent of the players in our experiment actually said their current rating reflected their true strength. About 4 percent thought they were overrated, and the other 75 percent believed they were underrated. The magnitude of their overconfidence in their own playing ability was stunning: On average, these competitive chess players thought they were ninety-nine points underrated, which means they believed that they would win a match against another player *with the exact same rating as their own* by a two-to-one margin—a crushing victory. Of course, in reality the most likely outcome of a match against a player with the same rating as their own would be a tie.

What explains this extreme overconfidence in the face of concrete evidence for their actual skills? Not a lack of familiarity with chess:

These players had played the game for an average of twenty years. Not a lack of feedback about their competitive skill levels: They had been playing in rated tournaments for thirteen years, and their average rating was 1751, well above the average player's. Not being out of touch with their own skill level (from being out of practice): Over half had played at least one other tournament within the two months before we surveyed them.

Perhaps the players interpreted our question slightly differently than we had intended. Maybe they were predicting what their ratings *would be* once the system caught up to their true strength. Because ratings are adjusted only after tournaments, and the updated ratings sometimes take a month or two to be published, it is possible for rapidly improving players to be systematically underrated in the official lists, because they are improving at a rate too fast for their ratings to keep up. We checked our subjects' ratings a year later, and the players were rated almost exactly as they had been when we first did the experiment: one hundred points lower than their own estimates of their skill. In fact, even after five years, they still hadn't reached the levels they had estimated as their actual strength. The overconfidence that players displayed cannot be explained by a reasonable expectation of future improvement.[3] Our tournament chess players, despite their long and intimate experience with competitive chess ratings, overestimated their abilities. They suffered from our third everyday illusion: the *illusion of confidence.*

The illusion of confidence has two distinct but related aspects. First, as with the chess players, it causes us to overestimate our own qualities, especially our abilities relative to other people. Second, as Chris experienced in the doctor's office, it causes us to interpret the confidence—or lack thereof—that other people express as a valid signal of their own abilities, of the extent of their knowledge, and of the accuracy of their memories. This wouldn't be a problem if confidence in fact had a close relationship with these things, but the reality is that confidence and ability can diverge so far that relying on the former becomes a gigantic mental trap, with potentially disastrous consequences. Thinking you're better at chess than you really are is only the beginning.

"Unskilled and Unaware of It"

Charles Darwin observed that "ignorance more frequently begets confidence than does knowledge."[4] In fact, those who are the least skilled are the most likely to think better of themselves than they should—they disproportionately experience the illusion of confidence. Some of the most striking examples of this principle come from criminals, an idea captured in Woody Allen's first feature film, *Take the Money and Run*.[5] Allen stars as Virgil Starkwell, a boy raised in difficult circumstances who turns to a life of crime as a teenager. But Virgil never manages to achieve success in his profession. As a child he tries to steal gumballs but gets his hand stuck and has to run down the street carrying the entire machine. As an adult he tries to rob a bank, but the tellers can't read his holdup note and the police arrive before he can explain it to them. He tries to break out of jail by carving a gun out of soap and coating it with black shoe polish, but as he leaves, it pours rain and the guards notice suds frothing from his weapon.

Stupid criminals are a staple of film and television comedy in part because they violate the stereotype of the criminal mastermind—the genius-turned-psychopath James Bond villain. But this stereotype is not representative of actual criminals, at least not those who get caught. Smut Brown, the murder suspect whom Kenneth Conley chased down in Boston, was a high school dropout who was arrested eight times in a single year.[6] People convicted of crimes are, on average, less intelligent than noncriminals.[7] And they can be spectacularly foolish. A high school classmate of Dan's decided to vandalize the school—by spray-painting his own initials on the back wall. A Briton named Peter Addison went one step further and vandalized the side of a building by writing "Peter Addison was here." Sixty-six-year-old Samuel Porter tried to pass a one-million-dollar bill at a supermarket in the United States and became irate when the cashier wouldn't make change for him.

In a brilliant article entitled "Unskilled and Unaware of It," social psychologists Justin Kruger and David Dunning of Cornell University tell the story of McArthur Wheeler, who robbed two banks in

Pittsburgh in 1995 without using a disguise.[8] Security camera footage of him was broadcast on the evening news the same day as the robberies, and he was arrested an hour later. According to Kruger and Dunning, "When police later showed him the surveillance tapes, Mr. Wheeler stared in incredulity. 'But I wore the juice,' he mumbled. Apparently, Mr. Wheeler was under the impression that rubbing one's face with lemon juice"—a substance used by generations of children to write hidden messages—"rendered it invisible to videotape cameras."[9]

Kruger and Dunning wondered whether Wheeler's combination of incompetence and obliviousness was unusual (perhaps a profile peculiar to failed criminals) or whether it might be a more general phenomenon. In their first experiment, they zeroed in not on criminal ability, which is (we hope) uncommon, but on a quality that most people believe they possess: a sense of humor. They asked whether people who are bad at understanding which jokes are funny and which are not mistakenly believe they have a perfectly good sense of humor. But how to measure sense of humor?

Unlike chess, there is no rating system for sense of humor, but one clear lesson of the past century of psychology research is that almost any quality can be measured well enough to be studied scientifically. We don't mean to say that it's easy to capture the ineffable qualities that make something funny. If it were, then someone with no sense of humor could write a computer program to generate good jokes. What we mean is that people are remarkably consistent in judging what's funny and what's groan-worthy. The same is true for many other seemingly immeasurable qualities. You might think that beauty is in the eye of the beholder, but it isn't—when asked to judge the attractiveness of a set of faces, people give remarkably consistent ratings despite individual differences in tastes and preferences. This is the reason why most people will never be models.[10]

To create their sense-of-humor test, Kruger and Dunning selected thirty jokes written by Woody Allen, Al Franken, Jack Handey, and Jeff Rovin, and e-mailed them to professional comedians, eight of whom agreed to rate how funny the jokes were. Kruger and Dunning had them use a funniness scale that ranged from 1 to 11, with 1 meaning "not at all funny" and 11 meaning "very funny." You can test your own sense of humor right now. Decide which of these two jokes is funnier:

1. Question: What is as big as a man, but weighs nothing? Answer: His shadow.

2. If a kid asks where rain comes from, I think a cute thing to tell him is "God is crying." And if he asks why God is crying, another cute thing to tell him is "Probably because of something you did."

The experts generally agreed about which jokes were funny and which were not. That's not surprising, considering that expert comedians succeed as comedians because they know what most people will find humorous. The first joke listed above received the lowest rating (1.3) of the thirty that were tested, and the second one, from Jack Handey's "Deep Thoughts" on *Saturday Night Live,* received the highest rating (9.6). Kruger and Dunning then asked undergraduate students at Cornell to rate the same jokes. The idea was that people with a good sense of humor would rate the jokes similarly to the professional funny people, but people with a bad sense of humor would rate them differently. The top scorers agreed with the comedians 78 percent of the time on whether or not a joke was funny. The bottom scorers—those in the bottom quarter of the subjects on the sense-of-humor test—actually *disagreed* with the comedians about whether a joke was funny more often than they agreed with them. They thought only 44 percent of the funny jokes were funny, but that 56 percent of the unfunny jokes were.[11]

Next, Kruger and Dunning asked their subjects to assess their own "ability to recognize what's funny" by writing down the percentage of other Cornell students they thought were worse than themselves in this skill. The average student is, by definition, better than 50 percent of other students. But 66 percent of the subjects thought they had a better sense of humor than most of their peers.[12] Where did that sixteen-percentage-point overconfidence effect come from? Almost exclusively from those participants with the worst sense of humor! People who scored in the lowest 25 percent on the sense-of-humor test thought they had an above-average sense of humor.

The same pattern held in our study of chess players who thought they should have been more highly rated than they actually were. The players who considered themselves most underrated were disproportionately found in the *bottom half* of the ability range. On average, these weaker players thought they were underrated by 150 points, whereas the players in the top half in ability claimed to be only 50 points underrated.[13] Stronger players thus were somewhat overconfident, but weaker players were extremely overconfident.

These findings help to explain why competitive reality shows like *America's Got Talent* and *American Idol* attract so many people who audition but have no hope of qualifying, let alone winning. Many are just trying to get a few seconds of TV time, but some, like William Hung with his famously awful rendition of Ricky Martin's "She Bangs," seem to believe that they're much more skilled than they actually are.

In other experiments, Kruger and Dunning showed that this unskilled-and-unaware effect can be measured in many areas besides humor, including logical reasoning and English grammar skills. It probably applies to any area of human experience. Whether in real life or on the television comedy *The Office*, we have all encountered obliviously incompetent managers. People who graduate last in their medical school classes are still doctors—and probably think they are pretty good ones.

Aside from showing that the depth of a stupid criminal's plight can be quantified, can psychology offer any help to the McArthur Wheelers of the world? The answer to this depends on the source of their problem. The incompetent face two significant hurdles. First, they are below average in ability. Second, since they don't realize that they are below average, they are unlikely to take steps to improve their ability. McArthur Wheeler didn't know that he needed to become a better criminal before taking on the challenge of robbing banks. But what kept him from that realization? Why couldn't he imagine executing his plan for robbing a bank and realize that he didn't fully grasp everything involved? Why didn't he question his own competence?

Our colleague Brian Scholl, the Yale psychology professor who worked with us on some of the inattentional blindness studies described in Chapter 1, tells an anecdote that might shed some light on the reasons why the illusion of confidence is so powerful. In his graduate school days at Rutgers University in New Jersey, he learned to play the ancient and challenging board game Go. Brian found that with some practice, he could beat all of his friends. While visiting New York, he had an opportunity to test his skills against an acquaintance who was a top-notch Go player. To his own surprise, the match was close and he ended up losing by just half a point. He came away from the game with a newfound sense of confidence in his skills. Unfortunately, his confidence came crashing to Earth when he talked with a professor in his department who was an expert Go player. When he described his success against the Go expert, she just shook her head and rolled her eyes. "Brian," she said, "don't you know that when a good Go player is facing a much weaker player, they sometimes challenge themselves by trying to win by as few points as possible?"

Brian's error of ascribing his Go results to his own skill, although reasonable, reflects a general tendency we all have to interpret feedback about our abilities in the most positive possible light. We tend to think that our good performances reflect our superior abilities, while our mistakes are "accidental," "inadvertent," or a result of circumstances beyond our control, and we do our best to ignore evidence that contradicts these conclusions. If incompetence and overconfidence are linked, would training incompetent people to be more skilled improve their understanding of their own skill levels? Kruger and Dunning found just that in a later experiment: Teaching the people who did worst on a logical reasoning task to perform the task better significantly (although not completely) reduced their overconfidence. Making people more competent is the way—or at least one way—to make them better judges of their competence.[14]

The finding that incompetence causes overconfidence is actually re-assuring. It tells us that as we study and practice a task, we get better at both performing the task and knowing how well we perform it. Think of it this way: When people start learning a new skill, their skill level is low and their confidence is often higher than it should be—they are overconfident. As their skills improve, their confidence also increases, but at a slower rate, so that eventually, at a high level of skill, their confidence levels are appropriate for their skill levels (or, at least, they are closer to the appropriate levels). The most dangerous kind of overconfidence in our abilities comes not when we are already skilled at a task but when we are still unskilled.

Once you know about this aspect of the illusion of confidence, you can start to pay more attention to what confidence really means, for yourself and for others. If you are just learning a new task, you now know that you should hedge your estimate of how well you are doing. You can also recognize that other people are most likely to be overconfident when they are first learning a task. When your children are learning to drive, they will be more confident of their skill than they should be. Managers who have just been promoted to new positions are likely to display unwarranted certainty in their own actions. And keep in mind that it is gaining real skill in a task, not just doing it more and more, that makes confidence a truer signal of ability. Experience does not guarantee expertise.

Brian Scholl's Go anecdote shows how we tend to assume the best of our abilities (and the worst of our adversary's abilities). Unwarranted certainty about our own competence spans ability, gender, and nationality. According to our national survey, 63 percent of Americans consider themselves to be above average in intelligence. Perhaps unsurprisingly, men were more confident in their intelligence than women, with 71 percent judging themselves to be smarter than average. But even among women, significantly more than half—57 percent—thought themselves to be smarter than the average person. This overconfidence isn't limited to arrogant Americans; according to a recent survey of a representative sample of Canadians, approximately 70 percent considered themselves "above average" in intelligence too. Nor is this overconfidence a new phenomenon, a reflection of some ambiguity in the concept of intelligence, an artifact of North American narcissism, or an inflated twenty-first-century notion of self-esteem: A 1981 study found that 69 percent of Swedish college students estimated themselves to be superior to 50 percent of their peers in driving ability, and 77 percent believed they were in the top 50 percent in safety. Most people also consider themselves to be above average in attractiveness.[15]

This illusion of confidence occurs automatically, without our actually reflecting on the situation. Only when direct, incontrovertible evidence forces us to confront our limitations can we see through the illusion. The disillusionment that Brian Scholl experienced after learning that he'd been played by the Go expert forced him to recalibrate his beliefs in his own skills, diminishing his overconfidence. If Brian kept playing Go, his ability would improve and his level of confidence would move closer to his level of skill. Competence helps to dispel the illusion of confidence. The key, though, is having definitive evidence of your own skills—you have to become good enough at what you do to recognize your own limitations.

We don't want you to think we believe that people are nothing but bluster and bravado, always overstating their abilities and trying to deceive others. In fact, people who are highly skilled occasionally suffer from the opposite problem. Almost all of the new teachers or professors we have met, especially those who achieved some early success in their careers, are convinced that they are fooling people—that they aren't really as good as people think they are.[16] Recall Kruger and Dunning's humor experiment. We didn't tell you this before, but the subjects in the top 25 percent in sense of humor didn't fully realize how good their senses of humor were—they actually *underestimated* the number of their peers who were less funny.[17] Overconfidence is more common—and more dangerous—but underconfidence like this does exist.

A Crisis of Confidence

The combination of incompetence and overconfidence gives us hilarious stories of stupid criminals and entertaining video clips of deluded *American Idol* aspirants, but misplaced confidence can have more insidious effects as well. Western society places extraordinary value on individual self-confidence; a life lived without confidence is not a worthy life. David Baird's self-help book *A Thousand Paths to Confidence* begins by declaring, "Every moment of our life is absolutely precious and is not to be wasted in self-doubt. The wish to be confident and to live life with confidence is the vital first step. If you are prepared to take it, congratulate yourself—you have begun your journey on the path to confidence."[18] A popular business book by Harvard professor Rosabeth Moss Kanter, not coincidentally titled *Confidence,* argues that maintaining confidence perpetuates winning streaks, while losing it can trigger losing streaks, and that "confidence shapes the outcomes of many contests of life—from simple ball games to complex enterprises, from individual performance to national culture."[19]

The central premise of the Albert Brooks movie *Defending Your Life* is that only those who acted confidently while they were alive can proceed to the next level in the afterlife. The power of confidence pervades parenting advice as well, with a recent cover story in *Parents* magazine offering tips on how to "raise a confident child," promising "the most effective ways to help your child become happy, self-assured, and successful."[20] Actress Tina Fey echoed this sentiment upon accepting an Emmy Award for her television comedy *30 Rock:* "I thank my parents for somehow raising me to have confidence that is disproportionate with my looks and abilities. Well done. That is what all parents should do."

President Jimmy Carter thought that confidence had even broader significance. On national television in July 1979 he gave his most famous presidential speech, in which he reported the grave lesson he had learned from a series of private meetings with politicians, businesspeople, clergy, and other citizens. After quoting nineteen of these people (including, though without attribution, first-term Arkansas

governor Bill Clinton), many of whom were sharply critical of his leadership and gloomy about the country's economic prospects, he diagnosed the problem not as one of politics or policy, but of psychology:

> I want to talk to you right now about a fundamental threat to
> American democracy. . . . The threat is nearly invisible in ordi-
> nary ways. It is a crisis of confidence. It is a crisis that strikes
> at the very heart and soul and spirit of our national will. . . . The
> erosion of our confidence in the future is threatening to destroy
> the social and the political fabric of America.[21]

The president was especially troubled by polls that suggested "a majority of people believe that the next five years will be worse than the
past five years," and by what he perceived as growing consumerism and
disrespect for traditional institutions. He went on to propose a series of
new energy-related policies intended to gradually reduce the country's
use of imported oil. Whether or not his diagnosis of America's mood was
correct, and regardless of whether changing energy sources was the right
prescription, after an initially positive reaction and an 11-percent jump
in his job-approval ratings, many commentators assailed Carter for seemingly blaming the government's failings on the people.[22] This speech became known as the "malaise speech" because of comments Clark Clifford,
a Democratic party wise man, had made to journalists before the speech
about what he perceived to be Carter's concerns about the country.
Carter's pollster, Patrick Cadell, had also used the word in a memo to the
president that was later leaked to the press. Ironically, Carter never once
used the word "malaise," but he did mention "confidence" fifteen times.
In his mind, a sort of collective self-confidence was the key ingredient in
the recipe for the nation's success.

Time and again, people embrace certainty and reject tentativeness,
whether in their own beliefs and memories, the counsel of an adviser, the
testimony of a witness, or the speech of a leader during a crisis. Indeed,
we pay great attention to confidence—in ourselves, our leaders, and those
around us—particularly when the facts or the future are uncertain. In
the 1980s, the investment bank Drexel Burnham Lambert and its star

financier Michael Milken were able to catalyze hostile corporate take-overs merely by claiming in a letter to be "highly confident" that they could raise the necessary funds.[23] Before they invented the aptly named "highly confident letter," Milken and his colleagues had to spend weeks or months making financial arrangements, work that might prove wasted if the deal didn't go through. Expressing their confidence in advance turned out to be just as effective—not to mention faster and cheaper—once Drexel and Milken's reputations preceded them into battle.

According to journalist Bob Woodward, in late 2002 President George W. Bush had doubts about launching an invasion of Iraq, so he asked CIA director George Tenet directly about the strength of the evidence that Saddam Hussein possessed unconventional weapons. Tenet said, "It's a slam dunk case!" Bush repeated, "George, how confident are you?" Tenet's reply: "Don't worry, it's a slam dunk!" Weeks into the war, White House spokesman Ari Fleischer expressed "high confidence" that weapons of mass destruction would yet be found. As of this writing, they are still missing, and an exhaustive government investigation has concluded that they were not there to be found.[24]

Why does confidence have such a hold on us? Why do we have such an overwhelming and often unnoticed inclination to take another person's outward confidence as an honest signal of his or her inner knowledge, ability, and resolve? As we have seen, the most incompetent among us tend to be the most overconfident, yet we still rely on confidence as an indicator of ability.

Sometimes the Cream Doesn't Rise to the Top

Imagine being asked to work together with three other people—call them Jane, Emily, and Megan—to solve challenging math problems. You don't know who in your group is good at math; you have only your (imperfect) knowledge of your own abilities. On the first problem, Jane is the first to suggest an answer, and Emily chimes in with her own thoughts. Megan is initially quiet, but after a while, she comes up with the correct answer and explains why the other answers were wrong. This happens several times, so it becomes clear to all that Megan is good at solving problems like these. The group comes to defer to her as their de facto leader, and it does very well on its task. In an ideal world, group dynamics would always work this way: The cream would rise to the top; all members would contribute their unique knowledge, skills, and competence; and group deliberation would lead to better decisions. But the reality of group performance too often diverges from this ideal.

Chris once interviewed a U.S. government intelligence agent about group decision processes. The agent described a method his group sometimes used to arrive at a shared estimate for an unknown quantity: The members went around the room, each giving his or her own estimate, *in descending order of seniority.*[25] Imagine the false sense of consensus and confidence that cascades through a group when one person after another confirms the boss's original guess. Although each staff member could have offered an independent, unbiased, uninfluenced opinion by secret ballot, the chances of that happening in practice are virtually nil. The very process of putting individuals together to deliberate before they reach a conclusion almost guarantees that the group's decision will *not* be the product of independent opinions and contributions. Instead, it will be influenced by group dynamics, personality conflicts, and other social factors that have little to do with who knows what, and why they know it.

Rather than producing better understanding of abilities and more realistic expressions of confidence, group processes can inspire a feeling akin to "safety in numbers" among the most hesitant members, decreasing realism and increasing certainty. We think that this reflects another illusion people have about the mind—the misguided intuition that the best way for a group to use the abilities of its members in solving a problem is to deliberate over the correct answer and arrive at a consensus.

Suppose you are in a group of people asked to estimate an unknown quantity, such as the number of jelly beans in a large jar. You might think the best approach would be to discuss the options with other members until you agree on an estimate, but you'd be wrong. A different strategy consistently outperforms all others: With no prior discussion, each person should write down his or her best estimate, and then the group should simply average together all the independent estimates.[26] We asked Richard Hackman, a Harvard professor and expert on the psychology of groups, if he had ever heard of a group spontaneously deciding to use this procedure, as opposed to immediately launching into discussion and debate.[27] He had not.

Of course, in some contexts, the overconfidence derived from group consensus has value. In the midst of a military battle, nervous, low-confidence soldiers can draw strength from their comrades and leaders and take necessary risks—including the ultimate risk, their own lives—that they might choose not to take if they were alone in the decision. But the illusion of confidence can have tragic consequences when independent analysis and judgment of the highest quality are required. And just like individuals, groups appear to be totally unaware that they have this tendency to overstate their collective abilities.

Cameron Anderson and Gavin Kilduff at Berkeley's Haas School of Business actually conducted the math problem–solving experiment we asked you to imagine.[28] They formed groups of four students who had never met one another and asked them to solve math questions from the GMAT, a standardized test used for admission to graduate business schools. An advantage of using math problems as the group task was that Anderson and Kilduff could objectively measure how well each group member performed by assessing (from the videos) how many good and bad solutions each member suggested. And they could compare group members' perceptions of each person's math competence with an objective measure of the person's actual competence: scores on the math section of the SAT college admission test.

Anderson and Kilduff recorded all of the group interactions on video and reviewed them later to determine who the group leaders were. They also asked outside observers to make the same determination, and they polled the members of each group to see whom they thought had taken the leadership roles. All parties identified the same people as group leaders. The important question was what factors determined which of the four members of each group became its leader. In the hypothetical example we used to start this section, the cream rose to the top and the best mathematician, Megan, emerged as the go-to group member.

As you've probably anticipated, in the actual experiment, the group leaders proved to be no more competent than anyone else. They became leaders by force of personality rather than strength of ability. Before starting the group task, the participants completed a short questionnaire designed to measure how "dominant" they tended to be. Those people with the most dominant personalities tended to become the leaders. How did the dominant individuals become the group leaders even though they were no better at math? Did they bully the others into obeying, shouting down meek but intelligent group members? Did they campaign for the role, persuading others that they were the best at math, or at least the best at organizing their group? Not at all. The answer is almost absurdly simple: They spoke first. For 94 percent of the problems, the group's final answer was the first answer anyone suggested, and people with dominant personalities just tend to speak first and most forcefully.

So in this experiment, group leadership was determined largely by confidence. People with dominant personalities tend to exhibit greater self-confidence, and due to the illusion of confidence, others tend to trust and follow people who speak with confidence. If you offer your opinion early and often, people will take your confidence as an indicator of ability, even if you are actually no better than your peers. The illusion of confidence keeps the cream blended in. Only when confidence happens to be correlated with actual competence will the most able person rise to the top.

The Trait of Confidence

Psychologists use the term *trait* to describe a general characteristic of a person that influences his or her behavior in a wide variety of situations. In Anderson and Kilduff's study of group leadership, dominance was taken to be a trait—people scoring high on the researchers' dominance test were thought to assert control and assume power across a wide range of situations. Similarly, if you score high on a test of extraversion, you are probably more outgoing than the average person, and your tendency to approach and engage with other people will manifest itself more often than not.

Personality traits don't determine your behavior all the time—many other factors, especially ones particular to the situation you are in, have powerful influences as well. An extraverted person who knows nothing about *Star Trek* might be more shy at a science-fiction convention than an introvert who attends these events all the time. However, extraverted people tend toward more social engagement in the absence of other overriding situational factors. By default, they are more socially gregarious than are introverted people.

Confidence itself doesn't show up in most of the lists of traits compiled by psychologists. It isn't one of the so-called "big five" dimensions, which include neuroticism, extraversion, openness to experience, agreeableness, and conscientiousness. Confidence is related to, but is not the same as dominance, and even dominance isn't typically measured in studies of personality. We think that differences among people in their tendency to express confidence are vitally important for understanding how we make decisions and influence one another. So do these differences exist? Is confidence a trait?

The "con" part of "con man," "con artist," and "con game" is short for confidence. The original "confidence man" was a grifter in the 1840s named William Thompson, who had the audacity to approach strangers on the streets of Manhattan and simply ask them to hand over their watches. Attempting this gambit required Thompson to somehow gain the confidence of his marks; amazingly, he was able to do this while explicitly asking them, "Have you confidence in me to trust me with your watch until tomorrow?"[29]

The most inherently confident person in history might have been Frank Abagnale, who was portrayed by Leonardo DiCaprio in Steven Spielberg's movie *Catch Me If You Can*. Abagnale started early: While still a high school student, he successfully impersonated a high school teacher, and he conned his father out of $3,400. By the age of eighteen, pretending to be a Pan Am pilot, he had tricked the airline into letting him fly over one million miles as a "deadhead"—riding in unsold seats or as a guest in the cockpit. He expertly forged checks worth millions of dollars. When he was finally arrested in France, at the age of twenty-one, he was wanted in twelve countries. After being tried and serving time in France and Sweden, he was extradited to the United States, where he repeatedly escaped and eluded authorities, on one occasion by pretending to be an undercover investigator looking into allegations of poor conditions for prisoners. Eventually he was recaptured and convicted. As part of a deal with American prosecutors, he agreed to assist the FBI in future investigations of other frauds in exchange for early parole. The diversity, ease, and precociousness of his con games attest to his ability to display levels of confidence that people expect to see only in those who are telling the truth.[30]

Chris and some of his colleagues wondered whether confidence is a stable trait, as the careers of Abagnale and Thompson suggest.[31] They conducted a simple experiment to find out. Subjects were asked to answer a series of challenging true/false trivia questions, such as "the O.J. Simpson murder trial ended in 1993" (false—it ended in 1995), and to express their confidence in each answer as a percentage (between 50% and 100%). On this test, most people express considerable overconfidence: They get about 60 percent of the answers correct, but their average confidence is about 75 percent.

The critical element in the design of this experiment was the creation of two trivia tests that were equally difficult but included entirely different questions. Each subject first completed one of the tests, and then several weeks later, completed the other one. Remarkably, just by knowing how confident someone was on the first test, it was possible to predict how confident they would be on the second test. Of those people who scored in the top half on confidence in the first test they took, 90 percent scored in the top half on the second test. Yet confidence did not predict accuracy; the more confident people were no more accurate than the less confident people. Confidence also was unrelated to intelligence.

Other experiments have shown that confidence is a general trait: People who are highly confident of their skills in one domain, such as visual perception, also tend to be highly confident of their skills in other domains, such as memory.[32] In short, confidence appears to be a consistent quality that varies from one person to the next, but has relatively little to do with one's underlying knowledge or mental ability. One thing that does appear to influence confidence is genes. According to a recent study by a group of economists in Sweden, identical twins are more similar to each other in how confident they are of their own abilities than are fraternal twins.[33] Since identical twins have essentially the same genes, but fraternal twins are no more similar genetically than ordinary siblings, confidence must have at least some genetic basis. Your confidence isn't entirely determined by your genetic makeup, but it's not entirely independent of it. As it turns out, Frank Abagnale's father was also a con man; he lost the family home in a failed tax-fraud scheme.

Why David Took on Goliath

In August 2008, the tiny nation of Georgia provoked a military conflict with its northern neighbor Russia over two provinces whose separatist movements were being encouraged and supported by the Russian government. Georgia's army was overwhelmed after less than one week of fighting, and Russia was left in control of the provinces. All that Georgia obtained from the war was some sympathy among Western governments. Incredibly, Georgia's leaders actually believed their forces would quickly overtake the key points in South Ossetia and Abkhazia and that, once entrenched, they would be able to repel Russian counterattacks. "Several Georgian officials said that night that seizing South Ossetia would be militarily easy," according to the *New York Times*. "Some administration officials said the Georgian military had drawn up a 'concept of operations' for a crisis in South Ossetia that called for its army units to sweep across the region and rapidly establish such firm control that a Russian response could be pre-empted."[34]

The Georgians were woefully overconfident in provoking war with the second-strongest military power in the world. In his book *Overconfidence and War,* political scientist Dominic Johnson of Princeton University analyzes a range of military turning points, from World War I to Vietnam to Iraq, and although he doesn't use our terminology, he makes the point that almost any country that voluntarily initiates a war and then loses must have suffered from the illusion of confidence, since negotiation is always an option.[35] When Mikheil Saakashvili was elected president of Georgia in 2004, he was only thirty-six years old. He stocked the government with loyal ministers who were also in their thirties and lacked military experience but sympathized with their leader's views about the importance of reclaiming the breakaway regions from Russian influence. Over the next four years they managed to convince themselves that it was a good idea to fight an army that outnumbered theirs by twenty-five to one. It's not hard to imagine how a group of like-minded government officials could take a set of opinions that none of them held with great confidence individually and aggregate them, by deliberating among themselves and reinforcing one another's public statements, into a high-confidence conclusion.[36]

Chris and his colleagues at Harvard tried to capture this process of confidence inflation in groups through an experiment. They began by giving seven hundred people one of the true/false trivia tests we just described. As usual, people thought they knew more than they did, averaging 70 percent confidence in their answers even though their actual scores averaged only 54 percent correct. Chris's team used each person's confidence on the first test to select members for three different types of two-person groups: groups with two high-confidence members, groups with two low-confidence members, and groups with one high- and one low-confidence member. Each pair then visited the laboratory, where they worked together on the second trivia test—one that was just as difficult but had different questions from the first one. The members of each group could share their thoughts, deliberate about the best answer, and make a collective judgment about how likely they were to be right.

Our intuition tells us that groups should be more accurate and less overconfident than individuals. When two people come up with different answers to a trivia question, one of them must be wrong. Such discrepancies should lead to two changes. First, they should spur further discussion, which should sometimes result in more accurate answers. Second, they should provide a signal to both individuals that their certainty in their own opinion may be too high, so the group's collective certainty should decrease when there is disagreement.

At least for this sort of trivia task, though, two heads weren't better than one: The groups were no better at solving the trivia questions than were the individuals. But being part of a group did swell the heads of the subjects. Even though they were no more accurate, they were more confident![37] Confidence increased the most for pairs composed of two low-confidence people. The members of groups like this apparently reinforced each other, leading to an 11-percent increase in confidence despite no improvement in performance. This experiment illustrates why the Georgian government's high-confidence decision to provoke war with Russia did not necessarily stem from the overconfident beliefs of any one individual. The people making these decisions might each have had low confidence, perhaps so low that they would not have given the order by themselves. In a group, however, their confidence could have inflated to the point where what were actually risky, uncertain actions seemed highly likely to succeed.

The Fault Lies Not in Our Confidence, But in Our Love of Confidence

In the hit Fox TV show *House, M.D.,* Dr. Gregory House and his medical fellows encounter one rare case after another, solving each one by the end of an episode, after first testing several false leads. House, like many other television doctors, is overbearingly confident and self-assured. He has an uncanny ability to diagnose rare disorders that others miss. Although the character of Dr. House is fictional, Dr. Jim Keating plays the same role in his work at St. Louis Children's Hospital. Like House, he solves the cases that nobody else can. Unlike House, he is gregarious, friendly, quick to laugh, and willing to admit when he doesn't know the answer. Dr. Keating runs a clinic for infants and children with undiagnosed (and often undiagnosable) problems. Dr. Keating typically sees patients only after they have been to many other doctors and specialists and undergone countless tests. He's called in as a last resort—somebody who might be able to see what everyone else missed.

As you might expect, Dr. Keating has an impressive educational pedigree—undergraduate and medical degrees from Harvard, specialties in pediatrics, pediatric critical care, and pediatric gastroenterology, a master's in epidemiology and biostatistics from London, and a stint in Vietnam when he treated civilians during the war, even diagnosing one patient with bubonic plague. Only after accumulating decades of experience across a broad range of medical subspecialties did he start the diagnostic clinic that he's been running for more than ten years now. Now that he is in his early seventies, he told Dan, "It was time not to be doing all of those things. The diagnostic center fits well because I have the breadth of experience with a whole range of problems and the confidence that comes from doing clinical medicine intensely with patients."

Keating recognizes the role that confidence plays in medicine. "Doctors need to have some level of confidence to be able to interact with patients and everybody else, the nurses . . . In the emergency room, when everything is happening at once and the patient's in shock, I like to hear a voice that's steady and calm." Patients trust doctors, perhaps more than they should, and that trust reinforces the confidence that doctors already have. As Keating puts it, "When people go to the doctor, they often believe that the doctor has an ability to make the right decisions for them. That goes beyond the scientific reality. They trust your decision-making more than their own. That's a problem because it encourages doctors to not be honest about what they know and what they don't know. It builds your ego to have people think that you know."

In medicine, the confidence cycle is self-perpetuating. Doctors learn to speak with confidence as part of their training process (of course, there may also be a tendency for inherently confident people to become doctors). Then patients, mistaking confidence for competence, treat doctors more as priests with divine insight than as people who might not know as much as they profess to. This adulation in turn reinforces the behavior of doctors, leading them to be more confident. The danger comes when confidence gets too far ahead of knowledge and ability. As Keating notes, "Equanimity is something we should aspire to, but we ought to get there by building skills, and it should always have a 'not sure' component to it so you can continue to learn. There's still a lot of room for humility in our profession." Doctors have to be able to listen to the evidence, admit when they don't know, and learn from their patients. Not all of them are able to overcome their overconfidence.

Psychology professor Seth Roberts of Berkeley described the experience of being told by his doctor that he had a small hernia and that he needed surgery. Roberts asked the surgeon whether the risk of side effects from anesthesia and surgery, as well as the costs in time and money, justified the benefits of correcting a "problem" that wasn't actually bothering him at all. Yes, he was told, there are clinical trials showing the value of the surgery, and you can find them easily online. Roberts couldn't find them, nor could his mother, a former medical-school librarian. The surgeon insisted that the studies existed and promised to find and send them. They never arrived. We don't have any special insight into whether the surgery was a good idea for Roberts—it might or might not have been. Our focus is on the surgeon's extreme confidence that her decision was not only correct, but justified by clinical trials. Even after learning that an experienced medical researcher couldn't find this evidence, she continued to insist on its existence.[38]

An obdurate certainty in the face of conflicting evidence is perhaps the best indication that you need a different doctor. The best doctors show a range of confidence—they admit when they don't know and are more confident when they do know. Doctors who willingly consult people with greater knowledge than their own are likely to provide much better care than those who think they can handle any situation on their own. When Dan met with potential pediatricians for his son, one of the first things he mentioned was that his own father is a pediatrician. He then gauged their reactions. Did they seem to be threatened by this fact? Did they express willingness to take input from other doctors, including Dan's father? Dr. Keating advises looking for the following trait in a doctor: "They need to be able to say 'I don't know' and mean it."

Adopting this strategy for evaluating doctors requires consciously overriding our tendency to trust that confidence corresponds to knowledge—to assume that doctors who express certainty in their knowledge are better than those who express doubt. A study conducted in 1986 at the University of Rochester demonstrates the power of this misguided assumption.[39] The researchers asked patients who were waiting for their own appointments to view a videotape of a simulated meeting between a doctor and a patient and to rate their satisfaction with the doctor. The patient had a heart murmur and had been told by his dentist that he should talk to his doctor about possibly taking antibiotics before having oral surgery (taking antibiotics prior to dental surgery is a common step to prevent heart valve infections in people with heart disease).

In the video, the doctor took a history, performed a physical exam, confirmed the existence of a heart problem, and wrote a prescription for antibiotics. In some versions of the tape, the doctor expressed no uncertainty whatsoever about the diagnosis or treatment. In other versions the doctor acknowledged uncertainty about the need for antibiotics but prescribed them nonetheless. In one of these tapes, the doctor just said, "You have nothing to lose," and went ahead with the prescription. In another, he consulted a reference book before writing the prescription. The patients viewing these videos found the confident doctors most satisfying, and they rated the one who looked in a book to be the least satisfying of all. At least in medicine, an expert is evidently expected to have all relevant knowledge stored in memory; consulting a reference is even worse than effectively saying "what the hell" and charging ahead.

Recall Chris's encounter with the doctor who diagnosed and treated his Lyme disease. This doctor would have received the lowest rating from the subjects in the videotape study, and at the time, Chris probably would have given her a low rating too. But he filled his prescription, took all of the antibiotic as directed, and was cured in short order. Looking back, he realizes that the doctor had the self-awareness to know the limits of her knowledge and the true competence to look information up rather than charge ahead with a decision in a false show of bravado.

Doctors who express doubt are probably more self-aware than those who don't, but people rarely notice that sign of actual competence in an expert. Instead, we focus on personality and appearances. A number of studies show that patients are more likely to trust and confide in doctors who are dressed formally and wear a white lab coat than those who dress more casually.[40] Yet the worst doctor is just as able to put on a lab coat as the best doctor, so what doctors wear should have no bearing on our estimation of their abilities.

The self-help literature focuses extensively on the importance of appearing confident. Rightly so: You will persuade more people and consequently you will have more success (at least in the short term) if you present your ideas confidently. If your goal is to convince patients to accept your diagnoses without questioning, by all means wear a lab coat. Faking confidence can be beneficial (although those who can convincingly feign confidence are likely to be fairly confident people to begin with). Unfortunately, if everyone takes the advice of the self-help books and "fakes it till they make it," the already limited signaling value of confidence will be further eroded, which will make the illusion of confidence even more dangerous. In the extreme, we will be relying on something that has no predictive validity rather than something that—at present—at least occasionally does improve our judgments. Increasing your own confidence might help you, but at the cost of hurting all of us.

One question still remains: Why do we tend to trust the pronouncements of confident doctors more than those of more hesitant doctors? One reason is self-knowledge. When we know more about a topic, we tend to be more confident in our judgments about it. (As we mentioned earlier, our confidence increases as we gain skill, but our *overconfidence* decreases.) When dealing with people we know well, we can judge whether their confidence is high or low *for them*. With knowledge of the range of confidence someone exhibits, you can use confidence as a reasonable predictor of that person's knowledge; just like you, people generally act more confident when they know more about a topic and less confident when they know less. For example, if you observe that your close friend is more confident about his ability to write a good wedding toast than about his ability to fix a flat tire, you can reasonably infer that he is better at being a best man than at repairing cars.

The problem, though, is that confidence is also a personality trait, which means that the baseline level of confidence people express can vary dramatically from one person to the next. If you don't know how much confidence someone expresses across a range of situations, you have no way to judge whether the confidence you see at any particular moment reflects their knowledge or personality. If during your first encounter with someone, he expressed confidence in his ability to give wedding toasts, you would have no way to know whether he is truly skilled at giving toasts or whether he is just confident in general. If he is a confident person but an inexperienced toast-giver, then his confidence level would likely be even higher in a different area where he actually had some expertise.

We all encounter hundreds or even thousands of people whom we don't know well, but whose confidence we can observe—and draw conclusions from. For such casual acquaintances, confidence is a weak signal. But in a smaller-scale, more communal society, such as the sort in which our brains evolved, confidence would be a much more accurate signal of knowledge and abilities. When close-knit groups and families spend their entire lives together, people come to know almost everyone they ever interact with, and they can adjust for baseline differences in confidence when interpreting other people's behavior. In these conditions it is entirely reasonable to rely on confidence; if your brother shows more confidence across a range of situations than your sister, you know to discount his bravado when assessing his true competence. Unfortunately, this otherwise useful mechanism becomes a potentially catastrophic everyday illusion when we deal with people we hardly know—like eyewitnesses testifying in court.

Her Confidence and His Convictions

In July 1984, Jennifer Thompson was a twenty-two-year-old student at Elon College in North Carolina. She lived in an apartment complex in Burlington, a town about five miles from the college. Late one night, Thompson was startled awake by a noise and saw a black man in her bedroom. He jumped on her and pinned her down by her arms. She screamed. He produced a knife, held it to her throat, and told her that if she made any more noise he would kill her.[41]

At first Thompson thought this might be a joke played on her by a friend (a friend with an appalling sense of humor). But she realized it wasn't once she got a look at the intruder's face. She said he could take whatever he wanted from her apartment. The man pulled off her underwear, held her legs down, and performed oral sex. Thompson later recalled, "At that point I realized that I was going to be raped. And I didn't know if this was going to be the end, if he was going to kill me, if he was going to hurt me, and I decided that what I needed to do was to outsmart him." The attack went on for half an hour, and during that time Thompson turned on lights to get a better look at the rapist. Each time, he ordered her to turn them off right away. The rapist turned on her stereo, and a blue light illuminated his face. Gradually, Thompson assembled a sense of what he looked like. "It was just long enough for me to think, OK, his nose looks this way, his shirt is navy blue, not black."

At one point the rapist tried to kiss Thompson. She told him that she would "feel so much more at ease" if he would just put his knife outside the apartment. Surprisingly, he did. Then she asked to get a drink in the kitchen. Once there, she saw that the back door was open and realized that the rapist must have entered the apartment through it. She ran outside and found a neighbor—a professor at Elon who recognized her from campus—who let her in. She fainted and was taken to the hospital.

Later that same night, less than a mile away, another rape took place. The attacker appeared in the victim's bedroom, fondled her breasts, and briefly left before returning to rape her. The victim tried to telephone for help, but the line was cut (as it had been at Thompson's home). The rapist spent as much as thirty minutes in the apartment and left by the front door. The police quickly inferred that the same man committed both crimes.

Just hours after her ordeal, Jennifer Thompson described her attacker to a police composite artist. Detective Mike Gauldin, who investigated the case, said later that he "had great confidence in her ability to identify her assailant." According to the bulletin the police issued, the suspect was a "black male with a light complexion, around six feet tall, 170 to 175 pounds . . . with short hair and a pencil-type mustache." After publicizing the sketch, Gauldin received a tip that Ronald Cotton, who worked at a nearby seafood restaurant, resembled the person in the picture. Thompson readily picked a photograph of Cotton out of an array that included five other potential suspects, all black males, mentioned by tipsters. Only then did the police tell her that Cotton had a prior conviction for attempted rape. He'd also been convicted for breaking and entering and was said to have touched some of the waitresses at his workplace and made inappropriate comments to them. Thompson later identified Cotton in a "live" lineup, in which the suspects also spoke words she remembered her attacker saying. Ronald Cotton was arrested and imprisoned while he awaited trial.

During the trial, which took place in January 1985, no definitive physical evidence was offered, nor was it mentioned that the victim of the other rape that night could not identify Cotton (and thus that he was not being tried for that crime). The case was decided on the contrast between Cotton's shaky and inconsistent alibis for the night of the rape, and Thompson's confident, consistent identification of Cotton, from the photo array, to the lineup, to the courtroom. Thompson proved to be a compelling witness: She told the jury that during the rape, she had the presence of mind to focus her efforts on memorizing "every single detail on the rapist's face" in order to make sure he was caught later. "Jennifer, are you absolutely sure that Ronald Junior Cotton is the man?" asked the prosecutor. "Yes," she replied. The jury convicted Cotton after four hours of deliberation. He was sentenced to life plus fifty years in prison.

Two years later, Ronald Cotton received a new trial after another prisoner named Bobby Poole told other inmates that *he,* not Cotton, was the one who had raped Jennifer Thompson. Cotton and Poole looked similar, so much so that some prison workers mistook them for each other. Cotton tricked Poole into posing side by side with him for a photograph, which he sent to his lawyer with a letter describing his claim that Poole was the real rapist. But in court during Cotton's second trial, Thompson looked at Bobby Poole and said, "I have never seen him in my life. I have no idea who he is." A more categorical—and confident—statement is hard to imagine. The jury was convinced, and Cotton went back to prison with an even harsher sentence, this time having been convicted of both rapes.

As the years passed, Thompson gradually managed to put the entire matter behind her. In 1995, ten years after the first trial, she was contacted again by Mike Gauldin and the district attorney, who told her that lawyers for Cotton had requested DNA testing to determine whether he might have been wrongly convicted. DNA recovered from her body at the hospital would be compared with fresh samples provided by Ronald Cotton, Bobby Poole, and Thompson herself. She cooperated enthusiastically, convinced that the test "would allow me to move on once and for all." But the test proved that Thompson, despite her inner and outward confidence in her memory, had been wrong all along. Cotton had been right in protesting his innocence, as had the jailhouse braggart Poole in boasting of his own guilt—his DNA matched that left by the rapist.

Thompson accepted Cotton's innocence, but she was racked with guilt over the responsibility she felt for taking away his freedom. She wrote later that "for so many years, the police officers and the prosecutors told me I was the 'best witness' they ever put on the stand; I was 'textbook.'" Jurors believe confident witnesses, and investigators and prosecutors know this. The U.S. Supreme Court stated that the "level of certainty of the witness" was an important factor in a 1972 case where a victim expressed "no doubt" in court that she recognized her own rapist.[42] By contrast, most psychologists who testify as experts on eyewitness memory say that "an eyewitness's confidence is *not* a good predictor of his or her identification accuracy."[43] In fact, mistaken eyewitness identifications, and their confident presentation to the jury, are the main cause of over 75 percent of wrongful convictions that are later overturned by DNA evidence.[44]

In a powerful demonstration of the extent to which confidence sways juries, psychologist Gary Wells and his colleagues conducted an elaborate experiment that resembled the entire criminal law process, from the initial witnessing of a crime to the jury's decision on guilt or innocence. First, the researchers staged a crime for each of 108 different subjects: An actor pretended to steal a calculator from the room where each subject was completing some forms.[45] Wells varied the amount of time that the perpetrator was in the room, how much he said to the subject, and whether he wore a hat (which made his face harder to see). Shortly after the "criminal" left the room, the experimenter entered and asked the subject to select the criminal from a photographic lineup and to state a level of confidence in that selection. Not surprisingly, subjects who had viewed the criminal only briefly were more than twice as likely to make an incorrect selection from the lineup as those who viewed the perpetrator for a long time. Yet they were nearly as confident in their selection as those who saw the perpetrator for a long time.

The most interesting part of this experiment wasn't the finding of overconfidence, which had been demonstrated before. After selecting a person from the lineup and judging their confidence in their selection, the subjects were then "cross-examined" by another experimenter who had no information about which choice they had made or how confident they were. Videotapes of these cross-examinations were shown to a new group of subjects—the "jurors"—who were asked to judge whether the witness had made an accurate identification. The jurors trusted the selections of highly confident witnesses 77 percent of the time and less confident witnesses 59 percent of the time. More important, the jurors were disproportionately swayed by a highly confident witness when the witness experienced poor viewing conditions (only a brief exposure to a hat-wearing perpetrator). That is, confidence had the most detrimental effect on juror judgments when the witnesses had the least information to go on.

At Ronald Cotton's trials, the juries relied on confidence as a way to distinguish an accurate witness from an inaccurate one. A group of scientists led by Siegfried Sporer, a psychologist at the University of Giessen in Germany, reviewed all of the studies done on the identification of suspects from lineups—a crucial step in the investigation of Cotton for the Thompson rape. Several of these studies showed no relationship between the accuracy of witnesses and the level of confidence they expressed, but others found that higher confidence is associated with greater accuracy. Considering all of the relevant studies, they found that on average, high-confidence witnesses are accurate 70 percent of the time, whereas low-confidence witnesses are accurate just 30 percent of the time.[46] So, all other things being equal, a confident witness is more likely—much more likely—to be accurate than an unconfident one.

But there are two problems here. First, the level of confidence witnesses express depends as much on whether they are confident in general as on whether they are accurate in a given instance. If jurors could observe the confidence of a particular witness under a wide variety of situations, they could better judge whether that witness's testimony was unusually confident. In the absence of any information about whether or not a witness generally acts with confidence, we tend to trust people who appear confident. The effect of a confident witness holds so much sway that 37 percent of respondents in our national survey agreed that "the testimony of one confident eyewitness should be enough evidence to convict a defendant of a crime."

Second, and even more important, is that while higher confidence is associated with higher accuracy, the association is not *perfect*. Highly confident witnesses are right in their identifications 70 percent of the time, which means they are wrong the other 30 percent of the time; a criminal conviction based entirely on a confident eyewitness identification has a 30 percent chance of being erroneous. As eyewitness testimony expert Gary Wells and his colleagues at Iowa State University put it, "We would expect to encounter a highly confident mistaken eyewitness (or a nonconfident accurate eyewitness) about as often as we would encounter a tall female (or a short male)."[47] This should make us question verdicts that rely exclusively on eyewitness memories, no matter how confidently they are recalled in court.

The Ronald Cotton case is often described as one of mistaken eyewitness identification due to the fallibility of memory. It is. But if the illusion of confidence did not exist, the authorities and the jurors would not have given Thompson's identifications and recollections the inordinate weight they did. They would have recognized that her lack of doubt still left much room for error, and that physical and even circumstantial evidence are necessary backstops for eyewitness testimony—no matter how articulate, persuasive, and confident its delivery.[48] The illusion of confidence obscures all of this, often with disastrous consequences.

For Ronald Cotton, the consequence was eleven years in prison for crimes he didn't commit, but it could easily have been his entire life. At his second trial, on the basis of new testimony by the second victim, he was convicted of both rapes that were committed on that July night. His lawyers later wanted to test his DNA against samples from each crime scene, but the material from the second rape had deteriorated too much. If the samples taken from Jennifer Thompson were not testable—or were gone entirely—there would have been no way to prove Cotton's innocence. Instead, he was set free on June 30, 1995. He was offered $5,000 in compensation by the state of North Carolina, an amount later raised to over $100,000 by changes to the law. These days, he travels and speaks on the issue of false convictions, often in tandem with Jennifer Thompson, who is now a married mother of triplets and an advocate for criminal justice reform.

In our view, what is most in need of reform is the legal system's understanding of how the mind works. The police, the witnesses, the lawyers, the judges, and the jurors are all too susceptible to the illusions we have discussed. Because they are human, they believe that we pay attention to much more than we do, that our memories are more complete and faithful than they are, and that confidence is a reliable gauge of accuracy. The common law of criminal procedure was established over centuries in England and the United States, and its assumptions are based precisely on mistaken intuitions like these.

The mind is not the only thing we think we understand much better than we actually do. From physical mechanisms as simple as a toilet or a zipper, to complex technologies like the Internet, to vast engineering projects like Boston's "Big Dig," to abstract entities like financial markets and terrorist networks, we easily deceive ourselves into thinking that we understand and can explain things that we really know very little about. In fact, our dangerous tendency to overestimate the extent and the depth of our knowledge is the next everyday illusion we will discuss. The *illusion of knowledge* is like the illusion of confidence, but it is not a direct expression of one's level of certainty or ability. It doesn't involve telling someone else that you are "confident," "certain," "better than the average person," and so on. It involves implicitly believing that you understand things at a deeper level than you really do, and it lurks behind some of the most dangerous and misguided decisions we make.

should you be more like
a weather forecaster or a
hedge fund manager?

N JUNE 2000, U.S. president Bill Clinton and British prime minister Tony Blair jointly announced the completion of the initial phase of the Human Genome Project, the celebrated international effort to de-code the DNA sequence of all twenty-three human chromosomes. The project ultimately spent about $2.5 billion over ten years to produce a "first draft" of the sequence, and over $1 billion more to fill in the gaps and polish the results.[1] One of the most intriguing questions that biolo-gists hoped the project would answer seemed to be a simple one: How many genes are there in the human genome?[2]

Before the sequence was completed, prevailing opinion held that the complexity of human biology and behavior must be the product of a large number of genes, probably between 80,000 and 100,000. In Sep-tember 1999, a high-flying biotech company called Incyte Genomics proclaimed that there were 140,000 genes in the human genome. In May 2000, top geneticists from around the world converged at the

"Genome Sequencing and Biology" conference at the Cold Spring Harbor Laboratory in New York, and a lively debate about the true count ensued. Yet no consensus estimate emerged; some agreed with counts as high as those claimed by Incyte, and others argued that the number might be lower than 50,000.

With so many different opinions on offer, Ewan Birney, a geneticist at the European Bioinformatics Institute, started a betting pool for his fellow researchers to predict the final count. Each participant put in a dollar, and the winner would receive the total amount collected, plus a signed, leather-bound copy of Nobel Prize–winner James Watson's memoir, *The Double Helix*. Incyte's Sam LaBrie came in with the highest initial estimate: 153,478 genes. The average of the first 338 predictions entered was 66,050. Birney raised the entry fee to five dollars in 2001, and then to twenty dollars in 2002—it wouldn't really be fair to let later bettors in for the same amount as earlier ones, since the late bettors could use the earlier estimates as well as their own research findings to guide their guesses. The 115 later entries averaged 44,375, and the pot grew to $1,200. Over the full two-year betting period, the lowest entry was 25,747, submitted by Lee Rowen from the Institute for Systems Biology in Seattle.

The terms of the competition, set in 2000, required Birney to declare a winner in 2003. However, to Birney's surprise, there was still no consensus "final count" at that point. Based on evidence available at the time, Birney estimated the total count to be about 24,500. He decided to award portions of the pool to the three entrants who bet on the lowest numbers, with Rowen getting the largest prize. The final number is still in dispute, but the most accepted value has dropped to 20,500, squarely in the range between the roundworm called *C. elegans* (19,500) and the mustard plant called *Arabidopsis* (27,000).

The bettors all were leaders in the field of genetics, and they were sure that the number was higher than it actually was; the range of their 453 predictions, from the highest to the lowest estimate, did not even include the correct count. Francis Collins of the National Institutes of Health and Eric Lander of the Massachusetts Institute of Technology, leaders of the Genome Project, were each off by more than 100 percent, no better than the average guess. The collective also had a pretty poor idea of how quickly the gene-count question would be resolved (predicted: 2003, actual: 2007 or later). Collins reacted stoically: "Oh well, live and learn."

This is far from the only example of scientists overestimating their knowledge in their own fields of expertise. In 1957, two of the pioneers of computer science and artificial intelligence, Herbert Simon and Allen Newell, publicly predicted that within ten years a computer would be able to defeat the world chess champion in a match.[3] By 1968 no one had come close to creating a machine capable of that feat. David Levy, a Scottish computer programmer and chess player who would later achieve the title of international master (one level below grandmaster), met with four other computer scientists and bet them £500 of his own money—an amount equal to about one-half of his annual income at the time—that no computer would be able to beat him in a match within the *next* ten years. In 1978, with the pot sweetened to £1250 by further wagers, Levy in fact defeated the best computer program by a score of 3½–1½. Together with *Omni* magazine, he then offered a new prize of $5,000 to anyone whose computer could beat him, with no time limit on the bet. Finally, in 1989, Levy lost to Deep Thought, a predecessor of IBM's Deep Blue computer. Only in 1997 did Deep Blue, with its multiple processors and custom-designed chess chips, defeat world champion Garry Kasparov 3½–2½ and fulfill the Simon-Newell prophecy—thirty years behind schedule.[4]

In 1980, ecologist Paul Ehrlich, a professor at Stanford University, and his colleagues John Harte and John Holdren of the University of California at Berkeley, were convinced that global overpopulation would lead to drastic increases in the prices of food and other commodities that were in finite supply. Indeed, Ehrlich had been convinced that this threat was dire for some time, having written in 1968, "In the 1970s the world will undergo famines—hundreds of millions of people are going to starve to death."[5] He and Holdren predicted the imminent "exhaustion of mineral resources."[6]

Julian Simon, an economist at the University of Maryland, had the opposite view. He published an article in the journal *Science* titled "Resources, Population, Environment: An Oversupply of False Bad News."[7]

Simon, whose previous claim to fame was inventing the system under which airlines reward passengers for giving up their seats on overbooked flights, proceeded to challenge the doomsayers to put their money where their mouths were: Pick five commodities and bet that their prices would increase over the next ten years, as one would expect if demand were always increasing and supply were constant or decreasing. Ehrlich was outraged by the apostasy displayed by Simon (whom he referred to as the leader of a "space-age cargo cult"), so he got Harte and Holdren to join him in accepting the wager proposed by the economist. They selected five metals—chrome, copper, nickel, tin, and tungsten—and calculated the amount of each that could be purchased for $200 in 1980. If these metals' prices were higher ten years later, Simon would pay Ehrlich, Harte, and Holdren the difference; if the prices were lower, they would pay him. By 1990, all five commodities had gone down in price. In fact, they had collectively dropped more than 50 percent. Simon received an envelope containing a check in the amount of his winnings. There was no cover note.[8]

You might object that we've cherry-picked examples in which experts made their most horribly errant predictions. We agree that these examples are atypical, and we're not arguing that experts know nothing and are always wrong. Especially in scientific domains, they know a lot more and are right much more often than the average person. But these stories show that even scientific experts can dramatically overestimate what they know. Every single geneticist guessed high on the gene count, and some were off by a factor of five; the computer scientists were off by a factor of four; and the ecological doomsayers were wrong about every one of the metals they selected. If expert judgments can be so misguided, the rest of us must also be capable of overestimating what we know. Whenever people think they know more than they do, they are under the influence of our next everyday illusion: the *illusion of knowledge*.

The Virtue of Being Like an Annoying Child

Spend a moment now and try to form an image in your mind of a bicycle. Even better, if you have a piece of paper, draw a sketch of a bicycle.

Don't worry about making a great piece of art—just focus on getting all the major parts in the right place. Sketch out the frame, the handlebars, the wheels, the pedals, and so on. For simplicity, just make it a single-speed bicycle. Got it? If you had to rate your understanding of how a bicycle works on a 1 to 7 scale, where 1 means "no understanding" and 7 means "complete understanding," what score would you give yourself?

If you are like most of the people who participated in a clever study by British psychologist Rebecca Lawson, you thought you had a pretty good understanding of bicycles; her subjects rated the level of their knowledge at 4.5 out of 7, on average.[9] Now either look at your drawing or refresh your mental image and then answer the following questions: Does your bicycle have a chain? If so, does the chain run between the two wheels? Does the frame of your bicycle connect the front and back wheels? Are the pedals connected to the inside of the chain? If you drew a chain connecting the two wheels of your bicycle, think about how the bicycle would turn—the chain would have to stretch whenever the front wheel rotated, but chains aren't stretchy. Similarly, if a rigid frame connected both wheels, the bicycle could only go straight. Some people draw pedals outside the loop of the chain, making it impossible to turn the chain by pedaling. Errors like these were common in Lawson's study, and they are not trivial details of the functioning of a bicycle—the pedals turn the chain, which causes the back wheel to rotate, and the front wheel must be free to turn or the bicycle cannot change direction. People are much better at making sense of a bicycle's workings when the thing is sitting right in front of them than they are at explaining (or drawing) a bicycle purely from memory.

This example illustrates a critical aspect of the illusion of knowledge. Because of our extensive experience and familiarity with ordinary machines and tools, we often think we have a deep understanding of how they work. Think about each of the following objects and then judge your knowledge of it on the same 1 to 7 scale: a car speedometer, a zipper, a piano key, a toilet, a cylinder lock, a helicopter, and a sewing machine. Now try one more task: Pick the object that you gave the highest rating, the one you feel you best understand, and try to explain how it works. Give the kind of explanation you would give to a persistently inquisitive child—try to generate a detailed step-by-step description of how it works, and explain why it works. That is, try to come up with the causal connections between each step (in the case of the bicycle, you would have to say something about *why* pedaling makes the wheels turn, not just *that* pedaling makes the wheels turn). If you aren't sure how two steps are causally connected, you've uncovered a gap in your knowledge.

This test is similar to a series of ingenious experiments that Leon Rozenblit conducted as part of his doctoral research at Yale University with Professor Frank Keil (who, incidentally, was also Dan's graduate school adviser).[10] For his first study, Rozenblit approached students in the hallways of the psychology building and asked them if they knew why the sky is blue or how a cylinder lock works. If they answered yes, he then played what he calls the "why boy" game, which he describes as follows: "I ask you a question and you give me an answer, and I say 'why is that?' Channeling the spirit of a curious five-year-old, I then just keep following each explanation with another 'why is that?' until the other person gets really annoyed."[11] The unexpected result of this informal experiment was that people gave up really quickly—they answered no more than one or two "why" questions before they reached a gap in their understanding. Even more striking were their reactions when they discovered that they really had no understanding. "It was clearly counterintuitive to them. People were surprised and chagrined and a little embarrassed." After all, they had just claimed to know the answer.

Rozenblit pursued this illusion of knowledge in more than a dozen experiments over the next few years, testing people from all walks of life (from undergraduates at Yale to members of the New Haven community), and the results were remarkably consistent. No matter whom you talk to, you will eventually reach a point where they can no longer answer the why question. For most of us, our depth of understanding is sufficiently shallow that we may exhaust our knowledge after just the first question. We know that there is an answer, and we feel that we know it, but until asked to produce it we seem blissfully unaware of the shortcomings in our own knowledge.

Before you tried this little test, you might have thought intuitively that you understood how a toilet works, but all you really understand is how to work a toilet—and maybe how to unclog one. You likely understand how the various visible parts interact and move together. And, if you were looking inside a toilet and playing with the mechanism a bit, you might be able to figure out how it works. But when you aren't looking at a toilet, your impression of understanding is illusory: You mistake your knowledge of *what* happens for an understanding of *why* it happens, and you mistake your feeling of familiarity for genuine knowledge.

We sometimes encounter students who come to our offices and ask how they could have worked so hard but still failed our tests. They usually tell us that they read and reread the textbook and their class notes, and that they thought they understood everything well by the time of the exam. And they probably did internalize some bits and pieces of the material, but the illusion of knowledge led them to confuse the familiarity they had gained from repeated exposure to the concepts in the course with an actual understanding of them. As a rule, reading text over and over again yields diminishing returns in actual knowledge, but it increases familiarity and fosters a false sense of understanding. Only by testing ourselves can we actually determine whether or not we really understand. That is one reason why teachers give tests, and why the best tests probe knowledge at a deep level. Asking whether a lock has cylinders tests whether people can memorize the parts of a lock. Asking how to pick a lock tests whether people understand *why* locks have cylinders and what functional role they play in the operation of the lock.

Perhaps the most striking aspect of the illusion is how rarely we bother to do anything to probe the limits of our knowledge—especially considering how easy it is to do this. Before telling Leon Rozenblit that you know why the sky is blue, all you have to do is simulate the "why boy" game with yourself to see whether you actually know. We fall prey to the illusion because we simply do not recognize the need to question our own knowledge. According to Rozenblit,

In our day-to-day lives, do we stop and ask ourselves, "Do I know where the rain is coming from?" We probably don't do it without provocation, and it only happens in appropriate social and cognitive contexts: a five-year-old asks you, you're having an argument with someone, you're trying to write about it, you're trying to teach a class about it.

And even when we do check our knowledge, we often mislead ourselves. We focus on those snippets of information that we do possess, or can easily obtain, but ignore all of the elements that are missing, leaving us with the impression that we understand everything we need to. The illusion is remarkably persistent. Even after completing an entire experiment with Rozenblit, repeatedly playing the "why boy" game, some subjects still did not spontaneously check their own knowledge before proclaiming that they would have done better with different objects: "If you had just asked me about the lock, I could have done that."

Our tendency to make this error isn't limited to our thoughts and beliefs about physical devices and systems. It happens whenever we have a big project to complete, a problem to solve, or an assignment to do. We must overcome the temptation to dive in and get started rather than examine our understanding of the task and its requirements. Avoiding this aspect of the illusion of knowledge was the key for Tim Roberts, who won the $25,000 top prize in the 2008 edition of a computer programming tournament called the TopCoder Open. He had six hours to write a program that met a set of written specifications. Unlike his competitors, Roberts spent the first hour studying the specs and asking questions—"at least 30"—of their author. Only after verifying that he completely understood the challenge did he start to code. He completed a program that did exactly what was required, and nothing more. But it worked, and it was finished on time. The time he spent escaping the illusion of knowledge was an investment that paid off handsomely in the end.[12]

The Best-Laid Plans . . .

The illusion of knowledge makes us think we know how common objects work when we really don't, but it is even more influential and consequential when we reason about *complex systems*. Unlike a toilet or a bicycle, a complex system has many more interacting parts, and the system's overall behavior cannot be easily determined just by knowing how its individual parts behave. Large-scale innovative engineering projects, like the construction of the iconic Sydney Opera House or the "Big Dig" in Boston, are classic examples of this sort of complexity.

The Big Dig was a project intended to reorganize the transportation network in downtown Boston.[13] In 1948, the Massachusetts government developed a plan to build new highways through and around the city in an attempt to address growing traffic volume on local roads. As part of this highway expansion, a thousand buildings were destroyed and twenty thousand residents were displaced to erect a two-level elevated highway cutting through downtown Boston. Although it was six lanes wide, the highway had too many on- and off-ramps and it was subject to chronic stop-and-go congestion for eight or more hours every day. It was also an eyesore. Disappointment with these results caused a companion project to be cancelled, further increasing the load on the elevated highway.

The main goals of the Big Dig, which entered the planning stage in 1982, were to move the downtown portion of the elevated highway underground and to build a new tunnel under Boston Harbor to connect the city to Logan International Airport. Several other roads and bridges were added or improved. In 1985, the entire operation was projected to cost $6 billion. Construction began in 1991, and by the time it was completed in 2006, the total cost was nearly $15 billion. Since much of the money was borrowed by issuing bonds, the ultimate cost by the time all loans are repaid will include an additional $7 billion in interest, resulting in a total expense more than 250 percent higher than originally planned.

The Big Dig's cost grew for many reasons. One was the constant need to change plans as the project progressed. Officials considered stacking elevated highways one hundred feet high at one location in order to get traffic to where it needed to be; in the end that problem was solved by constructing a bridge that was the largest of its type ever built. Another factor driving up costs was the need to develop new technologies and engineering methods to meet the challenges of submerging miles of highway in an area already dense with subway lines, railroad tracks, and buildings. But why weren't these engineering complications foreseen? Everybody involved knew that the Big Dig was a public works effort of unprecedented size and complexity, but nobody realized, at least early on, that their estimates of the time and cost to complete it were little more than shots in the dark, and optimistic shots at that.

It is not as though this sort of underestimate had never happened before. The history of architecture is replete with examples of projects that turned out to be more difficult and costly than their designers— and the businessmen and politicians who launched them—ever expected. The Brooklyn Bridge, built between 1870 and 1883, cost twice as much as originally planned. The Sydney Opera House was commissioned by the Australian government in 1959 and designed by Danish architect Jørn Utzon over six months in his spare time. It was forecast in 1960 to cost 7 million Australian dollars. By the time it was finished, the bill came to AU$102 million. (Another AU$45 million will need to be spent to bring the building in line with aspects of Utzon's original design that were not realized.) Antoni Gaudi began to direct the construction of the Sagrada Familia Church in Barcelona in 1883, and he said in 1886 that he could finish it in ten years. It is expected to be completed in 2026, a mere one hundred years after his death.[14]

It is said that "the best-laid plans of mice and men often go awry" and that "no battle plan survives contact with the enemy." Hofstadter's law tells us: "It always takes longer than you expect, even when you take into account Hofstadter's Law."[15] The fact that we need these aphorisms to remind us of the inherent difficulty of planning demonstrates the strength of the illusion of knowledge. The problem is not that our plans go awry—after all, the world is more complex than our simple mental models and, as Yogi Berra explained, "it's tough to make predictions, especially about the future."[16] Even expert project managers don't get it right: They are more accurate than amateurs, but they are still wrong one-third of the time.[17] We all experience this sort of illusory knowledge, even for simpler projects. We underestimate how long they will take or how much they will cost, because what seems simple and straightforward in our mind typically turns out to be more complex when our plans encounter reality. The problem is that we never learn to take this limitation into account. Over and over, the illusion of knowledge convinces us that we have a deep understanding of what a project will entail, when all we really have is a rough and optimistic guess based on shallow familiarity.

By now you may be sensing a pattern to the everyday illusions we have been discussing: They all tend to cast an overly favorable light on our mental capacities. There are no illusions of blindness, amnesia, idiocy, and cluelessness. Instead, everyday illusions tell us that we perceive and remember more than we do, that we're all above average, and that we know more about the world and the future than is justified. Everyday illusions might be so persistent and pervasive in our thought patterns precisely because they lead us to think better of ourselves than we objectively should. Positive illusions can motivate us to get out of bed and optimistically take up challenges we might shrink from if we constantly had the truth about our minds in mind. If these illusions are in fact driven by a bias toward overly positive self-evaluation, then people who are less subject to this bias also should be less subject to everyday illusions. Indeed, people suffering from depression do tend to evaluate themselves more negatively and less optimistically, possibly resulting in a more accurate view of the relationship between themselves and the world.[18]

A larger dose of realism in planning ought to help us make better decisions about how to allocate our time and resources. Since the illusion of knowledge is an inherent barrier to realism in any plans we draw up for our own use, how can we avoid it? The answer is simple to learn, but not so simple to execute, and it works only for the kinds of projects that have been done many times before—it works if you are writing a report, developing a piece of software, renovating your house, or even putting up a new office building, but not if you are planning a one-of-a-kind project like the Big Dig. Fortunately, most of the projects you do are not as unique as you may think they are. For us, planning this book was a unique and unprecedented task. But for a publisher trying to estimate how long it would take us to write it, it was similar to all the other nonfiction, two-author, three-hundred-page books that have come out in the last few years.

To avoid the illusion of knowledge, start by admitting that your personal views of how expensive and time-consuming your own seemingly unique project will be are probably wrong. It can be hard to do this, because you truly do know much more about your own project than anyone else does, but this familiarity gives the false sense that only you understand it well enough to plan it out accurately. If instead you seek out similar projects that other people or organizations have already completed (the more similar to yours, the better, of course), you can use the actual time and cost of those projects to gauge how long yours will take. Taking such an "outside view" of what we normally keep inside our own minds dramatically changes the way we see our plans.[19]

Even if you don't have access to a database of renovation project timelines or software engineering case studies, you can ask other people to take a fresh look at your ideas and make their own forecast for the project. Not a forecast of how long it would take *them* to execute the ideas (since they too will likely underestimate their own time and costs), but of how long it will take *you* (or your contractors, employees, etc.) to do so. You can also imagine rolling your eyes as someone else excitedly tells you about their own plans to get a project like yours done. Such mental simulations can help you adopt an outside view. As a last resort, just calling to mind occasions when you were wildly optimistic (if you can be objective enough to recall them—we've all been foolish in this way more than once in our lives) can help you to reduce the illusion of knowledge that distorts your current predictions.[20]

"Every Time You Think You Know . . . Something Else Happens"

Thirty-two-year-old Brian Hunter was paid at least $75 million in 2005. His job was to trade futures contracts in energy, especially natural gas, for a Greenwich, Connecticut, hedge fund called Amaranth Advisors. His trading strategy involved placing bets on the future price of gas by buying and selling options. In the summer of 2005, when gas was trading at $7–9 per million BTUs, he predicted that prices would rise considerably by early fall, so he loaded up on cheap options to buy at prices like $12 that seemed outrageously high to the market at the time. When hurricanes Katrina, Rita, and Wilma devastated oil plat-forms and processing plants along the coast of the Gulf of Mexico in late summer, prices went over $13. Suddenly, Hunter's previously over-priced options were valuable. With trades like this he generated profits of more than $1 billion that year for Amaranth and its investors.

By August of the next year, Hunter and his colleagues had racked up gains of $2 billion. Gas prices had peaked at over $15 the previous De-cember, post-Katrina, but were now in decline. Hunter again placed a huge bet that they would reverse course and rise again. Instead, prices plunged, falling below $5. In a single September week, Hunter's trades lost $5 billion, approximately one-half of Amaranth's total assets. After a total loss of approximately $6.5 billion, which at the time was the largest publicly disclosed trading loss in history, the fund was forced to liquidate.

What went wrong at Amaranth? Brian Hunter, and others at the firm, believed that they knew more about their world (the energy markets) than they actually did. Amaranth's founder, Nick Maounis, thought that Hunter was "really, really good at taking controlled and measured risk." But Hunter's success was due at least as much to unpredictable events like hurricanes as to his understanding of the markets. Just be-fore the blowup, Hunter himself even said, "Every time you think you know what these markets can do, something else happens." But risk was apparently not being managed, and Hunter had not fully accounted for the unpredictability of the energy markets. He had actually made the same mistake earlier in his career at Deutsche Bank, blaming a one-week December 2003 loss of $51 million on "an unprecedented and unforeseeable run-up in gas prices."[21]

Throughout the history of financial markets, investors have formed theories to explain why some assets go up and others go down in value, and some writers have promoted simple strategies derived from these models. The Dow theory, based on the late-nineteenth-century writings of *Wall Street Journal* founder Charles Dow, was premised on the idea that investors could tell whether an upswing in industrial stocks was likely to continue by looking for a similar upswing in transportation company shares. The "Nifty Fifty" theory of the 1960s and early 1970s claimed that the best growth would be achieved by fifty of the largest multinational corporations traded on the New York Stock Exchange, and those were therefore the best and—by virtue of their size—safest investments. The 1990s saw the "Dogs of the Dow" and the "Foolish Four"—models that advocated holding particular proportions of the stocks from the Dow Jones Industrial Average that paid the highest dividends as a percentage of their share prices.[22]

Just as a lightweight model airplane keeps a few key features of a real airplane but leaves out all the rest, each of these theories represents a particular *model* of how the financial markets work, one that strips down a complex system into a simple one that investors can use to make decisions. Behind most patterns of behavior in our everyday lives are models. They aren't stated explicitly like the stock market models; rather they consist of implicit assumptions about how things work. When you are walking down a staircase, your brain automatically maintains and updates a model of your physical surroundings that it uses to determine the force and direction of your leg movements. You only become aware of this model when it is wrong—which it is when you expect one more step, only to feel a sudden thud when your foot hits the floor instead of slicing through empty space.

Albert Einstein is said to have recommended that "everything should be made as simple as possible, but not simpler." The Foolish Four, the Nifty Fifty, and their ilk unfortunately fall into the "simpler" category. They can't adapt to changes in market conditions, they don't account for an inevitable decrease in their profitability when more people adopt the same strategies, and they often assume that trends in historical financial data will recur in the future. By basing their projections so closely on past data patterns (a statistical foible known as "overfitting"), they are almost guaranteed to go wrong once conditions change.

Even worse are investment strategies that appear to start with a target value, usually a nice round marketable number, and then calculate the rate of growth in stock prices needed to reach the target. Arguments are then retrofitted to the numbers to explain why such a high rate of growth is plausible, or even likely. The stock market bubble of the dot-com era generated a bumper crop of this nonsense. In October 1999, with the Dow Jones Industrial Average at 11,497 after a long run-up, James K. Glassman and Kevin Hassett published *Dow 36,000*, which forecast that stock prices would more than triple within six years. Their optimism surpassed that of *Dow 30,000* but was no match for *Dow 40,000*, let alone *Dow 100,000*. (All of these are real books, by different authors, and every one of them was selling for just one cent—plus shipping and handling, of course—on Amazon.com's used-book marketplace as of April 2009.) The sheer number of these titles testifies to the large market for simple models that investors can easily assimilate and act on because they give a false sense of understanding. By the time the stock market began to recover from the dot-com bust, more titles appeared, including *Dow 30,000 by 2008: Why It's Different This Time*.

Illusory Knowledge and a Real Crisis

With hindsight we can see that the implosion of Amaranth in 2006 was a harbinger of the much larger financial crisis that came to a head two years later. Venerable companies like Bear Stearns and Lehman Brothers went out of business, others like AIG were driven into government control, and the economy plunged into a deep recession. The world financial system is perhaps the ultimate complex system: It reflects decisions made by literally billions of people every day, and those decisions are all based on beliefs about how much, or how little, various investors know. Any time you buy an individual stock, you are acting on an implicit belief that the market has undervalued the stock. Your purchase represents a claim that you have better knowledge than most other investors about the future value of that stock.

Consider the biggest investment that most people make: their house.[23]

Most people view the decision about what house to buy as, at least in part, an investing decision. They wonder whether a house will have good "resale value" or whether it is in an "up-and-coming" or "declining" neighborhood. Some people make a business of buying, improving, and selling the houses they live in, a practice called "flipping" that was promoted heavily by television shows like *Property Ladder* and *Flip That House* in the mid-2000s. At that time, the number of people who thought houses were a good investment was rising dramatically.[24] Even if you have never been a house flipper, you may still think of your house in part as a savings account, an asset you expect to appreciate in value over the medium-to-long term. Flipping is based on a model of the real estate market in which the prices of houses can also be counted on to increase in the short term, and the demand for them is always strong.

Acting on this model, people with no experience investing in real estate started buying houses on credit with the intent of selling them quickly at a profit. The speculative cycle was exacerbated, of course, by the willingness of banks to make loans that would probably never be repaid. Alberto Ramirez, a strawberry picker who lived in Watsonville, California, and earned about $15,000 a year, was able to buy a house for $720,000 without putting any money down; naturally he soon found that he couldn't afford the payments. The apotheosis of subprime lending gimmicks was mortgage company HCL Finance's "ninja" loan—no income, no job, no assets. Harvard economist Ed Glaeser, explaining why he did not foresee the bubble and ensuing crash in the housing market, said, "I underestimated the human capacity to think rosy thoughts about the value of a house."[25]

Flawed models of the housing market extended well beyond individual homeowners and speculators, of course. Large banks and government-backed corporations purchased mortgages and resold them in groups to other investors as mortgage-backed securities, which were themselves packaged together into the infamous collateralized debt obligations (CDOs). The bond-rating agencies—Moody's, Standard & Poor's, and Fitch—used complex statistical models to evaluate the riskiness of these new securities. But behind these models lay simple assumptions that—when they no longer applied—undermined the entire edifice. As late as 2007, Moody's was still using a model that had been built using data from the period before 2002—before the era of massive overbuilding, ninja loans, and strawberry pickers buying luxury homes. That is, despite the changes in the market, the model assumed that mortgage borrowers of 2007 would default at about the same rate as the mortgage borrowers of 2002. When the housing bubble burst, a general recession ensued, and the rate of mortgage defaults diverged from historical norms. As a result, many CDOs turned out to be riskier than the models had predicted, and firms that had invested in them lost a lot of money.

It can be difficult to determine how well our simple models correspond to the realities of complex systems, but it is easy to determine three things: (1) how well we understand our simple models; (2) how familiar we are with the surface elements, concepts, and vocabulary of the complex system; and (3) how much information we are aware of, and can easily access, about the complex system. We then take our knowledge of these particular things as signals that we understand the system as a whole—an utterly unwarranted inference that can quickly land us in hot water. Analysts understood their models, they were familiar with the vocabulary of subprime mortgages, CDOs, and the like, and they were swimming in a river of financial data and news, giving them the illusion that they understood the housing market itself—an illusion that persisted until the market collapsed.[26] With more and more financial information available at higher speed and lower cost (think CNBC, Yahoo! Finance, and online discount stockbrokers), the conditions for this illusion have spread from professional market participants to ordinary individual investors.

In a brilliant article for *Condé Nast Portfolio,* journalist Michael Lewis tells the story of a hedge fund manager named Steve Eisman who was one of the few to see through the smoke and mirrors of the housing boom and the CDO markets. Eisman looked into some complicated mortgage securities and had trouble understanding their terms, despite his many years of experience as a trader. Dan Gertner, a writer for *Grant's Interest Rate Observer,* had a similar experience; he actually read through the several hundred pages that constituted the complete documentation for a CDO—something none of its investors probably ever did—and after days of study still couldn't figure out how it really worked.

The central issue for any complex investment is how to properly determine its value. In this case, the value was obscured by layer upon layer of untestable assumptions, but buyers and sellers deceived themselves into thinking they understood both the value and the risk. Eisman would go to meetings and ask CDO salespeople to explain their products to him, and when they spouted some gobbledygook, he would ask them to explain what exactly they meant. Essentially, he played Leon Rozenblit's "why boy," gradually exposing whether the CDO vendors really knew their own products. "You figure out if they even know what they're talking about," said one of Eisman's partners. "And a lot of times, they don't!" He might just as well have asked them to explain how their toilets worked.

You don't have to be a seller of newfangled securities to let the surface familiarity of financial terms and concepts blind you into thinking you know more about the markets than you really do. For a few years, Chris made a specialty of investing in small biotechnology and pharmaceutical companies that focused on developing treatments for brain diseases. A couple of his stocks did well for a time, increasing by over 500 percent in one case. He started to believe that he actually had some talent for picking stocks in this sector, and easily came up with reasons why: He knew a lot of neuroscience and some genetics, and he was competent at designing experiments and analyzing data, which is the core discipline behind the clinical trials that are used to decide whether drugs can jump over all the regulatory hurdles to reach patients. But the sample of his stock-picking experience was orders of magnitude too small to demonstrate any real skill—luck was the most likely explanation for his success. That interpretation seems to have been confirmed: Most of his picks lost three-quarters or more of their value in the end.

If you can't escape the illusion entirely and still think of yourself as a knowledgeable stock picker, you might try to limit how much the illusion can affect you by allocating just a small proportion of your assets to active investment decisions, and thinking of those investments at least partly as a hobby. The rest of your money could be dedicated to strategies that are less subject to the illusion of knowledge, such as passively investing in index funds that just track the movements of the overall market. That's also a reasonable plan for a gambler who wants to keep his or her hobby under control: Set aside a small bankroll and focus on the entertainment that comes from the practice rather than counting on it to generate significant income. Chris has abandoned stock picking entirely, and he keeps his poker money in a separate bank account.

Sometimes More Is Less

Imagine that you are a subject in the following experiment, conducted by pioneering behavioral economist Richard Thaler and his colleagues.[27] You are told that you are in charge of managing the endowment portfolio of a small college and investing it in a simulated financial market. The market consists entirely of just two mutual funds, A and B, and you start with a hundred shares that you must allocate between the two. You can put all of your shares into A, all of them into B, or some into A and the rest into B. You will be running the portfolio for twenty-five simulated years. Every so often, you will be informed of how each fund has performed, and thus whether your shares have gone up or down in value, and you will then have the opportunity to change how your shares are allocated. At the end of the simulation, you will be paid an amount that is proportional to how well your shares have performed, so you have an incentive to do as well as you can. Before the game begins, however, you have to choose how often you would like to receive the feedback and have the chance to change your allocations: every month, every year, or every five years (of simulated time).

The correct answer seems obvious: Give us information, and let us use that information, as often as possible! Thaler's group tested whether this intuitive answer is right—not by giving people the choice, but by randomly assigning them to receive feedback monthly, yearly, or every five years. Most people initially tried a 50/50 allocation between the two funds since they knew nothing about which might be better. As they got information about the performance of the funds, they shifted their allocations. Since the simulated length of the experiment was twenty-five years, the subjects in the five-year condition got feedback and could change their allocations only a few times, compared with hundreds of times for the subjects in the monthly condition. By the end of the experiment, subjects who only got performance information once every five years earned *more than twice as much* as those who got monthly feedback.

How could having sixty times as many pieces of information and opportunities to adjust their portfolios have caused the monthly-feedback investors to do *worse* than the five-year ones? The answer lies partly in the nature of the two funds the investors had to choose from. The first had a low average rate of return but was fairly safe—it didn't vary much from month to month and rarely lost money. It was designed to simulate a mutual fund consisting of bonds. The second was like a stock mutual fund: It had a much higher rate of return, but also a much higher variance, so that it lost money in about 40 percent of the months.

In the long run, the best returns resulted from investing all of the money in the stock fund, since the higher return made up for the losses. Over a one-year or five-year period, the occasional monthly losses in the stock fund were canceled out by gains, so the stock fund rarely had a losing year and never had a losing five-year stretch. In the monthly condition, when subjects saw losses in the stock fund, they tended to shift their money to the safer bond fund, thereby hurting their long-term performance. Subjects who received feedback every year or every five years saw that the stock fund outperformed the bond fund, but they did not see the difference in variability. At the end of the experiment, the subjects in the five-year condition had 66 percent of their money in the stock fund, compared with only 40 percent for the subjects in the monthly condition.

What went wrong for the subjects who got monthly feedback? They got a lot of information, but it was short-term information that was not representative of the true, long-term pattern of performance for the two funds. The short-term information created an illusion of knowledge—knowledge that the stock fund was too risky, in this case. The monthly-feedback subjects had all the information they needed to generate actual knowledge—that the stock fund was the better long-term investment—but they didn't manage to do so.

The same thing happens in the real world of investing decisions. Brad Barber and Terrance Odean managed to obtain six years of trading records for sixty thousand accounts from a brokerage firm and compared investment returns between people who bought and sold stocks frequently and those who traded rarely. Presumably investors who make lots of trades believe that they have lots of knowledge and good ideas about stocks—that each of their trades will make money because it is anticipating a market move. But once their returns were adjusted for the costs and tax payments generated by all the trades they made, the most active traders earned one-third less per year than the least active ones.[28]

Professional and amateur investors alike should seek the best rates of return they can get, balanced against the level of risk they are taking. Individual investors in particular may be better off paying more attention to the riskiness of their portfolios than they currently do. Earning an extra few percentage points on your money may not be worth the anxiety, lost sleep, and bad temper that can accompany the volatility of large price swings. To make truly informed financial decisions, you must have an accurate picture of the long-term returns *and* short-term volatility you should expect from each of your investment options, and you must evaluate these factors in light of your own ability to tolerate risk.

We are generally taught that it is better to have more information than to have less. Who wouldn't want to consult *Consumer Reports* before purchasing a car or a dishwasher? Who wouldn't want to know the price of a flat-screen TV at three different stores rather than just one? And in these cases, more information does make for better decisions (at least up to a point). The studies we just presented, and others like them, suggest that investors who have more information also believe that they have better knowledge. But when that information is in fact uninformative, it only feeds the illusion of knowledge. In reality, most short-term fluctuations in value are unrelated to longer-term rates of return and should not determine your investment decisions (unless you are investing money that you might need in the near future, of course). When it comes to assessing the long-term characteristics of an investment, sometimes having more information can result in less real understanding. What the Thaler group's experiment showed was that paradoxically, people who got the most feedback about the short-term risks were least likely to acquire knowledge of the long-term returns.

The illusion of knowledge can't predict the timing and magnitude of each financial bubble—in fact, knowing about the illusion should make us just as wary of attempts to predict price drops as price increases. The illusion of knowledge does appear to be a necessary ingredient for the formation of bubbles, though. Each historical bubble has been associated with a piece of new "knowledge" that was disseminated so widely that it eventually reached people who knew nothing else about finance except for that one piece of information (tulip bulbs are a can't-lose investment, the Internet will fundamentally change what companies are worth, the Dow is going to 36,000, real estate never loses value, and so on). The proliferation of information about finance, from cable news networks to websites to business magazines, is a recipe for the illusory feeling that we know how the markets work, when all we really have is a lot of information about what they are doing at the moment, what they have done in the past, and how people *think* they work, none of which necessarily predicts what they will do in the future. Familiarity with the language of finance and the immediacy of market changes often masks a lack of deep knowledge, and the increasingly rapid flow of information may even shorten the cycle of booms and busts in the future.

The Power of Familiarity

Much as we cannot focus attention on more than a limited subset of our world and we cannot remember everything around us, the illusion of knowledge is a by-product of an otherwise effective and useful mental process. We rarely need to explain why something works. Rather, we just need to understand how to work it. We need to understand how to unclog a toilet, but we don't need to know how flushing the toilet causes water to empty from the bowl and then to fill it back up. Our ability to operate a toilet when we need to—and to do so without even thinking about the process—gives us a sense that we understand it. And for most practical purposes, that is all the understanding we really need.

In Chapter 2, we discussed the error of "change blindness blindness"—the idea that people think they will notice changes that, in reality, they rarely do. People easily confuse what they actually remember with what they potentially *could* remember if given the chance to study things further. Stop reading now and draw a picture of the face of a penny, or form an image of one in your mind. Odds are that your image has at least a couple of errors—you might have Lincoln facing the wrong direction, or you might have put the date in the wrong place, or you might have forgotten to include the date altogether. You have seen pennies every day for years, and before now you probably thought you knew what a penny looked like. You do know enough to tell a penny apart from other coins, which is the only knowledge you really need.[29]

Ronald Rensink, a vision scientist at the University of British Columbia and a leader in the study of change blindness, has made the interesting proposal that the mind works much like a Web browser. Chris's father, a smart man born long before the digital computer was invented, has asked Chris several times over the years to explain how all the information from the Internet gets into his "set," his quaint name for his iMac. Most of us know that the contents of the Internet are distributed across millions of computers around the world, rather than being duplicated inside every desktop computer. But if you had a fast enough Internet connection and there were fast enough servers on the network, you would not be able to see any difference between these two accounts of how the Internet works. From your perspective, the information you want arrives as soon as you request it; you follow a link with your Web browser, and the contents of the page appear almost immediately. The perception that the Web is stored locally on your computer is a reasonable misunderstanding, and in most cases, one that would make no difference to you. When your Internet connection goes down, though, your "set" no longer has access to the information you thought was inside it. Similarly, the experiments in which we don't notice people changing into other people reveal how little information we store in our memories. We don't need to store this information any more than our computers need to store the contents of the Web—in each case, under normal circumstances, we can obtain the information on demand, whether by looking at the person standing in front of us or by accessing sites on the Internet.[30]

Neurobabble and Brain Porn

Companies often prey on the illusion of knowledge to hawk their wares, emphasizing technical details in a way that leads people to think they understand how a product works. For example, audiophiles and audio cable manufacturers regularly wax poetic about the quality of the cables that connect different system components. Cable manufacturers tout the superior shielding on their cables, greater dynamic range, higher-quality copper, gold-plated connectors, and cleaner sound. Reviewers say that the cables make their old speakers sound like new ones, and that there is simply no comparison between the high-end cables and regular cables. In at least one informal experiment, though, audiophiles in a blind test could not distinguish one expensive set of cables from wire coat hangers used as speaker cables![31] All of the high-tech cable technology made little difference in the sound of the music. Of course, it is possible that the other components in their stereo systems might have been of insufficient quality to reveal the difference, but most people listening to music or watching movies on a home theater system wouldn't have the sort of equipment necessary to detect the difference either.

The hype is much funnier in the case of cables that transmit digital signals. As long as a cable is able to transmit the 0s and 1s that make up a digital signal, the quality of the wire doesn't matter one bit. The factor that matters is the protocol used to generate and interpret those 0s and 1s. Modern stereo systems and video systems use digital standards such as HDMI to transfer information from one component to another. Yet prices on HDMI cables vary by more than a factor of ten: A cable that costs $5 will transmit the signal just as well as a cable that costs $50. Denon even sells a 1.5-meter Ethernet cable for audio systems that is priced at $500. Here is the product description at Amazon.com:

> Get the purest digital audio you've ever experienced from multi-channel DVD and CD playback through your Denon home theater receiver with the AK-DL1 dedicated cable. Made of high-purity copper wire, it's designed to thoroughly eliminate adverse effects from vibration and helps stabilize the digital transmission from occurrences of jitter and ripple. A tin-bearing copper alloy is used for the cable's shield while the insulation is made of a fluoropolymer material with superior heat resistance, weather resistance, and anti-aging properties. The connector features a rounded plug lever to prevent bending or breaking and direction marks to indicate correct direction for connecting cable.

Apparently, some people have actually bought this product, but as reviewers on Amazon.com point out, since the signal is digital rather than analog, there is no reason to expect any difference in sound quality between this cable and an ordinary Ethernet cable you can get from your local dollar store. It's not even clear what "jitter" and "ripple" mean, why vibration matters for a stream of 0s and 1s, or how fluoropolymers prevent aging. Most of the hundreds of reviews of this product on Amazon.com are facetious, and the five most commonly associated customer tags for it include "snake oil," "ripoff," "waste of money," "throwing your money away," and "unconscionable."[32]

A group of researchers in the Yale psychology department, including Dan's graduate school adviser, Frank Keil, and our friend Jeremy Gray, conducted a mischievous experiment in which subjects read passages of text that included some uninformative babble like the description of Denon's cable. Each passage began with a straightforward summary of a psychology experiment like the following:

> Researchers created a list of facts that about 50% of people knew. Subjects then read the list and noted which ones they already knew. They then judged what percentage of other people would know those facts. When subjects knew a fact, they thought that an inaccurately large percentage of others would know it, too. For example, a subject who already knew that Hartford was the capital of Connecticut might think that 80% of other people would know it, even though only 50% actually do. The researchers call this finding "the curse of knowledge."

After reading this passage, subjects would then read either a good or a bad explanation for the "curse of knowledge." The "bad" explanation for the curse of knowledge was the following: "This 'curse' happens because subjects make more mistakes when they have to judge the knowledge of others. People are better at judging what they themselves know." Note that this explanation doesn't actually tell us anything about the "curse of knowledge." The experiment showed that people judge the knowledge of others differently depending on whether they themselves have the knowledge. It said nothing about whether we are better at judging our own knowledge or the knowledge of others.

In contrast, a "good" explanation read as follows: "This 'curse' happens because subjects have trouble switching their point of view to consider what someone else might know, mistakenly projecting their own knowledge onto others." This explanation is good because it explains the curse of knowledge in terms of a broader principle about our minds—the difficulty we have in adopting another person's perspective. The explanation may or may not be scientifically correct, but at least it is logically relevant.

Each subject read a series of these passages and explanations and rated how satisfying each explanation was. Generally, people rated the good explanations as more satisfying—they recognized that the good explanations actually said something to explain the experimental result, and the bad ones were largely irrelevant.

The twist in the experiment came from a third condition, in which irrelevant information about the brain was added to the bad explanation: "Brain scans indicate that this 'curse' happens because of the frontal lobe brain circuitry known to be involved in self-knowledge. Subjects make more mistakes when they have to judge the knowledge of others. People are much better at judging what they themselves know."

Much as the technobabble in the cable description on Amazon.com doesn't turn a $2 bundle of wires into a $500 gadget, this superfluous brain-talk, which we like to call "neurobabble," does nothing to rescue the validity of the bad psychological explanation. But the subjects rated the bad explanations that included neurobabble as more satisfying than those that did not. The neurobabble induced an illusion of knowledge; it made the bad explanations seem like they imparted more understanding than they actually did. Even students in an introductory neuroscience course were influenced. Fortunately, neuroscience graduate students had enough actual understanding to immunize them to the neurobabble.[33]

The cousin of neurobabble is "brain porn," the colorful images of blobs of activity on brain scans that can seduce us into thinking we have learned more about the brain (and the mind) than we really have. Neuroscientists have recognized that these pictures can sometimes be more of a sales tool for their research than a true aid to understanding. In one clever experiment, David McCabe and Alan Castel had subjects read one of two descriptions of a fictitious research study. The text was identical, but one description was accompanied by a typical three-dimensional brain image with activated areas drawn in color, while the other included only an ordinary bar graph of the same data. Subjects who read the version with the brain porn thought that the article was significantly better written and made more sense. The kicker is that none of the fictitious studies actually made any sense—they all described dubious claims that were not at all improved by the decorative brain scans.[34]

Neurobabble has crept into advertising, alongside technobabble and other irrelevant information that makes consumers feel that they understand something better than they really do. In a ubiquitous magazine ad, Allstate Insurance asks, "Why do most 16-year-olds drive like they're missing a part of their brain?" and answers, "Because they are." The company attributes their risky driving to an immature dorsal lateral prefrontal cortex, a region critical for "decision making, problem solving and understanding future consequences of today's actions." Beneath the headline, a cartoon depicts a brain with a car-shaped hole right in this location.[35] The ad copy might be right about the science, but the information about the brain is entirely irrelevant to its point. Teenagers are indeed risky drivers, but that's all you need to know to be persuaded that parents should talk more to their children about road safety, which is the point of Allstate's ad. If you're more likely to talk to your kids (or to buy Allstate's insurance) because you know what part of the brain is responsible for risk-taking, you are a victim of the illusion of knowledge—courtesy of neurobabble and brain porn.

There's a 50 Percent Chance the Weather Will Be Great, Sort of Wish You Were Here

In the 2005 comedy-drama *The Weather Man,* the title character (played by Nicolas Cage) is paid well but receives little respect for his job, which consists entirely of acting authoritative while reading forecasts prepared by others. It's easy to mock a class of professionals whose work comes to mind mainly when a game is rained out or a flight is delayed. There are some places, though, where the weather really is important news, and accurate weather forecasts can make millions or even billions of dollars of difference in people's lives. Dan lives in Champaign, a college town in east-central Illinois. The University of Illinois, where he teaches, is the largest employer in the area, but the dominant economic force in the region is large-scale farming of corn and soybeans. Illinois produces a larger soybean crop than any other state and is the second-largest corn producer.[36] The weather influences all of the important decisions a farmer makes, including when to plant and harvest, what to plant, and how to plan ahead for future supply and demand. Farmers in Illinois monitor conditions far outside their own region. A bumper corn crop during Argentina's summer can affect which crops Illinois farmers plant in the spring. Even the world markets for oil and other forms of energy affect planting decisions, since Illinois corn is responsible for 40 percent of the ethanol produced in the United States.

Few National Public Radio stations have more than one weather forecaster on staff, and even fewer have one with a meteorology degree. The Champaign NPR station, WILL, has one full-time meteorologist, two part-time meteorologists, and another weather forecaster on staff. WILL gives detailed weather forecasts throughout the day, devoting as much time to the weather as any station in the United States. It has to, because farmers depend on weather forecasts for their livelihood.[37] If weather forecasters really know how much they know—in technical terms, if they are "well calibrated"—then farmers can rely on their predictions when making major decisions.

Although people have attempted to predict the weather for millennia, the first published forecast appeared in print less than 150 years ago, in Cincinnati on September 1, 1869: "Cloudy and warm this evening. Tomorrow clear."[38] The addition of probabilities expressed as percentages didn't begin until 1920, when Cleve Hallenbeck, the head of the U.S. Weather Bureau office in Roswell, New Mexico, published an article advocating their use. Hallenbeck had tested his method with an informal experiment that lasted 220 days. On each day he estimated the probability of rain and then recorded whether it rained. His forecasts turned out to be remarkably well calibrated: It rained on most of his high-probability days and on few of his low-probability days. However, only in 1965 did the U.S. National Weather Service begin to regularly include percentage probabilities of rain in its forecasts. In 1980, meteorologists Jerome Charba and William Klein undertook a massive examination of more than 150,000 precipitation forecasts during the two years from 1977 to 1979. The forecasted likelihood of rain matched the actual probability of rain almost perfectly. Tellingly, the only systematic errors happened when the forecasters assigned a 100 percent chance of rain—it turned out to rain on only about 90 percent of those days. Beware of certainty!

What makes weather forecasts, at least good ones, different from other forms of reasoning and prediction? When meteorologists say that there is a 60 percent chance of rain, they are estimating the probability that, given the existing atmospheric conditions, it actually will rain. And these estimates are highly accurate over a long series of forecasts. Meteorologists continually adjust their predictions—and the mathematical and statistical models and computer programs that generate those predictions—based on feedback from previous predictions. If a 60 percent probability of rain is attached to certain climate patterns, but it only rains 40 percent of the time, then the models are refined so that the next time those atmospheric conditions occur, the estimated probability of rain will be lower. Weather forecasting is unusual in that forecasters receive immediate and definitive feedback about their predictions, and their knowledge of probabilities accumulates over time. For example, during the period from 1966 through 1978, skill at forecasting precipitation thirty-six hours in advance nearly doubled.[39]

Like weather forecasters, when we receive appropriate feedback, we can sometimes calibrate our judgments and eliminate the illusion of knowledge. In a demonstration Dan has used in an introductory psychology class, students are each given a playing card, which they proceed to hold to their forehead so that they can't see it, but everyone else can.[40] Then each person in the class tries to get the person with the highest possible card to pair up with him or her. Remember, the students can't see their own card, but they can see everyone else's—so they can see who rejects them.

Initially, most people in the class will try to pair up with an Ace or King (the highest cards), but most will be rejected. Only those who have a really high card are likely to be accepted by someone who has an Ace or a King. People with an Ace or King don't know what they have, but they know that they really can't do better than an Ace or King and they aren't likely to accept an invitation from someone with a 6 or 7—they hope to match with someone higher. Surprisingly, people pair off quite quickly with others who have cards comparable to their own. They are able to rapidly use the feedback they get from rejection to calibrate their expectations. The same principle can be used to explain why people of widely different attractiveness rarely end up as couples[41]— people reach for the best they can get, and dating allows for some calibration of your self-impressions.

The card-matching game and the real world of dating and mating provide immediate and direct (and sometimes painful) feedback in the form of rejection. Unfortunately, for most of the judgments that we make in our lives, we never receive the precise feedback that weather forecasters do of seeing the next morning whether we were right or wrong, day after day, year after year. This is an important difference between meteorology and fields like medicine. Information about the correctness of a diagnosis, or the outcome of a surgical procedure, is available *in principle*. In practice, though, it is rarely collected systematically, stored, and analyzed the way data about the weather is; a doctor who diagnoses pneumonia and prescribes a treatment will have to wait awhile to learn—or may never learn—whether the treatment worked. Even then it may be difficult to distinguish the effects of the treatment from improvements that happened spontaneously. If you've recently switched from a film camera to a digital camera, you have experienced the benefits of instant feedback. You no longer have to wait for your film to be developed before you know what you did wrong (or right) in composing your shots. And when you do make a mistake, you can fix it right away. As any student knows, whether in photography, psychology, or business, it's harder to improve if you don't get immediate feedback about your mistakes.

Why Does the Illusion of Knowledge Persist?

Scientists, architects, and hedge fund managers are respected, but weather forecasters are parodied. Yet weather forecasters have fewer illusions about their own knowledge than do members of these other professions. In Chapter 3 we saw that doctors who consulted books and computers were underappreciated by patients, whereas a rape victim who expressed no doubt in her testimony was praised as a model witness. There we argued that our love of confidence can reward people for acting as though they are more skilled and accurate than they really are. The illusion of knowledge has similar consequences: We seem to prefer the advice of experts who act like they know more than they really do—or who honestly believe their knowledge is greater than it is.

Do people actually prefer expressions of knowledge that exude more certainty to more tentative statements, even when the tentative ones are better calibrated? Try answering the following simple question devised by the Dutch psychologist Gideon Keren:

Listed below are four-day weather forecasts for the probability of rain, made by two meteorologists, Anna and Betty:

	MONDAY	TUESDAY	WEDNESDAY	THURSDAY
Anna's Forecast:	90%	90%	90%	90%
Betty's Forecast:	75%	75%	75%	75%

As it turned out, it rained on three out of the four days. Who, in your opinion, was a better forecaster: Anna or Betty?

This question pits our preferences for accuracy and certainty against each other. Betty said it should rain 75 percent of the time, and it did, so her predictions reflected no illusion of knowledge. Anna thought she knew more about the likelihood of rain than she really did: It would have to have rained on all four days for her forecasts to be more accurate than Betty's. When we conducted an experiment using a variant of this question, nearly half of our subjects, however, preferred Anna's forecast.[42]

The conditions of this experiment differ from most real-world situations, in which we rarely get to choose among experts with such clear track records of success or failure in prediction. A study of experts on international politics—a field in which it can take years or decades to see whether predictions are borne out—found that their forecasts were significantly less accurate than those of simple statistical models. The way the forecasts were worse was revealing: In general, the experts predicted that political and economic conditions would change (for the better or the worse) more often than they actually did. So a strategy of simply assuming that the future will be the same as the present would have yielded more accurate predictions (but probably less airtime for the pundit). Unlike the weather forecasting experiment, though, people listening to these political experts have no way to tell in advance how accurate their forecasts will be.[43] Compared to the laboratory, in the real world it's much harder to make a correct choice, precisely because we either lack the necessary information, or we have it but lack the time, attention, and insight we need to evaluate it properly.

The Anna/Betty experiment shows that even when we have all the necessary information to recognize which expert knows the limits of her own knowledge, we often prefer the one who does not. Self-help authors who say precisely what to do ("eat this, not that") have larger audiences than those who give a menu of reasonable options for readers to try out in order to find out what works best for them. TV stock-picking guru Jim Cramer tells you to "buy buy buy" or "sell sell sell" (with a hearty "Boo-yah!") rather than to analyze investment ideas in the context of your overall financial goals, weighting of different types of assets, and other nuanced considerations that might undermine the dazzling sense of conviction that he exudes.[44]

So the illusion of knowledge persists in part because people prefer experts who think they know more than they really do. People who know the limits of their knowledge say things like "there is a 75 percent chance of rain," while people who don't know those limits express undue certainty. Yet even those with the best understanding of their field can fall prey to the illusion of knowledge. Recall the scientists who made misguided predictions about the number of human genes, the limits of natural resources, and the promise of chess-playing computers. These scientists were far from marginal figures or failures in their fields. Eric Lander, who mispredicted the number of human genes, and John Holdren, who wrongly forecast ever-rising commodity prices, went on to become science advisers in Barack Obama's administration. Paul Ehrlich received a MacArthur Foundation "genius" award worth $345,000 in 1990, the same year he lost his bet about commodity prices. And Herbert Simon won the Nobel Prize in economics in 1978—for his "pioneering research on the decision-making processes within economic organizations," not for his ability to forecast the results of chess matches.[45]

In none of these cases did the illusion of knowledge cost people their livelihoods, but in others it has. The archetype of the successful investor is not someone who hedges his bets carefully and makes sure that his asset allocation and leverage reflect an appropriate level of uncertainty about the future. It is one who makes bold moves—who gambles it all and wins. The illusion of knowledge is so strong that we eagerly welcome back into the fold people who win for a while and then go too far and lose it all. In 2007, despite his disastrous losses at Amaranth and Deutsche Bank, and despite having been formally charged with market manipulation by the U.S. government, Brian Hunter was raising capital for a new hedge fund—as did the disgraced founders of Long-Term Capital Management and other failed funds before him.[46]

jumping to conclusions

O N MAY 29, 2005, a six-year-old girl was hospitalized in Cincinnati, where she'd been visiting relatives. She was dehydrated, had a fever and a rash, and had to spend days in the hospital on a ventilator. The hospital sent a blood sample to the Ohio State Department of Health Laboratory for testing, and the result confirmed their initial diagnosis: She had measles.[1]

Measles is among the most infectious viruses affecting children. When a person with measles sneezes, another person can contract the disease just by breathing the air in the room or touching a contaminated surface—the virus remains active for up to two hours. The rash is the first visible evidence that distinguishes the measles infection from other viruses, but the disease is contagious for four days before the rash appears. Moreover, someone exposed to measles might show no symptoms at all for up to two weeks.

The combination of delayed onset of symptoms, the potential for carriers to spread the disease before they know they are infected, and the highly infectious nature of the virus itself creates a perfect recipe for epidemics. Before the 1970s, measles was so prevalent, even in the United States, that it was unusual for children *not* to get it. It's still prevalent throughout much of the world; according to the World Health Organization (WHO), nearly two hundred thousand people died from measles infection in 2007 alone, and it remains a leading cause of death in children worldwide.

Serious complications of the disease include blindness, severe dehydration, diarrhea, encephalitis, and pneumonia. In poorer, developing countries with inadequate health care and high rates of malnutrition, measles outbreaks can be catastrophic; the WHO estimates death rates as high as 10 percent from outbreaks in such regions. In wealthier countries with effective health care systems, measles rarely causes death, but it can cause serious complications for people with existing health problems like asthma.

The elimination of measles is one of the great success stories for programs of systematic vaccination. Cases of measles in the United States are exceptionally rare today because of the effectiveness of the combination MMR vaccine that inoculates against measles, mumps, and rubella. Mandatory MMR vaccination of children before they enter the public school system largely eliminated measles from the United States by the year 2000. Vaccination levels of 90 percent of the population are needed to effectively prevent epidemics, and the United States has exceeded that threshold for more than a decade. So how did a six-year-old girl in Cincinnati get the disease?

Measles is still endemic in parts of Europe where vaccination programs are voluntary, and full-scale epidemics are common in Africa and parts of Asia. Most cases of measles in the United States are isolated—an unvaccinated person visits a country where an outbreak is underway, is exposed to the virus, returns home, and then starts to show symptoms. The girl visiting Cincinnati lived in northwest Indiana and hadn't been out of the country. So how did she get it?

Because measles can be contagious for so long before symptoms appear, it can be transmitted by people who don't know they have it. Even if this girl hadn't been to a region where measles is endemic, she could have unknowingly encountered someone who had. She most likely was infected about two weeks earlier, on May 15, when she attended a large gathering with about five hundred members of her Indiana church. Her parents reported to Cincinnati hospital workers that one of the teenagers at the gathering was sick—she had a fever, a cough, and conjunctivitis (colloquially known as "pink eye"). As it turned out, that seventeen-year-old girl had just returned to Indiana following a church mission in Bucharest, the capital of Romania, where she'd worked in an orphanage and hospital. She had traveled on commercial flights to get back to the United States on May 14 and attended the church gathering the next day. She was the "index case"—the first person to be infected, and thus the source of the infections in all of the later patients—in what quickly became the biggest measles outbreak in the United States since 2000.

During May and June of 2005, another 32 people contracted measles. Of these 34 documented cases, 33 were church members who either came into direct contact with the seventeen-year-old index case or lived in the same house as someone who had. The only person who contracted measles outside of the church community worked at a hospital where one of the patients was treated. Fortunately, none of those infected died from the disease. In addition to the six-year-old girl in Cincinnati, a forty-five-year-old man needed intravenous fluids and the hospital worker needed six days of ventilator support because of pneumonia and respiratory distress. Through effective treatment and management of the outbreak—anyone exposed to the virus who hadn't yet shown symptoms had to be quarantined for eighteen days—the outbreak was contained by the end of July, with no new cases reported after then. By one estimate, the total cost of the containment and treatment efforts was nearly $300,000.[2]

Only two of the 34 patients had been vaccinated, and one of those two—the hospital worker—had only received one dose of the vaccine. The six-year-old girl hadn't been vaccinated, nor had the seventeen-year-old who had traveled to Romania. In the gathering of 500 people, 50 were unvaccinated, and 16 of those 50 subsequently got measles. The outbreak was containable because most of the community members had been vaccinated. In countries where vaccination is less common, the outbreak would have been much larger.

Why were 10 percent of the church members unvaccinated when the vaccination rate for school-age children in the United States is over 95 percent? Although vaccination is mandatory for all children attending public schools in the United States, in many states, parents can file a "personal belief exemption" that allows them to forgo vaccination for their children for religious or other reasons. And in fact, most of the measles cases occurred in a few families that had declined inoculation. Many of these families continued to refuse vaccination even as health authorities were trying to control the outbreak.

The 2005 Cincinnati outbreak was not unique. During the first seven months of 2008, the Centers for Disease Control (CDC) documented 131 cases of measles in the United States, more than double the yearly average from 2001 through 2007, and the highest number since 1996. Most of the cases occurred among schoolchildren who are eligible for vaccination but whose parents declined to have them vaccinated.

Why would parents knowingly reject a vaccine that could prevent a serious and highly contagious childhood illness, one that had been effectively eradicated by that same vaccine? Why would people knowingly violate CDC and WHO guidelines by traveling to foreign countries where measles and other preventable diseases are prevalent without first vaccinating themselves? Why would parents expose their children to potentially deadly diseases like measles when a safe and effective vaccine has been available for more than forty years?

This behavior, as we'll discover, is the result of another everyday illusion—the *illusion of cause*. Before we can understand why people would choose not to vaccinate their children, we must first consider three separate, but interrelated, biases that contribute to the illusion of cause. These biases arise from the fact that our minds are built to detect meaning in patterns, to infer causal relationships from coincidences, and to believe that earlier events cause later ones.

Seeing the God in Everything

Pattern perception is central to our lives, and skill in many professions is based almost entirely on the ability to rapidly recognize a large variety of important patterns. Doctors look for combinations of symptoms that form a pattern, allowing them to infer an underlying cause, make a diagnosis, select a treatment, and predict their patient's outcome. Clinical psychologists and counselors look for patterns in thoughts and behaviors to help diagnose mental dysfunction. Stock traders follow the ups and downs of the major indices, looking for consistencies that will give them an advantage. Baseball coaches decide where to position their players in the field based on regularities in where batters tend to hit the ball, and pitchers adjust their pitching based on the patterns they perceive in a batter's swings. All of us use pattern detection without even knowing that we're doing it. We can identify people we know from no more information than characteristic regularities in their gaits. Just by picking up patterns of movement and gesture from brief silent videos, students can even predict which teachers are likely to receive good ratings at the end of a semester.[3] We can't help but see patterns in the world and make predictions based on those patterns.

These extraordinary pattern detection abilities often serve us well, enabling us to draw conclusions in seconds (or milliseconds) that would take minutes or hours if we had to rely on laborious logical calculations. Unfortunately, they can also lead us astray, contributing to the illusion of cause. At times, we perceive patterns where none exist, and we misperceive them where they do exist. Regardless of whether a repeating pattern actually exists, when we perceive that it does, we readily infer that it results from a causal relationship. Much as our memory for the world can be distorted to match our conceptions of what we should remember, and just as we can fail to see the gorillas around us because they do not fit with our preexisting expectations, our understanding of our world is systematically biased to perceive meaning rather than randomness and to infer cause rather than coincidence. And we are usually completely unaware of these biases.

The illusion of cause arises when we see patterns in randomness, and we are most likely to see patterns when we think we understand what is causing them. Our intuitive beliefs about causation lead us to perceive patterns consistent with those beliefs at least as often as the patterns we perceive lead us to form new beliefs. Some of the most striking examples of pattern perception gone awry involve the detection of faces in unusual places.

One day in 1994, Diana Duyser saw something strange after she bit into a grilled cheese sandwich she had just made. Etched into the surface of the toasted bread, staring back at her, was a face. Duyser, a jewelry designer in South Florida, immediately recognized the face as that of the Virgin Mary. She stopped eating the sandwich and stored it in a plastic box, where it remained, miraculously mold-free, for ten years. Then, for unknown reasons, she decided to sell this religious icon on eBay. The Internet gambling site GoldenPalace.com put in the winning bid of $28,000 and sent its CEO to personally pick up the purchase. In handing it over, Duyser was quoted as saying, "I do believe that this is the Virgin Mary Mother of God."[4]

The human mind's tendency to promiscuously perceive meaningful visual patterns in randomness has a one-word name: *pareidolia*. Like the Virgin Mary Grilled Cheese, many examples of pareidolia involve religious images. The "Nun Bun" was a cinnamon pastry whose twisty rolls eerily resembled the nose and jowls of Mother Teresa. It was found in a Nashville coffee shop in 1996, but was stolen on Christmas in 2005. "Our Lady of the Underpass" was another appearance by the Virgin Mary, this time in the guise of a salt stain under Interstate 94 in Chicago that drew huge crowds and stopped traffic for months in 2005. Other cases include Hot Chocolate Jesus, Jesus on a shrimp tail dinner, Jesus in a dental x-ray, and Cheesus (a Cheeto purportedly shaped like Jesus). Islam forbids images of Allah, but followers in West Yorkshire, England, have noticed the word "Allah" written out, in Arabic, in the veiny material inside a sliced-open tomato.

You won't be surprised to learn that we favor a mundane explanation for all of these face sightings. Your visual system has a difficult problem to solve in recognizing faces, objects, and words. They can all appear in a wide variety of conditions: good light, bad light, near, far, oriented at different angles, with some parts hidden, in different colors, and so on. Like an amplifier that you turn up in order to hear a weak signal, your visual system is exquisitely sensitive to the patterns that are most important to you. In fact, visual areas of your brain can be activated by images that only vaguely resemble what they're tuned for. In just one-fifth of a second, your brain can distinguish a face from other objects like chairs or cars. In just an instant more, your brain can distinguish objects that look a bit like faces, such as a parking meter or a three-prong outlet, from other objects like chairs. Seeing objects that resemble faces induces activity in a brain area called the fusiform gyrus that is highly sensitive to real faces. In other words, almost immediately after you see an object that looks anything like a face, your brain treats it like a face and processes it differently than other objects. That's one reason why we find it so easy to see facelike patterns as actual faces.[5]

The same principles apply to our other senses. Play Led Zeppelin's "Stairway to Heaven" backward and you may hear "Satan," "666," and some other strange words. Play Queen's "Another One Bites the Dust" backward and the late Freddie Mercury might tell you "it's fun to smoke marijuana." This phenomenon can be exploited for fun and profit. A writer named Karen Stollznow noticed a faint outline on a Pop-Tart that could be interpreted as the miter-style hat traditionally worn by the pope. She snapped a digital photo, uploaded it to eBay, and opened up bidding on the "Pope Tart." Over the course of the auction she exchanged numerous entertaining e-mails with believers and skeptics. By the end, the winning bid was $46. She attributed the relatively low price paid for the Pope Tart to a lack of publicity, as compared with the press releases and television coverage received by the Virgin Mary Grilled Cheese.[6]

These examples represent just the tip of the iceberg that is the mind's hyperactive tendency to spot patterns. Even trained professionals are biased to see patterns they expect to see and not ones that seem inconsistent with their beliefs. Recall Brian Hunter, the hedge fund manager who lost it all (more than once) by betting on the future price of natural gas. He thought he understood the reasons for the movements of the energy markets, and his inference of a causal pattern in the markets led to his company's downfall. When pattern recognition works well, we can find the face of our lost child in the middle of a huge crowd at the mall. When it works too well, we spot deities in pastries, trends in stock prices, and other relationships that aren't really there or don't mean what we think they do.

Causes and Symptoms

Unlike the parade of unusual patients appearing on television dramas like *Grey's Anatomy* and *House,* or coming to Dr. Keating's St. Louis diagnostic clinic, the vast majority of the patients whom doctors see on a daily basis have run-of-the-mill problems. Experts quickly recognize common sets of symptoms; they're sensitized to the most probable diagnoses, learning quite reasonably to expect to encounter the common cold more often than an exotic Asian flu, and ordinary sadness more often than clinical depression.

Intuitively, most people think that experts consider more alternatives and more possible diagnoses rather than fewer. Yet the mark of true expertise is not the ability to consider more options, but the ability to filter out irrelevant ones. Imagine that a child arrives in the emergency room wheezing and short of breath. The most likely explanation might be asthma, in which case treating with a bronchodilator like albuterol should fix the problem. Of course, it's also possible that the wheezing is caused by something the child swallowed that became lodged in his throat. Such a foreign body could cause all sorts of other symptoms, including secondary infections. On shows like *House,* that rare explanation would of course turn out to be the cause of the child's symptoms. In reality, though, asthma or pneumonia is a far more likely explanation. An expert doctor recognizes the pattern, and likely has seen many patients with asthma, leading to a quick and almost always accurate diagnosis. Unless your job is like Dr. Keating's, and you know that you're dealing with exceptional cases, focusing too much on the rare causes would be counterproductive. Expert doctors consider first those few diagnoses that are the most probable explanations for a pattern of symptoms.

Experts are, in a sense, primed to see patterns that fit their well-established expectations, but perceiving the world through a lens of expectations, however reasonable, can backfire. Just as people counting basketball passes often fail to notice an unexpected gorilla, experts can miss a "gorilla" if it is an unusual, unexpected, or rare underlying cause of a pattern. This can be an issue when doctors move from practicing in hospitals during their residencies and fellowships to practicing privately, especially if they go into family practice or internal medicine in a more suburban area. The frequencies of diseases doctors encounter in urban teaching hospitals differ greatly from those in suburban medical offices, so doctors must retune their pattern recognizers to the new environment in order to maintain an expert level of diagnostic skill.

Expectations can cause anyone to sometimes see things that don't exist. Chris's mother has suffered from arthritis pain in her hands and knees for several years, and she feels that her joints hurt more on days when it is cold and raining. She's not alone. A 1972 study found that 80–90 percent of arthritis patients reported greater pain when the temperature went down, the barometric pressure went down, and the humidity went up—in other words, when a cold rain was on the way. Medical textbooks used to devote entire chapters to the relationship between weather and arthritis. Some experts have even advised chronic pain patients to move across the country to warmer, drier areas. But does the weather actually exacerbate arthritis pain?

Researchers Donald Redelmeier, a medical doctor, and Amos Tversky, a cognitive psychologist, tracked eighteen arthritis patients over fifteen months, asking them to rate their pain level twice each month. Then they matched these data up with local weather reports from the same time period. All but one of the patients believed that weather changes had affected their pain levels. But when Redelmeier and Tversky mapped the reports of pain to the weather the same day, or the day before, or two days before, there was no association at all. Despite the strong beliefs of the subjects who participated in their experiment, changes in the weather were entirely unrelated to reports of pain.

Chris told his mother about this study. She said she was sure it was right, but she still felt what she felt. It's not surprising that pain doesn't necessarily respond to statistics. So why do arthritis sufferers believe in a pattern that doesn't exist? What would lead people to think there was an association even when the weather was completely unpredictive? Redelmeier and Tversky conducted a second experiment. They recruited undergraduates for a study and showed them pairs of numbers, one giving a patient's pain level and the other giving the barometric pressure for that day. Keep in mind that in actuality, pain and weather conditions are unrelated—knowing the barometric pressure is of no use in predicting how much pain a patient experienced that day, because pain is just as likely when it's warm and sunny as when it's cold and rainy. In the fake, experimental data there was also no relationship. Yet just like the actual patients, more than half of the undergraduates thought there was a link between arthritis and pain in the data set. In one case, 87 percent saw a positive relationship.

Through a process of "selective matching," the subjects in this experiment focused on patterns that existed only in subsets of the data, such as a few days when low pressure and pain happened to coincide, and neglected the rest. Arthritis sufferers likely do the same: They remember those days when arthritis pain coincided with cold, rainy weather better than those days when they had pain but it was warm and sunny, and much better than pain-free days, which don't stand out in memory at all. Putative links between the weather and symptoms are part of our everyday language; we speak of "feeling under the weather" and we think that wearing hats in winter lessens our chances of "catching a cold." The subjects and the patients perceived an association where none existed because they interpreted the weather and pain data in a way that was consistent with their preexisting beliefs. In essence, they saw the gorilla they expected to see even when it was nowhere in sight.[7]

Beware of Belief Becoming "Because"

Many introductory psychology textbooks ask students to think about possible reasons why ice cream consumption should be positively associated with drowning rates. More people drown on days when a lot of ice cream is consumed, and fewer people drown on days when only a little ice cream is consumed. Eating ice cream presumably doesn't cause drowning, and news of drownings shouldn't inspire people to eat ice cream. Rather, a third factor—the summer heat—likely causes both. Less ice cream is consumed in winter, and fewer people drown then because fewer people go swimming.[8]

This example draws attention to the second major bias underlying the illusion of cause—when two events tend to happen together, we infer that one must have caused the other. Textbooks use the ice cream–drowning correlation precisely because it's hard to see how either one could cause the other, but easy to see how a third, unmentioned factor could cause both. Unfortunately, seeing through the illusion of cause is rarely so simple in the real world.

Most conspiracy theories are based on detecting patterns in events that, when viewed with the theory in mind, seem to help us understand why they happened. In essence, conspiracy theories infer cause from coincidence. The more you believe the theory, the more likely you are to fall prey to the illusion of cause.

Conspiracy theories result from a pattern perception mechanism gone awry—they are cognitive versions of the Virgin Mary Grilled Cheese. Those conspiracy theorists who already believed that President Bush would stage 9/11 to justify a preconceived plan to invade Iraq were quick to see his false memory of seeing the first plane hit the towers as evidence that he knew about the attack in advance. People who already thought that Hillary Clinton would say anything to get elected were quick to jump on her false memory of Bosnian snipers as evidence that she was lying to benefit her campaign. In both cases, people used their understanding of the person to fit the event into a pattern. They inferred an underlying cause, and they were so confident that they had the right cause that they failed to notice more plausible alternative ex-planations.

Illustrations of this illusion of cause are so pervasive that undergrad-uates in our research methods classes have no problem completing our assignment to find a recent media report that mistakenly infers a causal relationship from a mere association. One BBC article, provocatively titled "Sex Keeps You Young," reported a study by Dr. David Weeks of the Royal Edinburgh Hospital showing that "couples who have sex at least three times a week look more than 10 years younger than the aver-age adult who makes love twice a week."[9] The caption to an attached photo read, "Regular sex 'can take years off your looks.'" Although having sex could somehow cause a youthful appearance, it is at least as plausible that having a youthful appearance leads to more sexual en-counters, or that a youthful appearance is a sign of physical fitness, which makes frequent sex easier, or that people who appear more youth-ful are more likely to maintain an ongoing sexual relationship, or . . . the possible explanations are endless. The statistical association between youthful appearance and sexual activity does not imply that one causes the other. Had the title been phrased in the opposite way, "Looking Young Gets You More Sex," it would have been equally conclusory, but less surprising and therefore less newsworthy.

Of course, some correlations are more likely to reflect an actual causal relationship than others. Higher summer temperatures are more likely to cause people to eat ice cream than are reports of drownings. Statisticians and social scientists have developed clever ways to gather and analyze correlational data that increase the odds of finding a true causal effect. But the only way—let us repeat, *the only way*—to defini-tively test whether an association is causal is to run an experiment. Without an experiment, observing an association may just be the scien-tific equivalent of noticing a coincidence. Many medical studies adopt an epidemiological approach, measuring rates of illness and compar-ing them among groups of people or among societies. For example, an epidemiological study might measure and compare the overall health of people who eat lots of vegetables with that of people who eat few vegetables. Such a study could show that people who eat vegetables throughout their lives tend to be healthier than those who don't. This study would provide scientific evidence for an association between vegetable-eating and health, but it would not support a claim that eating vegetables causes health (or that being healthy causes people to eat vegetables, for that matter). Both vegetable-eating and health could be caused by a third factor—for instance, wealth may enable people to afford both tasty, fresh produce and superior health care. Epidemiological studies are not experiments, but in many cases—such as smoking and lung cancer in humans—they are the best way to determine whether two factors are associated, and therefore have at least a potential causal connection.

Unlike an observed association, though, an experiment systematically varies one factor, known as the independent variable, to see its effect on another factor, the dependent variable. For example, if you were interested in learning whether people are better able to focus on a difficult task when listening to background music than when sitting in silence, you would randomly assign some people to listen to music and others to work in silence and you would measure how well they do on some cognitive test. You have introduced a cause (listening to music or not listening to music) and then observed an effect (differences in performance on the cognitive test). Just measuring two effects and showing that they co-occur does not imply that one causes the other. That is, if you just measure whether people listen to music and then measure how they do on cognitive tasks, you cannot demonstrate a causal link between music listening and cognitive performance. Why not?

Paradoxically, properly inferring causation depends on an element of randomness. Each person must be assigned randomly to one of the two groups—otherwise, any differences between the groups could be due to other systematic biases. Let's say you just asked people to report whether they listen to music while working and you found that people who worked in silence tended to be more productive. Many factors could cause this difference. Perhaps people who are better educated prefer working in silence, or perhaps people with attention deficits are more likely to listen to music.

A standard principle taught in introductory psychology classes is that correlation does not imply causation. This principle needs to be taught because it runs counter to the illusion of cause. It is particularly hard to internalize, and in the abstract, knowing the principle does little to immunize us against the error. Fortunately, we have a simple trick to help you spot the illusion in action: When you hear or read about an association between two factors, think about whether people could have been assigned randomly to conditions for one of them. If it would have been impossible, too expensive, or ethically dubious to randomly assign people to those groups, then the study could not have been an experiment and the causal inference is not supported. To illustrate this idea, here are some examples taken from actual news headlines:[10]

- "Drop That BlackBerry! Multitasking May Be Harmful"— Could researchers randomly assign some people to lead a multitasking, BlackBerry-addicted life and others to just focus on one thing at a time all day long? Probably not. The study actually used a questionnaire to find people who already tended to watch TV, text-message, and use their computers simultaneously, and compared them with people who tended to do just one of these things at a time. Then they gave a set of cognitive tests to both groups and found that the multitaskers did worse on some of the tests. The original article describes the study's method clearly, but the headline added an unwarranted causal interpretation. It's also possible that people who do badly at the cognitive tests also think they can multitask just fine, and therefore tend to do it more than they should.

- "Bullying Harms Kids' Mental Health"—Could a researcher randomly assign some kids to be bullied and others not to be bullied? No—not ethically, anyway. So the study must have measured an association between being bullied and suffering mental health problems. The causal relationship could well be reversed—children who have mental health issues might be more likely to get bullied. Or some other factors, perhaps in their family background, could cause them both to be bullied and to have mental health issues.

- "Does Your Neighborhood Cause Schizophrenia?"—This study showed that rates of schizophrenia were greater in some neighborhoods than others. Could the researchers have randomly assigned people to live in different neighborhoods? In our experience people generally like to participate in psychology experiments, but requiring them to pack up and move might be asking too much.

- "Housework Cuts Breast Cancer Risk"—We doubt experimenters would have much luck randomly assigning some women to a "more housework" condition and others to a "less housework" condition (though some of the subjects might be happy with their luck).

- "Sexual Lyrics Prompt Teens to Have Sex"—Were some teens randomly assigned to listen to sexually explicit lyrics and others to listen to more innocuous lyrics, and then observed to see how much sex they had? Perhaps an adventurous experimenter could do this in the lab, but that's not what these researchers did. And it's doubtful that exposing teens to the music of Eminem and Prince in a lab would cause a measurable change in their sexual behavior even if such an experiment were conducted.

Once you apply this trick, you can see the humor in most of these misleading headlines. In most of these cases, the researchers likely knew the limits of their studies, understood that correlation does not imply causation, and used the right logic and terminology in their scientific papers. But when their research was "translated" for popular consumption, the illusion of cause took over and these subtleties were lost. News reporting often gets the causation wrong in an attempt to make the claim more interesting or the narrative more convincing. It's far less exciting to say that those teens who listen to sexually explicit lyrics also happen to have sex at earlier ages. That more precise phrasing leaves open the plausible alternatives—that having sex or being interested in sex makes teens more receptive to sexually explicit lyrics, or that some other factor contributes to both sexual precocity and a preference for sexually explicit lyrics.

And Then What Happened?

The illusory perception of causes from correlations is closely tied to the appeal of stories. When we hear that teens are listening to sexually explicit music or playing violent games, we expect there to be consequences, and when we hear that those same teens are *subsequently* more likely to have sex or to be violent, we perceive a causal link. We immediately believe we understand how these behaviors are causally linked, but our understanding is based on a logical fallacy. The third major mechanism driving the illusion of cause comes from the way in which we interpret narratives. In chronologies or mere sequences of happenings, we assume that the earlier events must have caused the later ones.

David Foster Wallace, the celebrated author of the novel *Infinite Jest,* committed suicide by hanging himself in the late summer of 2008. Like many famous creative writers, he suffered for a long time from depression and substance abuse, and he had attempted suicide before. Wallace was something of a literary prodigy, publishing his first novel, *The Broom of the System,* at the age of twenty-five while he was still studying for his master of fine arts (MFA) degree. The book was praised by the *New York Times,* but received mixed reviews elsewhere. Wallace worked on a follow-up short story collection, but could not help feeling like a failure. His mother brought him back to live at home. According to a profile in the *New Yorker* by D. T. Max,[11] things went downhill quickly:

> One night, he and Amy [his sister] watched "The Karen Carpenter Story," a maudlin TV movie about the singer, who died of a heart attack brought on by anorexia. When it was over, Wallace's

sister, who was working on her own M.F.A., at the University of Virginia, told David that she had to drive back to Virginia. David asked her not to go. After she went, he tried to commit suicide with pills.

What do you make of this passage about Wallace's earlier suicide attempt? To us, the most natural interpretation is that the movie upset Wallace, that he wanted his sister to stay with him but she refused, and that in despair over losing her companionship, he overdosed. But if you read the passage again, you will see that none of these facts are stated explicitly. Strictly speaking, even the idea that he wanted her to stay is only implied by the sentence, "David asked her not to go." Max is almost clinically sparing in his just-the-facts approach. But the interpretation we attach to these facts seems obvious; we come to it automatically and without conscious thought, indeed without even realizing that we are adding in information that is not present in the source. This is the illusion of cause at work. When a series of facts is narrated, we fill in the gaps to create a causal sequence: Event 1 caused Event 2, which caused Event 3, and so on. The movie made Wallace sad, which made him ask Amy to stay; she went, so she must have refused him, causing him to attempt suicide.

In addition to automatically inferring cause when it is only implied by a sequence, we also tend to remember a narrative better when we have to draw such inferences than when we don't. Consider the following pairs of sentences, taken from a study by University of Denver psychologist Janice Keenan and her colleagues:[12]

1. Joey's big brother punched him again and again. The next day his body was covered by bruises.

2. Joey's crazy mother became furiously angry with him. The next day his body was covered by bruises.

In the first case, no inference is needed—the cause of Joey's bruising is stated explicitly in the first sentence. In the second case, the cause of the bruises is implied but not stated. For this reason, understanding the second pair of sentences turns out to be slightly harder (and takes slightly longer) than understanding the first. But what you're doing as you read the sentences is crucial. To understand the second pair of sentences, you must make an extra logical inference that you don't need in order to make sense of the first pair. And in making this inference, you form a richer and more elaborate memory for what you've read. Readers of the *New Yorker* story likely will remember the implied cause of Wallace's early suicide attempt, even though it never was stated in the story itself. They will do so because they drew the inference themselves rather than having it handed to them.

"Tell me a story," children beg their parents. "And then what happened?" they ask if they hear a pause. Adults spend billions of dollars on movies, television, novels, short stories, works of biography and history, and other forms of narrative. One appeal of spectator sports is their chronology; every play, every shot, every home run is a new event in a story whose ending is in doubt. Teachers—and authors of books on science—are learning that stories are effective ways to grab and control an audience's attention.[13] But there is a paradox here: Stories—that is, sequences of events—are by themselves entertaining, but not directly useful. It's hard to see why evolution would have designed our brains to prefer receiving facts in chronological order unless there was some other benefit to be gained from that type of presentation. Unlike a specific story, a general rule about what causes what can be extremely valuable. Knowing that your brother ate a piece of fruit with dark spots on it and then vomited encourages you to infer causation (by food poisoning), a piece of knowledge that can help you in a wide variety of future situations. So we may delight in narrative precisely because we compulsively assume causation when all we have is chronological order, and it's the causation, not the sequence of events, that our brains are really designed to crave and use.

In the next paragraph of his David Foster Wallace profile, D. T. Max tells us that after recovering from his suicide attempt, "Wallace had decided that writing was not worth the risk to his mental health. He applied and was accepted as a graduate student in philosophy at Harvard." Again, the causation is implied: It was Wallace's fear of depression and suicide that drove him—perhaps ironically—to graduate study in philosophy. But what are we to conclude about how he went about it? One possibility is that he applied to Harvard, and only to Harvard. A much more common practice is to apply to a wide variety of graduate programs and to see which ones admit you. Applying just to Harvard is the act of someone who is either expressing supreme confidence or setting himself up to fail (or both); applying broadly is the act of someone who just wants to pursue his interests at the best school he can get into. The different actions signal different personalities and approaches to life.

It seems to us that Max is implying that Wallace applied *only* to Harvard, because if he had applied to other schools, that fact would have been relevant for our interpretation of Wallace's behavior, so the author would have mentioned it. We automatically make the assumption, when reading statements like this one, that we have been given all of the information we need, and that the most straightforward causal interpretation is also the correct one. Max's words don't explicitly say that Wallace applied only to Harvard; they just lead us, without our awareness, into concluding that he did.

The mind apparently prefers to make these extra leaps of logic over being explicitly told the reasons for everything. This may be one reason why the timeworn advice "show, don't tell" is so valuable to creative writers seeking to make their prose more compelling. The illusion of narrative can indeed be a powerful tool for authors and speakers. By arranging purely factual statements in different orders, or by omitting or inserting relevant information, they can control what inferences their audiences will make, without explicitly arguing for and defending those inferences themselves. D. T. Max, whether deliberately or not, creates the impression that Wallace's suicide attempt was precipitated by his sister's possibly callous refusal to stay with him, and that Wallace chose to apply only to Harvard for graduate school. When you know about the contribution of narrative to the illusion of cause, you can read his words differently, and see that none of these conclusions are necessarily correct. (Tip: Listen carefully for when politicians and advertisers use this technique!)

"I Want to Buy Your Rock"

A conversation between Homer and Lisa in an episode of *The Simpsons* provides one of the best illustrations of the dangers of turning a temporal association into a causal explanation.[14] After a bear is spotted in Springfield, the town initiates an official Bear Patrol, complete with helicopters and trucks with sirens, to make sure no bears are in town.

HOMER: Ahhh . . . not a bear in sight. The bear patrol must be working like a charm.

LISA: That's specious reasoning, Dad.

HOMER: Thank you, honey.

LISA (picking up a rock from the ground): By your logic, I could claim that this rock keeps tigers away.

HOMER: Ooooh . . . how does it work?

LISA: It doesn't work—it's just a stupid rock. But I don't see any tigers around here, do you?

HOMER: Lisa, I want to buy your rock.

Homer assumes that the bear patrol kept away bears, but it really did nothing at all—the first bear sighting was an anomaly that would not have recurred in any case. The scene is funny because the causal relationship is so outlandish. Rocks don't keep tigers away, but Homer draws the inference anyway because the chronology of events induced an illusion of cause. In other cases, when the causal relationship seems plausible, people naturally accept it rather than think about alternatives, and the consequences can be much greater than overpaying for an anti-tiger rock.

In April 2009, the Supreme Court of the United States heard oral arguments in the case of *Northwest Austin Municipal Utility District No. 1 v. Holder*. At issue was the Voting Rights Act, one of the federal civil rights laws enacted during the 1960s. Among other things, the law sought to prevent political jurisdictions (utility districts, cities, school boards, counties, etc.) in southern states from drawing boundaries and setting up election rules so as to favor the interests of white over black voters. Section 5 of the law required these states to obtain "preclearance" from the federal government before changing any election procedures. The Texas utility district argued that since the law imposed these requirements only on some of the states in the union (mostly those that had been—a hundred years earlier—part of the Confederacy), it unconstitutionally discriminated against them.

Chief Justice John Roberts asked Neal Katyal, the government's lawyer, about the import of the fact that just one out of every two thousand applications for an election rule change is rejected. Katyal answered, "I think what that represents is that Section 5 is actually working very well; that it provides a deterrent." Roberts might have had the bear patrol episode in the back of his mind when he replied: "Well, that's like the old elephant whistle—you know, I have this whistle to keep away the elephants. You know, well, that's silly. Well, there are no elephants, so it must work."[15]

Roberts's point, though he expressed it in the language of *The Simpsons* rather than that of cognitive psychology, is that the illusion of cause can make us assume that one event (the passage of the law) caused another event (the virtual end of discriminatory election rules), when the available data don't logically establish such a relationship. The fact that the government grants preclearance almost every time says nothing about whether the law caused compliance. Something other than the law—such as a gradual reduction of racism, or at least overtly racist practices, over time—might have caused the change.

We are taking no position on whether this part of the Voting Rights Act is necessary today; it may be or it may not be. But this is precisely the point: We have no way to know how useful it is if the only information we have is that virtually nobody is violating it. It's possible that they would behave consistently with the proscriptions of the law even if it were no longer on the books.

The problem illustrated by the arguments over the Voting Rights Act is endemic in public policy. How many laws are passed, renewed, or repealed on the basis of a truly causal understanding of their effects on behavior? We often speak of the clichéd danger of unintended consequences, but we rarely think about how little we can actually say about the *intended* consequences of government action. We know what was happening before the law or regulation went into effect, and we may know that something different happened afterward, but that alone does not prove that the law *caused* the difference. The only way to measure the causal effect of a law would be to conduct an experiment. In the case of the Voting Rights Act, the closest one could come would be to repeal Section 5 for a randomly selected group of jurisdictions and compare those with the rest over time, examining how many discriminatory electoral rules are enacted in each case. If the rate of discrimination differs between the two groups, then we could infer that the law has an effect.[16] Of course, the law might still violate the Constitution, but there are some questions that even clever experimentation and data analysis can't answer!

This tendency to neglect alternative paths to the same outcome in favor of a single narrative pervades many of the bestselling business books.[17] Almost every report claiming to identify the key factors that lead companies to succeed, from *In Search of Excellence* to *Good to Great*, errs by considering only companies that succeeded and then analyzing what they did. They don't look at whether other companies did those same things and failed. Malcolm Gladwell's bestseller *The Tipping Point* describes the remarkable reversal of fortune for the maker of unfashionable Hush Puppies after their shoes suddenly became trendy. Gladwell argues that Hush Puppies succeeded because they were adopted by a trendy subculture, which made them appealing and generated buzz. And he's right that Hush Puppies generated buzz. But the conclusion that the buzz caused their success follows only from a retrospective narrative bias and not from an experiment. In fact, it's not even clear that there's an association between buzz and success in the data. To establish even a noncausal association we would need to know how many other similar companies took off without first generating a buzz, and how many other companies generated similar buzz but remained grounded. Only then could we start worrying about whether the buzz caused the success—or whether the causation really ran in the other direction (success leading to buzz), or even in both directions simultaneously (a virtuous cycle).

There is one final pitfall inherent in turning chronology into causality. Because we perceive sequences of events as part of a timeline, with one leading to the next, it is hard to see that there are almost always many interrelated reasons or causes for a single outcome. The sequential nature of time leads people to act as though a complex decision or event must have only a single cause. We make fun of the enthusiasts of conspiracy theories for thinking this way, but they are just operating under a more extreme form of the illusion of cause that affects us all. Here are some statements made by Chris Matthews, host of the MSNBC news program *Hardball*, about the origins of the 2003 U.S. invasion of Iraq:

- "What is *the motive* for this war?" (February 4, 2003)

- "I wanted to know whether 9/11 is *the reason*, because a lot of people think it's payback." (February 6, 2003)

- "Do you believe the weapons of mass destruction was *the reason* for this war?" (October 24, 2003)

- ". . . *the reason* we went to war with Iraq was not to make a better Iraq. It was to kill the bad guys." (October 31, 2003)

- "President Bush says he wants democracy to spread throughout the Middle East. Was that *the real reason* behind the war in Iraq?" (November 7, 2003)

- "Why do you think we went to Iraq? *The real reason*, not the sales pitch." (October 9, 2006)

- "*Their reason* for this war, which they don't regret, was never *the reason* they used to sell us on the war." (January 29, 2009)

We added the emphasis in each statement to show how it presupposes that the war must have had a single motive, reason, or cause. In the mind of a decision maker (or perhaps a "decider," in this case), there might seem to be just one reason for a decision. But of course nearly every complex decision has multiple, complex causes. In this case, even as he searched for the one true reason, Matthews identified a wide variety of possibilities: weapons of mass destruction, Iraq's support of terrorism, Saddam Hussein's despotism, and the strategic goal of establishing democracy in Arab countries, to name only the most prominent. And they all arose against the backdrop of a new post-9/11 sensitivity to the possibility of enemies launching attacks on the U.S. homeland. Had one or some of these preconditions not been in place, the war might not have been launched. But it is not possible to isolate just one of them after the fact and say it was *the reason* for the invasion.[18]

This kind of faulty reasoning about cause and effect is just as common in business as in politics. Sherry Lansing, long described as the most powerful woman in Hollywood, was CEO of Paramount Pictures from 1992 to 2004. She oversaw megahits like *Forrest Gump* and *Titanic*, and films from her studio received three Academy Awards for Best Picture. According to an article in the *Los Angeles Times*, after a series of failed projects and declines in Paramount's share of box-office revenues, Lansing's contract was not renewed. She resigned a year early, and it was widely believed that she had effectively been fired for poor performance. But just as the hits weren't due solely to her genius, the duds couldn't have been due solely to her screwups—hundreds of other people have creative influence on each movie, and hundreds of factors determine whether a movie captures the imagination (and cash) of audiences.

Lansing's successor, Brad Grey, was lauded for turning the studio around; two of the first films released under his leadership, *War of the Worlds* and *The Longest Yard*, were top grossers in 2005. However, both movies were conceived and produced during Lansing's tenure. If she had just hung on for a few more months, she would have received the credit and might have remained in charge.[19] There's no doubt that a CEO is officially responsible for the performance of her company, but attributing all of the company's successes or failures to the one person at the top is a classic illustration of the illusion of cause.

The Vaccination Hypothesis

Let's return to the story that began this chapter, about the six-year-old girl who contracted measles at a church meeting in Indiana after an unvaccinated missionary returned from Romania and spread the disease. We asked why parents would forgo a vaccine that helped to eliminate a serious and extremely contagious childhood disease. Now that we have discussed the three biases underlying the illusion of cause—overzealous pattern detection mechanisms, the unjustified leap from correlation to causation, and the inherent appeal of chronological narratives—we can begin to explain why some people voluntarily choose not to vaccinate their children against measles. The answer is that these parents, the media, some high-profile celebrities, and even some doctors have fallen prey to the illusion of cause. More precisely, they perceive a pattern where none actually exists and confuse a coincidence of timing for a causal relationship.

Autism is a pervasive developmental disorder that currently affects about 1 in 110 children. The diagnosis of autism has become more common over the past decade in the United States.[20] The symptoms of autism include delayed or impaired language and social skills. Prior to age two, most children engage in "parallel play"—doing the same things as other children they play with, but not interacting directly with them. And many kids are not very verbal before age two. Autism is most frequently diagnosed during preschool, when typically developing children start playing interactively and their language development accelerates. Many parents of autistic children begin noticing that something isn't quite right with their kids around age two, and in some relatively rare cases, a child who had been developing normally starts to regress and loses the ability to communicate. These symptoms tend to be most noticeable to parents not long after their children have been vaccinated for measles, mumps, and rubella (MMR). In other words, the most clear-cut symptoms of autism become much more pronounced after childhood vaccinations.

By now, you should recognize the harbingers of the illusion of cause. Parents and scientists seeking a cause for the increase in autism rates spotted this association and inferred a causal relationship. Parents who saw no symptoms before the vaccinations noticed them afterward, a chronological pattern consistent with a causal narrative. They also noticed that increases in vaccination rates roughly coincided with increases in the diagnosis of autism. All three of the major contributors to the illusion of cause—pattern, correlation, and chronology—converged in this case. Of course, the increase in the frequency of the autism diagnosis also coincided with an increase in piracy off the coast of Somalia, but nobody argues that autism causes piracy (or that pirates cause autism, for that matter). The association has to have a plausible causal link, a connection that makes intuitive sense on its surface. It needs to provide an "Aha!" experience, one that taps our pattern perception mechanisms and triggers the illusion of cause. It needs more than the perception of an intuitive causal link to become a popular movement, though. It needs a credible authority to validate the causal link. In the case of vaccines and autism, it needed Dr. Andrew Wakefield.[21]

Andrew Wakefield was a prominent London physician who in 1998 announced the discovery of a link between autism and the MMR vaccine. He and a group of colleagues published an article in the medical journal *The Lancet* that suggested a link between the MMR vaccine and several cases of autism.[22] At a press conference on the day his paper was released, Wakefield explained how he came to this belief: "In 1995, I was approached by parents—articulate, well-educated, and concerned—who told me the stories of their children's deterioration into autism . . . Their children had developed normally for the first fifteen to eighteen months of life when they received the MMR vaccination. But after a variable period the children regressed, losing speech, language, social skills, and imaginative play, descending into autism."[23] Wakefield's announced link between autism and the so-called "triple jab" received extensive popular media attention, which likely led some parents to begin refusing MMR vaccination for their children, in turn contributing to reduced population immunity to measles in Great Britain.

Wakefield's report was based on claims by parents of eight of the twelve children in the study that their children developed autism after receiving the MMR vaccine. The *article* acknowledged that the study had not proven an association between the vaccine and autism. To do that, you would need to conduct a large-scale epidemiological study to examine rates of autism in children who had and who had not received the vaccine. Wakefield's promotion of an association in his *press conferences* prompted Paul Offit, a pediatrics professor at the University of Pennsylvania and a noted virologist, to comment sardonically in his book *Autism's False Prophets,* "It would have been more accurate if he had said he hadn't provided *any* evidence that MMR caused autism and had merely reported the convictions of the parents of eight autistic children."[24] Even if Wakefield had conducted a large-scale epidemiological study showing that vaccinated children had higher rates of autism, he still would not have demonstrated a causal link. Recall that to demonstrate causation, an experimenter must use random assignment to conditions. To make such an inference, Wakefield would have had to run a clinical trial in which some children were randomly assigned to receive a vaccine and others to receive a placebo, and he then would have had to show that the rates of autism differed significantly between these two groups.

Not only has no such clinical trial ever been conducted—nor could it ethically be conducted—but extensive epidemiological studies with hundreds of thousands of children have shown no association whatsoever. The rates of autism are no higher among children who have been vaccinated than among those who haven't. The link between vaccines and autism is illusory—there's actually no association whatsoever, let alone a causal one. People perceive a pattern that fits their beliefs and expectations, and they infer a causal relationship from a sequence of events. Yet the anecdotal evidence provided by a few patients inspired an international fear of a highly effective vaccine.[25]

What Mother Teresa, Quentin Tarantino, and Jenny McCarthy All Know

The extensive epidemiological evidence against a link between vaccines and autism and the lack of any experiments showing such a link establish that any inference of causality is an illusion. Vaccines can't cause autism if vaccinations aren't even statistically associated with autism. Given such incontrovertible evidence, rates of vaccination should return to the levels that effectively eliminated measles as a common disease. The vaccine is safe and effective in preventing measles, and it is entirely unrelated to autism. Game over, right?

Not exactly. As authors Chip and Dan Heath note in their engaging book *Made to Stick*, personal anecdotes are more memorable and stick in our minds much longer than abstract data.[26] They quote Mother Teresa: "If I look at the mass, I will never act. If I look at the one, I will." Anecdotes are inherently more persuasive than statistics. Precisely because anecdotes capitalize on the power of narrative, they hold considerable sway over all of us. You might know from reading *Consumer Reports* that Hondas and Toyotas have excellent reliability. Consumers Union, the publisher of *Consumer Reports*, surveys thousands of car owners and compiles their responses to generate their reliability ratings. But your one friend who complains that his Toyota is perpetually in the shop and insists that he would never buy another one can have more power than the aggregated reports of thousands of strangers. We can relate to the experiences—especially the suffering—of a single car owner. We can't relate to the statistical facts about thousands. And for a story to be powerful, persuasive, and memorable, we need to be able to empathize. Quentin Tarantino, maker of ultraviolent films, explains the importance of empathy this way: "A beheading in a movie doesn't make me wince. But when somebody gets a paper cut in a movie, you go, 'Ooh!'"[27]

It can be difficult to overcome a belief that is formed from compelling anecdotes. Recall the experiment in which people remembered pairs of sentences better when they had to infer a cause than when the cause was stated explicitly. Anecdotes work in much the same way—we naturally generalize from one example to the population as a whole, and our memories for such inferences are inherently sticky. Individual examples lodge in our minds, but statistics and averages do not. And it makes sense that anecdotes are compelling to us. Our brains evolved under conditions in which the only evidence available to us was what we experienced ourselves and what we heard from trusted others. Our ancestors lacked access to huge data sets, statistics, and experimental methods. By necessity, we learned from specific examples, not by compiling data from many people across a wide range of situations.

Prominent neuroscientist V. S. Ramachandran uses the following analogy to explain the power of examples: "Imagine that I cart a pig into your living room and tell you that it can talk. You might say 'Oh, really? Show me.' I then wave my wand and the pig starts talking. You might respond, 'My God! That's amazing!' You are not likely to say, 'Ah, but that's just one pig. Show me a few more and then I might believe you.'"[28] If you're convinced that you've seen a talking pig, no amount of scientific evidence that pigs are incapable of talking would convince you. Instead, scientists would need to prove to you that the pig *you* saw didn't actually talk—that Ramachandran used smoke and mirrors to create an illusion of a talking pig. And the more people circulate similar anecdotes, all equally fooled into believing the magic is real, the more science will struggle.

If a friend tells you, "I tried this new diet supplement and I now have more energy and fewer headaches," you will infer that the diet supplement caused those benefits. And having drawn that inference yourself (or trusting your friend who did), you will remember it better. A parent's story about how her son deteriorated after receiving the MMR vaccine and her expressed belief that the vaccine caused her son's autism is compelling, memorable, and hard to dismiss from our thoughts. Even in the face of overwhelming scientific evidence and statistics culled from studies of hundreds of thousands of people, that one personalized case carries undue influence. Parents know what they've experienced, but they usually don't know the science in the same way. Much as we intuitively think we know how a zipper works but never test that intuition, nothing impels us to test our anecdote-driven ideas. Like the illusion of knowledge, the illusion of cause can only be revealed by systematically testing our understanding, exploring the logical bases of our beliefs, and acknowledging that inferences of causality might derive from evidence that cannot really support them. That level of self-examination is one that we seldom reach.

Enter Jenny McCarthy, former *Playboy* centerfold, star of a hit MTV series, actress, and mother of a boy diagnosed with autism. With the best of intentions and a desire to help children like her own, she has inadvertently become a spokesmodel for an illusion. When McCarthy's son, Evan, was diagnosed with autism, she, like many parents, began looking for a cause. And despite overwhelming scientific evidence against a link between vaccinations and autism, she locked onto that false lead as the explanation: "It's an infection and/or toxins and/or funguses on top of vaccines that push children into this neurological downslide which we call autism." So convinced was she by her personal experience that she stated baldly in response to a question about whether parents should vaccinate their children, "If I had another child, there's no way in hell."[29] She made similar claims on the *Oprah Winfrey Show*, lending support to the unfounded fears of a vast audience of parents worried that vaccines can cause autism. Unfortunately, her advocacy, coupled with frequent media coverage of the illusory link, has been effective. The sad result is lowered population immunity to diseases like measles, which makes possible outbreaks like the one we described at the beginning of this chapter.

The powerful story of a mother who is convinced she understands the true reason for her son's illness is far more influential than literally dozens of studies with hundreds of thousands of children showing that her reason is bunk. (It also makes for more engaging television.) Just as Jennifer Thompson's powerful testimony about being raped led to the conviction of Ronald Cotton, the story of one mother's experience overwhelms our ability to properly weigh the evidence. It appeals to emotion, to our natural tendency to empathize with a person in pain, and to our tendency to give undue influence to anecdotes. Unfortunately, as we empathize with someone's experiences, we become less critical of the message those experiences convey. We also remember the message better. That is the basis of many advertising campaigns—if you can make the viewer empathize with the actors in the advertisement, people become less critical of what they have to say. In the case of autism, the consequences have been catastrophic.

If people want to eschew vaccinating their children, thereby putting them at risk of devastating illnesses, current law essentially gives them that right. However, that choice is not made in a vacuum. By not vaccinating your own children, you put other children at risk of exposure during an outbreak. As virus expert Paul Offit notes, "There are 500,000 people in the United States who can't be vaccinated. They can't be vaccinated because they're on cancer chemotherapy, or they've had a bone marrow transplant, or a solid organ transplant, or they're receiving steroids because they have severe asthma. They depend on those around them being vaccinated."[30] When such children come into contact with measles, they can die.

Vaccination enables a barricade against the rapid spread of the disease by making it possible to effectively quarantine a small number of people. The more unvaccinated people in a population, the greater the likelihood that an infection in one person will snowball into a broad outbreak. The relatively high levels of vaccination that still prevail in the United States are the reason why the outbreak in Indiana was easily halted. In Britain, where the media gave more coverage to Wakefield's publicity campaign, widespread outbreaks are increasingly common and measles is again considered endemic. That is what happens when the media gives airtime and weight to anecdotal claims of causality rather than proper epidemiological studies.

To some extent, we all must rely on secondary sources. We all put our trust in experts and the advice they give. Scientists, too, are affected by anecdotes and empathy. We tend to be more trusting of ideas from people close to us and more dismissive of those we know less well. Yet science has a way of filtering out unfounded conclusions: determine whether the studies behind them can be replicated. Anecdotes don't cumulate in the way that large scientific studies can. And scientific training does help in determining which sources to trust. McCarthy, for all of her good intentions, has devoted her energy and charm to attracting media coverage to a scientifically debunked explanation for autism, effectively diverting attention and resources from more promising research on the condition.

McCarthy's reliance on anecdotes over the scientific method and more rigorous statistical analysis has also fueled her belief in false cures for autism. She is convinced that she cured her son's autism through "a gluten-free, casein-free diet, vitamin supplementation, detox of metals, and anti-fungals for yeast overgrowth that plagued his intestines."[31] But she's astonished that the medical and scientific communities haven't jumped to investigate her son's miraculous recovery: "What might surprise a lot of you is that we've never been contacted by a single member of the CDC, the American Academy of Pediatrics, or any other health authority to evaluate and understand how Evan recovered from autism."

Could McCarthy be right that her special diet cured her son? Possibly. Is it likely? Not at all. Her regimen is just the latest in a long list of alleged cures for autism. Given the overwhelming scientific evidence that autism has strong genetic bases and that brain development in people with autism differs markedly from brain development in typical children, it's more likely that Evan's improvements resulted from extensive behavioral modification therapy that does help some children with autism. Or perhaps his symptoms just became less pronounced as he matured. It's even possible that Evan did not have autism in the first place, but instead had another disorder with similar symptoms that could have improved in response to medicines he was given for seizures.[32]

The tools of scientific reasoning can resolve questions like whether or not vaccines are linked to autism, but people do not necessarily accept the results of scientific studies, even when the data are overwhelming. An earlier false lead in the search for an autism cure focused on the hormone secretin, which plays a role in the digestive system. Anecdotal evidence from a small number of cases suggested that injection of secretin obtained from pigs led to the elimination of autistic symptoms. Yet more than a dozen small clinical trials showed it to be no more effective than a placebo injection of salt water. And a large-scale clinical trial examining multiple doses of synthetic secretin, sponsored by a drug company seeking FDA approval to market the synthetic hormone as an autism treatment, found no benefit.[33] That is science at work: Researchers test the hypothesis that a drug is effective by randomly assigning some people to receive the treatment and others to receive a placebo, and then they measure the outcome. The problem comes when people must reason about the outcome—do they trust the science, or do they trust their often flawed intuitions? Do they believe that they know better?

Adrian Sandler and his colleagues conducted one of these clinical trials. They randomly assigned 28 children to receive a dose of secretin and another 28 to receive a placebo. Not surprisingly (at least in hindsight), they found no benefit whatsoever from the secretin. The more interesting finding of this study came from interviews conducted afterward with the parents of the children: Even after learning that secretin had no benefit at all, 69 percent of them remained interested in injecting their child with it. In another double-blind study, parents were asked to guess whether their child had received secretin or the placebo. Parents often believe that they can detect effects that are missed by the more objective measures used in studies, and they use that belief to justify their continued faith in the efficacy of the treatment. In this case, though, the parents could not even guess successfully whether or not their child had received secretin—they had no idea whether their child had received the drug precisely because the drug had no detectable effect.

A central problem in combating medical anecdotes with hard data is that in any clinical trial, some people receiving the treatment will improve and some won't. Our tendency is to remember the cases where people improved and to assume that the treatment caused the improvement. What we usually fail to do is to compare the rates of improvement with the treatment and without the treatment. If the treatment has a causal effect, then a greater proportion of those who received the treatment should improve than those who didn't. If the treatment doesn't have a causal effect, then other, uncontrolled factors probably led some people to improve anyhow.

Just as business authors rarely consider how many companies follow the ideas they champion but still fail, or how many companies succeed with other approaches, people thinking about stories of vaccination and autism do not tally up the number of children who receive vaccines and do not develop autism, who show symptoms before vaccination, or who show symptoms without having been vaccinated. When these numbers *are* properly taken into account, it becomes clear that children tend to be diagnosed with autism at the same rates and at the same ages regardless of whether or not they received vaccinations.[34] The problem is exacerbated by the typical developmental trajectory of cognition and behavior. As any parent knows, development is not a continuous, gradual process. Just as children grow physically in spurts, they develop cognitively in spurts as well. Children with autism are much the same. For long stretches, they might show no improvement, only to show a big change in a short time frame. If parents happen to notice improvement while they are trying some new miracle cure, they will readily associate the treatment with the improvement.[35]

Accepting that a perceived cause is illusory can be difficult, and overcoming anecdotes with science and statistics can be even harder. Perhaps the best indication of the powerful hold of these anecdotal hypotheses comes from the emotions they inspire. Offit's authoritative book on the lack of scientific links between autism and vaccination has an average customer rating of 3.9 on the 1–5 scale at Amazon.com. However, in this case, the average is not typical of the individual reviews. Of the 102 reviewers at the time of this writing, not a single one gives the book the middle rating (three stars), whereas 70 give it the highest possible rating and 25 give it the lowest possible rating![36]

Despite the now-overwhelming evidence that vaccinations are not at all associated with autism, 29 percent of people in our national survey agreed with the statement "vaccines given to children are partly responsible for causing autism."[37] It's a bit reassuring that all the media attention to this illusory cause hasn't influenced more people, but science can only claim a partial victory at best. If 29 percent of parents follow through on such beliefs and do not vaccinate their children, population immunity could drop precipitously, leading to widespread measles outbreaks. Moreover, new autism "cures" relying on anecdotal evidence rather than careful experimentation continue to surface and lead parents down dangerous paths. We hope that reading this chapter has given you some immunity to these attempts to exploit the illusion of cause.

We have explored three ways the illusion of cause can affect us. First, we perceive patterns in randomness, and we interpret these repeating patterns as predictions of future events. Second, we look at events that happen together as having a causal relationship. Finally, we tend to interpret events that happened earlier as the causes of events that happened or appeared to happen later. The illusion of cause has deep roots. We humans are distinct from other primates in our ability to perform "causal inference." Even young children realize that when one object hits another, it can make the other object move. They can reason about hypothetical causes as well: If an object moved, something must have caused it to move. Our primate relatives generally do not make these inferences, and consequently, they have trouble learning about causes that they can't see.[38] On the timeline of evolution, therefore, the ability to infer the existence of hidden causes is quite recent, and new mechanisms often need refinement. We have no trouble inferring causes—the real trouble is that we are sometimes too good at inferring causes for our own good.

get smart quick!

BEFORE THE 2007 NATIONAL FOOTBALL League season, as before every season, the New York Jets made several adjustments to the team. Rookies arrived at training camp, some veterans left the team, other players had to compete for positions on the starting roster, and the playbook was updated. But one change was more unusual: Head Coach Eric Mangini ordered that the stadium loudspeakers play classical music—specifically, compositions by Wolfgang Amadeus Mozart— during team practices. "Mozart's music and brain waves are very similar, and it stimulates learning," explained Mangini, a coach known for meticulously preparing his team.[1]

Eric Mangini has much company in believing that listening to Mozart can make you smarter. An entrepreneur named Don Campbell trademarked the phrase "The Mozart Effect" and used it to market a series of books and CDs for adults and children alike. Campbell even consults with hospitals on the optimal design of sound systems to maximize the healing powers of music.[2] In 1998, Governor Zell Miller persuaded the Georgia legislature to spend public money to issue classical music tapes to all parents of newborn babies in the state. As part of his state-of-the-state speech, he played Beethoven's "Ode to Joy" to the legislators and asked, "Don't you feel smarter already?"[3] A hospital in Slovakia puts headphones on all of the infants in its nursery, within hours of their birth, to give them a true head start on building their brainpower. "Mozart's music has a very good effect on the development of the intelligence quotient," said the doctor who started the practice there.[4]

So far, we have discussed several everyday illusions that expose errors in the way people think about their own minds, and we have tried to convince you that these errors can have dramatic consequences for human affairs. We have also suggested ways to minimize the impact these illusions have on your own life. With our understanding of these illusions, we have found it possible—though far from easy—to change our mindset so as to recognize and escape them at least some of the time. But we would all be better off if there were a simple way to overcome everyday illusions, a way to increase our brainpower enough to make the illusions just disappear.

The *illusion of potential* leads us to think that vast reservoirs of untapped mental ability exist in our brains, just waiting to be accessed—if only we knew how. The illusion combines two beliefs: first, that beneath the surface, the human mind and brain harbor the potential to perform at much higher levels, in a wide range of situations and contexts, than they typically do; and second, that this potential can be released with simple techniques that are easily and rapidly implemented. The story of the Mozart effect is a perfect illustration of how this illusion can transform a claim with almost no scientific support into a popular legend that fuels multimillion-dollar businesses, so we will begin this chapter by going into it in depth.

"The Magic Genius of Mozart"

The Mozart effect burst into public consciousness in October 1993 when *Nature,* one of the top two scientific journals (the other being *Science*), published a one-page article by Frances Rauscher, Gordon Shaw, and Katherine Ky under the innocuous title, "Music and Spatial Task Performance."[5] Shaw, a physics professor who had shifted his interests to neuroscience, together with his student Xiaodan Leng, had developed a mathematical theory of how neurons in the brain work together. As a classical music enthusiast, Shaw noticed some similarities between the mathematical structure of classical pieces and the patterns his theory predicted would be found in the electrical activity of neurons. From this perceived similarity, he made the prediction that merely listening to music could enhance the function of one's brain—but only the right kind of music.[6] Shaw believed that Mozart had composed music that would "optimally resonate with the inherent internal neural language," and that it would have the greatest enhancing effect. As he later wrote, "The magic genius of Mozart perhaps displayed a supreme use of the inherent cortical language in his music."[7]

To help him test his theory, Shaw hired Frances Rauscher, a former concert cellist who had switched her profession to psychology, and together they conducted a simple experiment. Each of thirty-six college students performed three tests taken from a standard IQ test battery: "pattern analysis," "matrix reasoning," and "paper folding and cutting." In the pattern-analysis task, subjects constructed objects out of blocks according to patterns they were given. In the matrix-reasoning task, subjects selected which of several shapes would complete a pattern composed of other abstract shapes. In the paper-folding-and-cutting task, subjects viewed a picture of an origami-like design, with dashed and solid lines showing where one would fold and cut the pattern. Then the subjects chose which of several pictures accurately showed what the paper would look like after being unfolded.

Before taking these tests, the subjects listened to one of the following recordings: ten minutes of Mozart's "Sonata for Two Pianos in D Major (K.448)," ten minutes of "relaxation instructions designed to lower blood pressure," or ten minutes of silence. The sonata is described as "gallant from beginning to end . . . one of the most profound and mature of all Mozart's compositions."[8] According to the article, the subjects who did well on one of the tests did well on the others: There were significant correlations among all the tests, just as would be expected for the subparts of an IQ test, or any test of general cognitive ability like the SAT. So Shaw and colleagues combined the three tests into a single measure of what they called "abstract reasoning ability" and transformed it to the scale of IQ scores, which have an average of 100 points for the general population. Then they compared the three listening conditions, and found that the scores after sitting in silence were 110, after listening to relaxation instructions they were 111, and after listening to the Mozart sonata they were 119.

Thus, listening to Mozart appeared to make the students smarter, by eight to nine IQ points. Although nine points might seem small, it's not: An average person, who is by definition more intelligent than 50 percent of other people, would be more intelligent than 70 percent of other people after listening to the Mozart sonata. The simple tonic of ten minutes of classical music, if its effects could be harnessed, would propel a typical student past 20 percent of his or her relaxing or silence-enjoying peers, potentially turning Bs into As and failing grades into passing ones.

The media reported this new scientific finding with enthusiasm. "Mozart Makes You Smarter" read the headline in the *Boston Globe*. "Listening to Mozart is not only a music lover's pleasure. It's a brain tonic," the article began.[9] Less than a year after Rauscher, Shaw, and Ky published their article, music companies started creating new CDs to exploit the publicity, with titles such as *Mozart for Your Mind, Mozart Makes You Smarter,* and *Tune Your Brain with Mozart.* Ironically, most of these did not include the K.448 piano sonata that was used in the experiment, but it didn't matter. Sales ran into the millions.[10] In his address to the Georgia state legislature, Zell Miller cited the Rauscher article: "There's even a study that showed that after college students listened to a Mozart piano sonata for ten minutes, their IQ scores increased by nine points . . . no one doubts that listening to music, especially at a very early age, affects the spatial-temporal reasoning that underlies math, engineering, and chess."[11]

Subsequent research reports from the Mozart effect team also were covered extensively in the press. Just like the original, these new experiments found dramatic improvements in mental task performance immediately after the Mozart sonata, but not after silence or relaxation.[12] Meanwhile, psychologists interested in music and cognition began to examine this discovery, which was intriguing because no previous research had shown that merely listening to music could have such a large effect on mental ability.

The first independent research group to publish its findings was headed by Con Stough of the University of Auckland in New Zealand.[13] They used the same Mozart sonata and silence conditions as in the original study, and added a new one: dance music, specifically ten minutes of "Fake 88 (House Mix)" and "What Can I Say to Make You Love Me? (Hateful Club Mix)" by Alexander O'Neal. Thirty subjects participated in each listening condition and worked on part of the Raven's Advanced Progressive Matrices test after each one. This test is considered an excellent measure of general intelligence. Stough's team found that the Mozart group outperformed the control groups by only about one IQ point, not even close to the eight to nine points reported by Rauscher. A one-point difference is small enough that it could easily have arisen just from the random variations in the measures of cognitive abilities, or from accidental differences among the subjects assigned to the Mozart and control groups. Other researchers reported similar experiences.[14]

Along with two of his students, Kenneth Steele, a psychology professor at Appalachian State University in North Carolina, tried a Mozart experiment in 1997. They used a "digit span" test, which measures the longest list of digits that you can hold in short-term memory accurately enough to repeat it back, either forward or backward. This test is strongly associated with general intelligence: the smarter you are, the longer your backward digit span. But listening to Mozart had no effect on digit span. Steele tried again the next year, this time copying the design of Rauscher and Shaw's 1995 follow-up study, which had also produced a large Mozart effect. Steele used the paper-folding task rather than digit span, but again he found no benefits of Mozart.[15] The next year the American Psychological Society's flagship journal, *Psychological Science*, published these new results under the title "Mystery of the Mozart Effect: Failure to Replicate," and the society issued a press release headlined " 'Mozart Effect' De-Bunked." Almost immediately, the headline was changed to " 'Mozart Effect' Challenged" after Gordon Shaw threatened the APS with a lawsuit.[16]

Steele wrote later that when he started his experiments, he expected to replicate the Mozart effect.[17] Indeed, researchers rarely conduct experiments that they think will fail! Experiments can fail for many reasons even when the theory that motivated them is correct. In this case, the theory that listening to Mozart increases cognitive performance could be true, but any particular experiment intended to test the theory could fail to support it because of a variety of errors in design or execution, none of which have anything to do with the correctness of the theory. But after repeated failures to find any cognitive improvement after listening to Mozart, Steele came to believe that there was no Mozart effect to be found.

The Media and the Aftermath

The studies by Stough, Steele, and others received little notice, but the publications of the original discoverers continued to influence public perceptions and even public policy—Rauscher even testified about her findings before a committee of the U.S. Congress. The media gives tremendous weight and coverage to the *first* study published on a research question, and essentially ignores all of those that come later. This bias is unsurprising—fame goes to the discoverer, not to the person who got there a few months later, or who just followed up on the original work. But even in science, the judgment of greatness is a retrospective one that only history can render, and journalism is well known to be only the first draft of history. When a new finding is announced, journalists and other observers might be hard-pressed to say, "I won't report this story until I see it replicated by at least two other laboratories." And restraint is all the less likely when the impact might be as great as nine IQ points in ten minutes. The first report of a new scientific finding is analogous to the front-page coverage granted to a high-profile criminal indictment; the news that the results didn't hold up winds up in the back pages (if it is covered at all), next to the story about the suspect's eventual exoneration.

As the Mozart effect story evolved, it became even more fantastical. Even though all of the relevant studies had been conducted with college students or adults, the legend spread that Mozart was great for children, babies, and even fetuses. A Chinese newspaper columnist wrote, "According to studies conducted in the West, babies who hear Cosi Fan Tutte or the Mass in C Minor during gestation are likely to come out of the womb smarter than their peers."[18]

Social psychologists Adrian Bangerter and Chip Heath measured the news coverage devoted to the initial Rauscher-Shaw study and found that in 1993, the year of its publication, it received plenty of media attention, but no more than the other widely covered research studies published in *Nature* around the same time. (These concerned topics like schizophrenia, the orbit of Pluto, skin cancer, and even how many sexual partners men and women claim to have.) In the ensuing eight years, though, the Mozart effect paper received more than ten times as much coverage as those studies. The media's interest in the others diminished sharply after the initial reports, but coverage of the Mozart effect only grew.[19]

Chris's interest in the Mozart effect was piqued in early 1998 when he was writing an article about the concept of intelligence. The enthusiastic public reaction to the Mozart effect stems partly from the way that the concept of intelligence is presented in the media. Intelligence tests are thought by many to be a simplistic, arbitrary, inaccurate, and even racist way of understanding human cognition.[20] What better way to debunk IQ tests than to show that just listening to a few minutes of music can dramatically change your score? The reception of the Mozart effect among experts on cognition was different. Chris noticed that the failures to replicate the original Rauscher, Shaw, and Ky finding were piling up, and that almost all of the successful replications came from the original team, not from independent researchers. In science, whenever just one or a few labs can produce an effect, and others cannot (as in the celebrated case of cold fusion), scientists and skeptics begin to doubt the effect itself. Was the Mozart effect real, or just a myth?

Chris decided to conduct a meta-analysis, a statistical procedure that combines all of the available data from all of the studies on a research question to determine the best answer. The value of meta-analysis can perhaps be best understood by analogy to the classic carnival game of guessing the number of jelly beans in a jar that we discussed in Chapter 3. If you have a large group of people who want to come up with their best collective estimate of an unknown quantity, the way to do it is to have everyone make his or her guess privately, and then average together all the guesses. Each person's guess is unlikely to be right, but it is equally likely to be too high or too low. As a result, if you average all of the independent guesses, the estimates that are too large will cancel out the ones that are too small, and you will end up with a more accurate estimate of the actual total.[21]

The same principle applies to scientific research. Any individual study might be affected by inadvertent biases or errors that distort its results, leading to an imprecise estimate of the true effect (here, how much your IQ increases after listening to Mozart). By averaging across a number of studies, though, any random errors that led to over- or underestimates of the size of an effect will tend to average out, leaving a better estimate of the truth. Because they are based on *all* of the relevant studies, the results of a meta-analysis are not unduly influenced by a single memorable or well-publicized finding, such as the original Rauscher-Shaw article.

After scouring scientific journals for experiments like the original one, Chris noticed that—aside from Steele's article in *Psychological Science*—all of the followup studies were published in journals that most researchers never read, and many have never even heard of. He wrote to the authors of many of the articles to request additional data or information he needed to evaluate their results. In total, he found sixteen experiments (including the original) that tested the Mozart effect and were published in peer-reviewed scientific journals. All of them used the same sonata and compared it with silence, relaxation, or both. For each experiment, Chris calculated the size of the difference in performance between those subjects who had listened to Mozart and those who had not. When compared with silence, Mozart improved performance by the equivalent of 1.4 IQ points, only one-sixth as much as the Rauscher-Shaw team had found. For experiments comparing the sonata with relaxation, the advantage for Mozart turned out to be three IQ points, about a third as much as the original article reported, but still twice as large as in the comparison between Mozart and silence. There may be good reason for this small benefit: Relaxation reduces anxiety and arousal, but being in a "laid-back" state is not ideal for solving difficult problems on IQ tests. Nor is being excessively anxious, of course— a happy medium is best. Compared with relaxation, sitting in silence likely has a similar, but weaker effect—without external stimulation, your mind may wander, making you less prepared for hard work.

Chris concluded that the entire "Mozart effect" might have nothing to do with a positive effect of listening to music. Rather than Mozart making you smarter, sitting in silence or getting relaxed might make you dumber! Viewed this way, Mozart's music is a control condition that resembles the general level of mental stimulation we encounter during everyday life, and silence and relaxation are "treatments" that reduce cognitive performance. In either case, though, there is little or no Mozart effect to explain.

Several additional studies could not be included in Chris's meta-analysis because they did not include the relaxation or silence control conditions. However, they did reveal another possible explanation for the apparent benefit of Mozart. In one, British researcher Susan Hallam arranged for the BBC to conduct a massive experiment on *eight thousand* children in two hundred schools around the United Kingdom. The children listened to either a Mozart string quintet, a discussion about scientific experiments, or three popular songs ("Country House" by Blur, "Return of the Mack" by Mark Morrison, and "Stepping Stone" by PJ and Duncan), and then performed cognitive tests like those originally used by Rauscher. The children who listened to popular music did the best, and there was no difference in performance between those who listened to Mozart and those who heard the science discussion. An article on this finding cheekily dubbed it the "Blur Effect."[22]

A second study by Kristin Nantais and Glenn Schellenberg of the University of Toronto found no overall difference in cognitive task performance after listening to the Mozart sonata or the short story "The Last Rung on the Ladder" by Stephen King. But subjects did do better after listening to what they *liked* best.[23] The most sensible explanation for this finding, as well as for the "Blur Effect," is that your mood improves when you hear what you like, and you do modestly better on IQ tests when you are in a better mood. The effect has nothing to do with increasing your intelligence per se.

Chris submitted his meta-analysis to *Nature*, the journal that published the initial 1993 article. He did not expect the editors to accept it, because its conclusion—that any small benefits that do exist result from arousal and positive mood rather than any special property of Mozart's music—could be interpreted as questioning the journal's decision to publish the first paper. To his surprise and delight, they accepted the paper and published it in August 1999 alongside another report of a failure to replicate by Kenneth Steele and his colleagues. Rauscher was given space to reply, and *Nature* highlighted the exchange in its weekly press bulletin. The media, loving a good fight, even among staid academics, sprang into action: Chris was interviewed for CNN, CBS, and NBC news programs. Rauscher and Steele debated on the *Today* show, with Matt Lauer as referee. Chris's article even earned him a short appearance on an episode of *Penn and Teller: Bullshit!* entitled, charmingly, "Baby Bullshit."

Recall the media analysis done by Adrian Bangerter and Chip Heath. They found a spike in coverage of the Mozart effect in 1999, coincident with these articles in *Nature*, and then things died down again. Did Chris's meta-analysis, and the studies by Steele and Schellenberg, finally debunk the Mozart effect? Yes and no. Bangerter and Heath found that news articles mentioning the positive effect of listening to Mozart for adults became less and less frequent, but that articles falsely claiming that Mozart made babies smarter became more common! Indeed, this trend started just one year after the original Rauscher-Shaw report. To be clear, we repeat that no published studies had ever examined the effect with babies![24] Our national survey of fifteen hundred adults was conducted in 2009, ten years after Chris's meta-analysis was published. It found that 40 percent of people agreed that "listening to music by Mozart will increase your intelligence." A majority disagreed, but keep in mind that the scientific evidence does not support this claim at all. It would be better if almost everybody disagreed, as they would with a statement like "on average, women are taller than men."

Indeed, the Mozart effect still resonates with many. Eric Mangini must have been a believer in 2007 when he made classical music the new workout soundtrack for the New York Jets. Until we each had our first child, we didn't realize the extent to which the Mozart-for-babies myth has permeated the child-care industry. Intelligent, highly educated friends sent us toys that included—as a matter of routine, not a special feature—a "Mozart" setting that played classical music. The Baby Einstein company was founded in a basement with $5,000 in capital in 1997 (hot on the heels of the initial burst of Mozart effect publicity) and grew to sales of $25 million in 2001 before it was acquired by Disney.[25] The names of its DVDs—*Baby Mozart, Baby Einstein, Baby Van Gogh*, and so on—imply that by watching them, your child will become more like a genius and less like an ordinary baby. Videos designed to be watched by babies are now a $100-million-a-year business,[26] even though the American Academy of Pediatrics currently recommends that children younger than two years old watch no television or videos whatsoever.

A research group led by Frederick J. Zimmerman, a pediatrician at the University of Washington, attempted to test the effect of the products inspired by the Mozart effect on children's cognitive abilities. The researchers commissioned a telephone survey of parents of children less than two years old in the states of Washington and Montana. Each parent answered a series of questions about how much time his or her child spent watching educational television, movies, and other media, with a separate category for "baby DVDs/videos." Later in the survey, the parents were asked whether their children understood and/or used each of ninety words typically found in the vocabularies of young children. There were separate vocabulary lists for infants (age 8–16 months) and toddlers (age 17–24 months), so the researchers looked at these age groups separately. For the infants, each additional hour per day spent watching baby DVDs was associated with an 8 percent *reduction* in vocabulary. For the toddlers, there was no significant relationship between DVD viewing and vocabulary size.[27]

If you have become sensitive to the illusion of cause that we discussed in Chapter 5, you will notice that this is just a correlational study. The researchers couldn't randomly assign some babies to watch videos and others to not watch videos, so a headline of "Watching Baby DVDs Will Make Your Child Dumber" is not justified. The family environments of infants who watched more videos might be less conducive to vocabulary building in other ways. In their statistical analysis, Zimmerman and his colleagues accounted for some of the most likely factors that could make the DVD-watching children different, such as how much education their parents had, how much their parents read to them, how much other media they watched, whether they watched alone or with their parents, and so on. Even after all of those factors were accounted for, DVD watching was still associated with smaller vocabularies. Although we cannot make a strong causal inference from this study, it certainly provides no support for the belief that watching videos or listening to Mozart *improves* cognition.

Disney, which was getting $200 million in annual revenue from the Baby Einstein brand when the Zimmerman group published its article, reacted sharply. Its CEO, Robert Iger, publicly criticized the study as "flawed" for not differentiating between different baby DVD products, implying that other DVDs might lead to smaller vocabularies, but not those made by his company.[28] A Disney spokesman pounced on a statement by one of Zimmerman's coauthors, who told a newspaper that the study had found "harm" to children's vocabularies from baby DVDs. The company had a point here: As we have noted, the study was correlational, not causal, so strictly speaking, harm was not found.

Unfortunately, Disney's spokesman undermined his defense of scientific rigor by making an even more fallacious argument himself: " 'Baby Einstein' has been so well-received, and if properly used, they do have an impact on infants' health and happiness."[29] In other words, the product must be good for kids because it has been "well-received" (presumably by parents, many of whom might be understandably grateful for something that absorbs the attention of a crying baby for a few minutes, and who would like to believe that a product they spent money on with good intentions really did benefit their child). The spokesman offered no evidence, either correlational or causal, to support his claim that using the DVDs "properly" is beneficial.

In the end, Eric Mangini's own Mozart experiment did not succeed. In 2006, he had guided the Jets to a 10–6 record and a playoff appearance. He added classical music to the practices the next season, and his team went 4–12. Mangini lasted just one more year as the Jets' head coach before being fired.[30]

What Lies Beneath

Why does the Mozart effect find such a ready audience? Why do so many people buy classical CDs for their infants and DVDs for their toddlers? Why are people so willing to believe that music and videos can effortlessly raise their children's IQs? The Mozart effect masterfully exploits the illusion of potential. We all would like to be more intelligent, and the Mozart effect tells us that we can become more intelligent just by listening to classical music. The subtitle to Don Campbell's book *The Mozart Effect* directly appeals to the illusion: *Tapping the Power of Music to Heal the Body, Strengthen the Mind, and Unlock the Creative Spirit.*

We already mentioned that 40 percent of people still believe in the Mozart effect, despite the scientific evidence against it. Lest you think that this is just a silly belief that has no real importance, consider some of the implications. Parents holding this belief might think that they are doing just as much, if not more, for their children by sitting them in front of a baby DVD or playing classical music than by interacting with them. Daycare centers, schools, and other institutions might follow suit. The fad of playing Mozart to babies could substitute for much better practices, ones that might actually help the social and intellectual development of children. In other words, a belief in the Mozart effect might make children worse off than they would have been otherwise, as suggested by the Zimmerman group's study of baby DVDs.

If such a sizable number of people continue to believe in the Mozart effect despite its debunking, what about other beliefs in hidden mental powers that have not received as severe a public lashing as the Mozart effect? In our national telephone survey, we asked several questions that touched on other manifestations of the illusion of potential.

Sixty-one percent of our respondents agreed that "hypnosis is useful in helping witnesses accurately recall details of crimes." The idea that hypnosis can put the brain into a special state, in which the powers of memory are dramatically greater than normal, reflects a belief in a form of easily unlocked potential. But it is false. People under hypnosis do generate more "memories" than they do in a normal state, but these recollections are as likely to be false as true.[31] Hypnosis leads them to come up with more information, but not necessarily more accurate information. In fact, it might actually be people's beliefs in the power of hypnosis that lead them to recall more things: If people believe that they should have better memory under hypnosis, they will try harder to retrieve more memories when hypnotized. Unfortunately, there's no way to know whether the memories hypnotized people retrieve are true or not—unless of course we know exactly what the person should be able to remember. But if we knew that, then we'd have no need to use hypnosis in the first place![32]

Seventy-two percent of people agreed that "most people use only 10 percent of their brain capacity." This strange belief, a staple of advertisements, self-help books, and comedy routines, has been around so long that some psychologists have conducted historical investigations of its origins.[33] In some ways, it is the purest form of the illusion of potential: If we use only 10 percent of our brain, there must be another 90 percent waiting to be put to work, if we can just figure out how. There are so many problems with this belief that it's hard to know where to begin. Just as some laws cannot be enforced because they are written too imprecisely, this statement ought to be declared "void for vagueness." First, there is no known way to measure a person's "brain capacity" or to determine how much of that capacity he or she uses. Second, when brain tissue produces no activity whatsoever for an extended time, that means it is dead. So, if we only used 10 percent of our brain, there would be no possibility of increasing that percentage, short of a miraculous resurrection or a brain transplant. Finally, there is no reason to suspect that evolution—or even an intelligent designer—would give us an organ that is 90 percent inefficient. Having a large brain is positively dangerous to the survival of the human species—the large head needed to contain it can barely exit the birth canal, leading to a risk of death during childbirth. If we used only a fraction of our brain, natural selection would have shrunk it long ago.

This "10 percent myth" surfaced long before brain-imaging technologies like MRI and PET scanning even existed, but misunderstandings of neuroscience research might reinforce it. In the pictures of brain activity ("brain porn") that appear in media reports about neuroscience research, large areas of the brain are dark, or not "lit up" with blobs of color. However, the blobs don't indicate the "active" areas of the brain—they indicate areas that are *more* active in one situation or group of people than in another. For a neurologically normal person, the entire brain, including the dark areas, is always "on," with at least a baseline level of activity, and any task you can perform will raise activity in many brain areas. So, needless to say, "using more of your brain" will not help you avoid everyday illusions.

Sixty-five percent of people apparently believe that "if someone behind you is staring at the back of your head, you can sense that they are looking at you." Although it would be nice if we could reach out and touch someone with our eyes, our eyes do not emit any such rays, and there are no receptors in the back of our head that can detect someone's stare. This false belief rests on the idea that people have hidden, previously unmeasured perceptual abilities that function independently of our standard five senses, and that this sixth sense can prove useful. The idea has been thoroughly debunked, though. A prominent psychologist named Edward Titchener wrote, in the journal *Science,* "I have tested this . . . in a series of laboratory experiments conducted with persons who declared themselves peculiarly susceptible to the stare or peculiarly capable of 'making people turn round' . . . the experiments have invariably given a negative result."[34] We can't make people turn around by looking at them, and we can't tell when someone else is looking at us, at least not without first looking back at them.[35]

Why would people come to believe in such extrasensory perception? We tend to remember those cases when we turned around and saw someone, but not those cases when we turned around and nobody was there (nor the times when someone was there and we didn't notice, and certainly not the "times" when nobody was there and we didn't notice anyone). Recall from Chapter 5 that we are also prone to infer a causal pattern when the sequence of events is consistent with a narrative. If you start staring at someone and then they happen to turn around, the illusion of cause would lead you to the false inference that you caused them to turn. And when you infer a cause, you are especially likely to remember it.

Since it was utterly obvious to him that people actually couldn't feel the stares of others, Titchener felt the need to explain why he bothered to conduct studies to debunk the idea in the first place. He noted that the experiments "have their justification in the breaking-down of a superstition which has deep and widespread roots in the popular consciousness." He was absolutely right about the prevalence of the "sixth sense" belief. Unfortunately, Titchener's attempts to eradicate this superstition through experimentation were ineffective.[36] The prevalence of the false belief about feeling the stares of others has been remarkably stable over time— Titchener's article in *Science* was published in 1898.

Subliminal Pseudoscience

The most popular false belief in our survey was the idea that "subliminal messages in advertisements can cause people to buy things," which was endorsed by 76 percent of respondents. Subliminal persuasion, much like the belief that you can feel someone staring, is based on the idea that people are inordinately sensitive to weak signals, ones that we might not be able to detect using our normal sensory mechanisms. If we can change people's beliefs, attitudes, and behaviors through subtle and undetectable influences, then in principle we could use those same powers to allow ourselves to accomplish great things, releasing abilities and skills we didn't know we had. A belief in the power of subliminal persuasion underlies the idea that we can help ourselves quit smoking or learn a new language by listening to subliminal recordings while we sleep, unlocking the potential for change without exerting any conscious effort.

You might have heard of a famous experiment from the 1950s in which subliminal messages were shown during movies to drive up sales of soda and popcorn. You might also remember reading that advertisers embed sexual words and images in photographs to arouse greater desire for their products. In his 1973 bestseller *Subliminal Seduction,* Wilson Bryan Key described many examples of such subliminal "embeds" and his theories of the psychology behind them.[37] The first sentence of Key's book states: "Subliminal perception is a subject that virtually no one wants to believe exists, and—if it does exist—they much less believe that it has any practical application." If Key was right about public sentiment at that time, then our survey and others like it show that popular beliefs have changed dramatically in the years since. People now overwhelmingly believe that subliminal information affects how we think and act.

The movie experiment is one of the first exhibits Key offers to support his contention that subliminal advertising has vast power to manipulate our minds. According to Key's account, the experiment was conducted at a movie theater in Fort Lee, New Jersey, in 1957. The experiment ran for six weeks, during which time two messages were transmitted to viewers on alternate days: "Hungry? Eat Popcorn" and "Drink Coca-Cola." The messages were displayed for one three-thousandth of a second, once every five seconds. The results were a 58 percent increase in popcorn sales and an 18 percent increase in Coca-Cola sales, presumably compared with the period before the messages were inserted into the movies. When the study was reported in the press, the National Association of Broadcasters quickly banned its members from using the technique, and the United Kingdom and Australia enacted laws proscribing it.

The first color illustration in Key's book is now famous. It shows an ad for Gilbey's gin, featuring an open bottle next to a tall glass filled with ice cubes and clear gin. It looks like an ordinary image, but if you look closely, you can see three distorted letters making up the word "sex" faintly outlined in the ice cubes. Key showed this ad to a thousand college students, and 62 percent of them reported feeling aroused, romantic, excited, and the like. Nothing about this study demonstrates that the embedded "sex" caused these responses, because there was no control group of subjects who were asked to describe their feelings without being shown a liquor ad. It's possible that any kind of alcohol advertising would have induced a similar response, or that these college students were just perpetually horny.

Key reports a better-designed experiment in which two classes, each with one hundred students, were shown a *Playboy* magazine ad featuring a male model. The students were asked to rate how masculine the image was, on a scale of 1 to 5, with 1 standing for "very masculine," and 5 standing for "very feminine." One class saw just the ad and gave an average rating of 3.3 on the scale. The other class saw the ad with the word "man" subliminally presented on it, using the same technique as in the movie theater experiment. Their average rating was 2.4. Only 3 percent of the first class rated the image a 1 or 2, but 61 percent of the second class did. Merely pairing the image with a word that was compatible, but imperceptible, dramatically shifted the evaluations. Unfortunately, in light of everything else we now know about this kind of experiment, this shift was much too dramatic to be believable. Subliminal stimuli typically have tiny effects (if they have any effects at all), and larger effects likely result from stimuli that were not actually subliminal.[38]

What about the popcorn and Coke study? It may be directly responsible for the public's belief in the power of subliminal persuasion techniques. Just one year after the study's results were announced, a survey found that 41 percent of American adults had heard of subliminal advertising. By 1983, this number had increased to 81 percent, the majority of whom believed that it works, just as in our own poll. Wilson Bryan Key, writing in 1973, did not specifically mention that an advertising expert named James Vicary was behind the popcorn-Coke experiment. This could be because, more than ten years earlier, Vicary had publicly acknowledged that the study was a fraud. In an interview with *Advertising Age,* he confessed that his advertising business had not been going well, so he cooked up the "study" to help get more customers. Other researchers have attempted to replicate Vicary's purported findings, and none have succeeded. A Canadian television station flashed "phone now" repeatedly during one of its programs, but there was no increase in telephone calls. People who were watching at the time were later asked what they thought they'd seen. Nobody got the right answer, but many reported having felt hungry or thirsty.[39]

If you're like us, you probably first heard about the Vicary "results" in high school or college but were never told they were fabricated. By now you should sense a pattern that itself contributes to the persistence of beliefs in untapped potential: Initial claims for some new way of penetrating the mind's mysteries are heavily promoted and take on a life of their own, but the follow-up research that refutes those claims goes almost entirely unnoticed. Scientists have debated for over a century whether we can even process the meaning of words or images that we do not consciously see.[40] But even if we can, that doesn't mean that the information in ultrabrief stimuli can *cause* us to do things we wouldn't otherwise do, like buy more popcorn or soda. Despite the lack of evidence for subliminal persuasion, people nevertheless persist in their belief that such mind control is possible.[41] The makers of self-help recordings that purport to reprogram your mind and eliminate unwanted behaviors like smoking and overeating via subliminal messages are not deterred by the double-blind, controlled studies that find zero actual benefit from them.[42]

The premise of Key's *Subliminal Seduction* was the idea that subliminal communication might be even more powerful than more visible forms of persuasion, because if we aren't aware of an advertising message, we can't discount it or think carefully about how it is trying to influence our behavior. This belief in the powerful effects of subtle influences is a key part of the illusion of potential. During the 1984 presidential election campaign, ABC News anchor Peter Jennings smiled more when he spoke about Ronald Reagan, the Republican, than about Walter Mondale, the Democrat. (The anchors of NBC and CBS smiled about equally often for each candidate.) According to a small survey, ABC viewers in Cleveland were 13 percent more likely than NBC and CBS viewers to vote for Reagan in the 1984 election. In Williamstown, Massachusetts, the difference was 21 percent, and in Erie, Pennsylvania, it was an astonishing 24 percent.[43] Did Jennings's pattern of smiling cause his viewers to prefer Reagan? The researchers who conducted this study thought so, as did Malcolm Gladwell, who explained the results in his bestseller *The Tipping Point*: "It's not that smiles and nods are subliminal messages. They are straightforward and on the surface. It's just that they are incredibly subtle . . . the ABC viewers who voted for Reagan would never, in a thousand years, tell you that they voted that way because Peter Jennings smiled every time he mentioned the President." But exposure to Peter Jennings was just one tiny component of the election coverage experienced by American voters, and the way the press reported the election was just one of many factors that affected people's votes.

Think about what is really more likely: that Peter Jennings's facial muscles caused a jump of 13 to 24 percent in votes for Ronald Reagan, or that people who viewed ABC News had some preexisting characteristics that made them prefer that network to the others *and* made them more likely to vote for Reagan. To us, it is much more logical to think that the three broadcast TV networks drew different kinds of viewers because they broadcast different mixes of shows, and ABC's viewers at that time were just more conservative than those who watched CBS and NBC. Another possible explanation is that these percentage differences were just statistical blips arising from the small size of the surveys, which included only about one-tenth as many voters as modern-era political polls. One reason why many people, perhaps including the research team behind the study, prefer the causal explanation is that, like Wilson Bryan Key's claims about subliminal advertising, it invokes the mysterious power of influences that lie outside of our awareness.[44]

Training Your Brain?

If we can't unleash untapped mental powers through subliminal messages or hypnosis, perhaps there are other ways to enhance our abilities with relatively little pain. Unless you've been living in a cave for the past few years, you must have heard or seen advertisements like the following television commercial for Nintendo's Brain Age software for its gaming systems:[45]

ACTOR 1: How long has it been? [hugs his friend and then turns toward his wife] Honey, this is my old friend David. We went to high school together.

DAVID: [turns toward his wife] Honey, this is . . . uhh . . . uhh . . . uhhh . . .

NARRATOR: Has this ever happened to you? Exercise your mind with Brain Age. Train your brain in minutes a day. By completing a few challenging exercises and puzzles, you can help keep your mind sharp.

Cognitive training is a growing industry that capitalizes on the fear most people have of cognitive declines that come with aging. Brain Age and its sequel, Brain Age 2, have sold a combined 31 million copies since their release in 2005.[46] Many other cognitive training programs have appeared as well, often promoted with claims that they will help you overcome aging's negative effects on memory with just a few minutes of training each day. The website for Mindscape's Brain Trainer claims that "spending 10 to 15 minutes a day on a brain training workout using simple exercises and puzzles can improve the skills needed to achieve greater success academically and in everyday life."[47]

Now that you have read about the Mozart effect, the 10 percent myth, and subliminal persuasion, you can see why these advertisements are so effective, and you can begin to inoculate yourself against their power. They work by playing on our desire for the quick fix, the cure-all salve that will remedy all our problems. By playing these games for only minutes a day, you'll be better able to come up with that word or name on the tip of your tongue, you'll overcome the limits on your memory, and your entire brain will get younger. Just as those promoting the usefulness of listening to Mozart as an intelligence booster appeal to the desires of parents to help their children succeed, cognitive-training games capitalize on our desire to improve our own minds. These appeals are in some ways even more powerful because they promise a fountain of mental youth that can return our brains to a state when they gave us better memory and more efficient thinking powers.[48] We're already familiar with the "potential ability" these games purport to release, because we know that at some point in our lives, this ability was real rather than just potential.

These companies are smart to focus on aging. Most aspects of cognition, including memory, attention, processing speed, and the ability to switch between tasks, decline throughout adulthood.[49] These changes are noticeable and frustrating. The more often we forget conversations we've had with a spouse, or struggle to recall the name of a friend, the more we long to regain our previous abilities and skills. Just as competitive athletes normally experience a drop-off in skill as they approach their forties, the rest of us see many of our mental abilities go downhill in middle age. Even for games like chess, in which experts build up a mental database of patterns and situations over years of practice, the elite levels are dominated by young players; currently, only three of the top fifty players in the world are over forty years old, and approximately two-thirds are in their twenties.[50]

Not all aspects of thinking decline equally, though, and some don't decline at all. Aspects of cognition that are based on accumulated knowledge and experience are relatively preserved with age and can even improve, especially when speed of processing is not crucial. An expert diagnostician like Dr. Keating, the pediatric "House" we intro-

duced in Chapter 3, only gets better with age; the more unusual patients he encounters, the more able he is to spot similarities to his
increasingly large mental database of familiar cases. That said, a doctor
in his seventies, even if he's better able to identify a disorder, might have
more trouble recalling its name, and might be slower to learn the latest
procedures to treat it than would a doctor in his thirties. Old dogs *can*
learn new tricks—it's just a bit harder and takes a bit longer.

Since cognitive-training programs appeal directly to the illusion of
potential, at this point you might be inclined to dismiss them outright.
But that would be unwise. Just because a man is paranoid doesn't mean
that people aren't actually stalking him. We should be suspicious about
any simple cure for a complex problem, and we should be hesitant about
claims that we can acquire skills without effort. But there still could be
some truth in the adage "use it or lose it." So what, exactly, do the brain-
training programs offer?

Most of the programs provide a set of basic gamelike cognitive tasks,
such as arithmetic (with a time limit), word-finding, and Sudoku. They
are chosen to stress your reasoning and memory abilities, and they can
be fun and challenging. The programs show how your performance on
each task improves over time, and in some cases they provide a composite "brain fitness" score. Most of the programs justify their claims of
brain training by pointing to how much people can improve at these
simple tasks.

If you play these games and stick with them, you will get better at
them regardless of your age. Practicing anything diligently enough will
make you better. The real goal of the brain-training systems, though, is
broader than improving your performance on their specific tasks. Just
as you don't lift weights only to be able to lift bigger weights, you don't
play brain-training games to get better at playing brain-training games.
Even according to the marketers of these programs, you use them to
improve your ability to think and remember in your daily activities.
Brain Age is supposed to help you recall your old friends' names, find
your car keys, and do two things at once, not just get better at solving
Sudoku.

Few studies have even investigated whether training on simple perception and memory tasks has any consequences for our daily mental chores. Although many studies have shown that people who are more cognitively active when they're younger preserve their abilities better as they age, such studies are correlational.[51] Thinking about the illusion of cause reminds us that an association between two factors can occur even if neither one causes the other. The only way to study the effects of brain training on daily cognition is to conduct an experiment, randomly assigning some people to training conditions and others to control conditions, and then measuring the results of training. Over the past decade several clinical trials have done just that.

The largest experiment to date started in 1998 and randomly assigned 2,832 seniors to one of four groups: verbal memory training, problem solving, processing speed, or a control group that did no cognitive training.[52] This massive clinical trial, funded by the National Institutes of Health and conducted by researchers from many universities, hospitals, and research institutes, was known as the ACTIVE trial, which stands for "Advanced Cognitive Training for Independent and Vital Elderly." In the experiment, each group practiced one particular task for ten sessions of one hour each, spread out over about six weeks, and after the training, their performance was tested both on a set of laboratory tasks and on some real-world tasks. The hope was that training on the cognitive tasks would help to keep the brain sharp, leading to improvements on other cognitive tasks and on real-world functioning.

Not surprisingly, if you practice doing a visual search task for ten hours, you get better at visual search. If you practice a verbal memory task for ten hours, you get better at verbal memory. Many of the participants, particularly for the speed-of-processing training, showed improvements immediately after training, and the improvements lasted for years. However, the improvements were limited to the specific tasks they learned and did not carry over to the non-trained laboratory tasks. Practicing verbal memory buys you almost nothing for your processing speed, and vice versa.

Later followup surveys of participants in the ACTIVE study did show some evidence for transfer to real-world performance. Participants in the training groups reported fewer problems with daily activities than did people in the no-training control group. Of course, in this case, the participants knew they were in a training group and that they were expected to improve, so some of the self-reported benefits could be due to placebo effects.

Unfortunately, the results of the ACTIVE study are consistent with other studies. Training tends to be specific to the task that is trained. If you play Brain Age, you'll get better at the specific tasks included in the software, but your new skills won't transfer to other sorts of tasks. In fact, in the now vast cognitive-training literature, almost none of the studies document any transfer to tasks outside the laboratory, and most show only narrow transfer of skill between laboratory tasks—from the one practiced to those that are very similar.[53] If you want to get better at Sudoku, and especially if you like doing Sudoku, by all means, do more Sudoku. If you think that doing Sudoku will keep your mind sharp and help you avoid misplacing your keys or forgetting to take your medicine, you're likely succumbing to the illusion of potential. The same goes for solving crossword puzzles, a favorite recommendation of those who believe that mental exercise can keep the brain sharp and stave off dementia and the cognitive effects of aging: Unfortunately, people who do more crosswords decline mentally at the same rate as those who do fewer crosswords.[54] Practice improves specific skills, not general abilities.

The Real Way to Unlock Your Potential

Please don't get us wrong. We're not trying to argue that there is literally no potential for increasing our mental abilities. Our intellectual capacities are never frozen in place. We all have tremendous potential to learn new skills and to improve our abilities. Indeed, neuroscience research is showing that the plasticity of the adult brain—its ability to change in structure in response to training, injury, and other events—is much greater than previously believed. The illusion is that it is *easy* to unlock this potential, that it can be discovered all at once, or that it can be released with minimal effort. The potential is there, in everyone, to acquire extraordinary mental abilities. Most people, without any training, can remember a list of about seven numbers after hearing it only once. Yet one college student trained himself to be able to remember up to seventy-nine digits.[55] His feat was extraordinary, revealing a latent potential for exceptional digit memory, but it took hundreds of hours of practice and training. In principle, most people have the same potential ability, and could do the same thing with enough practice.

Genius is not born fully formed—it takes years to develop, and it follows a predictable trajectory. Mozart's early compositions were not masterpieces, and Bobby Fischer made plenty of mistakes when he was learning the game of chess. Both likely possessed exceptional talent to develop, but they did not become great without training and practice. And their greatness was limited to the domains they trained in. Training your memory for digits will not help you remember names. However, expertise in a domain does improve many other abilities *within that domain* that were not specifically trained.

A series of classic experiments conducted by the pioneering cognitive psychologists Adriaan de Groot, William Chase, and Herbert Simon demonstrated that chess masters can remember far more than seven items when the items tap into their expertise.[56] We repeated their studies ourselves by testing Chris's friend Patrick Wolff, a grandmaster who had won the U.S. championship twice. We brought Patrick into the lab and showed him a diagram of a chess position from an obscure master game for just five seconds. We then gave him an empty chessboard and a set of pieces and asked him to re-create the position from memory. Remarkably, he could reconstruct the position with nearly 100 percent accuracy even when it contained twenty-five or thirty pieces, far more than the typical seven-item limit for short-term memory.

After watching him perform this feat a few times, we asked him to explain how he did it. He first pointed out that the training of a chess grandmaster doesn't include practice in setting up chess positions after seeing them for just a few seconds. He said that he was able to quickly make sense of the positions and to combine pieces into groups based on the relationships among them. In essence, by recognizing familiar patterns, he stuffed not one but several pieces into each of his memory slots. As he became an expert in chess, he developed other skills that help in playing chess well—mental imagery, spatial reasoning, visual memory— all of which contributed to his ability to do this memory task better than other people. However, being an expert in chess did not make him an imagery, reasoning, or memory expert in general. In fact, when the chess positions we showed him had the same number of pieces ar- ranged on the board randomly, his memory was no better than that of a beginner, because his chess expertise and database of patterns were of little help. The same principle applies to the student who stretched his memory span to seventy-nine digits—his new memory capacity was specific to combinations of numbers, so even after several months of training with numbers, he still had a span of only six items when tested with letters.[57] In other words, he trained his potential ability to remem- ber numbers, but that training did not transfer to any other skills.

Chess grandmasters can apply their expertise to perform a wide vari- ety of chess tasks extremely well, even if they have never carried out those tasks before. One of the most dramatic examples is blindfold chess. Top players can play an entire game "blindfolded," without ever looking at the board—they are told (in chess notation) what moves their opponents have made, and they announce the moves they would like to make in reply. Grandmaster-level players can play two or more blindfold games simultaneously, at a high level of skill, even if they've never tried this before. The exceptional chess memory and imagery abilities needed to perform this feat accrue more or less automatically as players become experts.

Working with Eliot Hearst (another psychology professor who is also a chess master), Chris conducted a study to measure how much worse chess grandmasters play when they can't see the board and pieces.[58] You might think that they'd make more errors because of the additional memory load of remembering where every piece is. To find out whether this supposition is true, Chris took advantage of a unique chess tour- nament that has taken place in Monaco every year since 1992. In the tournament, twelve of the world's top players, including many world championship contenders, play each other twice: once under normal conditions, and once under blindfold conditions. Since the same players are involved in the normal and blindfold games, any difference in the number of errors must be due to the conditions, not the competitors.

In total, from 1993 to 1998 there were about four hundred regular games and four hundred blindfold games played in the tournament, with each lasting an average of forty-five moves by each player. Chris used a chess-playing program called Fritz, which was recognized as one of the best software chess players in the world, to find all the serious mistakes the humans made. Fritz undoubtedly missed some of the most subtle errors, but larger blunders and significant mistakes were easy for it to catch.

Under normal playing conditions, the grandmasters made an average of two mistakes for every three games. These were major blunders, ones that could have—and often did—cost them a game against top-level opposition. The surprise, though, was that the rate of errors in blindfold chess was virtually the same. The grandmasters had trained their potential so well that they could perform their art without even looking at its elements (look, Ma, no board or pieces!). For those interested in unlocking their potential, that's good news, of course. The bad news is that they didn't become chess grandmasters by just listening to the right music or reading the right self-help books. They did it by concentrated study and practice over a period of at least ten years. The brain's potential is vast, and you can indeed tap into it, but it takes time and effort.

Get Your Head in the Game

Practicing games like chess will enhance your ability to do chess-related tasks, but the transfer is relatively limited. Advocates for adding chess to school curricula argue that "chess makes you smarter," but there is no solid evidence for this claim from large, properly controlled experiments.[59] Is there any evidence for broad transfer of skill to tasks and domains other than the one you practice?

Cognitive psychologists were jarred into rethinking the limits of transfer by a striking set of experiments published in 2003 by Shawn

Green and Daphne Bavelier of the University of Rochester.[60] The central conclusion of these studies was that playing video games can improve your ability on a variety of basic cognitive tasks that are, at least on their surface, unrelated to the video games you play. Their first four experiments showed that expert video-game players, defined as people who had played at least four hours per week for the past six months, outperformed video-game novices on tests of some attention and perception abilities. Although this sort of comparison is interesting and provocative, as we discussed in Chapter 5, an association alone does not support a causal inference. It is quite possible that only people with superior abilities in attention and perception become video-game addicts, or that other differences between the experts and novices might contribute to the differences in cognitive performance. Dan's colleague Walter Boot, a psychology professor at Florida State University, suggests one such factor: "People who are able to handle college while also spending a lot of time playing video games are different from people who need to spend more of their time studying."[61] The only way to avoid such confounding factors and determine for sure whether playing video games improves attention and perception is to give novice players video-game training and then see whether their cognitive abilities have improved.

Green and Bavelier did exactly that in their final experiment. They recruited novice video-game players, defined as people who had spent little or no time playing video games in the past six months, and randomly assigned these subjects to one of two groups. One group spent one hour a day for ten days playing Medal of Honor, a fast-paced "first-person shooter" game in which players view and monitor their surroundings as if they were looking through the eyes of their character in the game's world. A second group played the two-dimensional puzzle game Tetris for the same amount of time. Before this practice, each completed a battery of basic cognition, perception, and attention tasks, and after training, they repeated the same battery of tasks. For example, in one of the tasks, known as *Useful Field of View*, a simple object appeared for just a fraction of a second right where the subject was looking, and subjects made a judgment about it (such as whether it was a car or a truck). At the same moment, another object appeared at some distance from where they were looking, and they had to determine where the peripheral object had appeared. The task measures how well people can focus attention on a central object while still devoting some attention to their periphery.

Green and Bavelier hypothesized that action video games would lead to better performance on this task because people have to focus on a wide field of view to do well in the games. In contrast, Tetris should not be of as much benefit because it doesn't require players to distribute their attention as broadly. Their results confirmed their prediction: Subjects who practiced Medal of Honor showed dramatic improvement on a number of attention and perception tasks, but the Tetris group showed no improvement at all. Following training on Medal of Honor, subjects were more than twice as accurate in the field-of-view task as they had been before training. Before training, they correctly reported the location of about 25 percent of the peripheral targets, but after training they got more than 50 percent right.

This finding was so surprising, and led to a publication in *Nature*, because it seemed to break down a wall between two ways that practice can improve our mental abilities. Suppose you work hard at becoming an expert Sudoku solver, spending all your free time doing nothing but solving Sudoku puzzles. You will, of course, get faster and more accurate at solving Sudoku. Moreover, you might find that your ability to solve KenKen puzzles—a new variant of Sudoku—also improves somewhat, even though you had not done a single one during the time you practiced Sudoku. Your improved performance on KenKen would be an example of "narrow transfer," where improvement on one mental skill transfers to other highly similar skills. It would be more surprising to find that practicing Sudoku improved your ability to calculate tips in your head, prepare your income taxes, or remember telephone numbers. Improvements on those skills would demonstrate "broad transfer," because they have little surface-level similarity to Sudoku. Playing Medal of Honor to get better at finding targets in a similar first-person-shooter video game would be an example of narrow transfer. Playing Medal of Honor to improve your ability to pay attention to your surroundings while driving your car is like solving Sudoku to get better at remembering telephone numbers. It's an example of broad transfer, which is valuable because it improves aspects of cognition that weren't specifically trained. Moreover, in this case, a different skill was improved by doing something fun and engaging. We'll bet that you're more likely to follow the adage "practice makes perfect" if the "practice" consists entirely of playing video games.

Green and Bavelier's experiment suggests that video-game training might actually enable people to release some untapped potential for broader skills without having to spend effort practicing those particular skills. It's far from obvious why passively listening to ten minutes of Mozart should change a cognitive ability (spatial reasoning) that has little or nothing to do with music or even hearing. But video games do require players to actively use a variety of cognitive skills, and it's not implausible that ten hours of training on a game that requires attention to a wide visual field could improve performance on a task that requires subjects to focus across a wide display, even though the game and the task are different in many other respects.

Perhaps the most astonishing aspect of this experiment was that it required *only ten hours of training*. Think about the implications of this: We all spend much of our lives focusing on our environment from a first-person perspective, making rapid decisions, and acting on them. Daily tasks like driving require us to focus on a wide visual field—you need to focus both on the road in front of you and on the side streets. And you most likely have driven for much more than ten hours in the past six months. Even if you haven't, you likely have done other things that require similar skills—playing any sport, or even walking down a crowded city street, requires similar rapid decisions and awareness of your surroundings. Why, then, should an additional ten hours of playing one video game have such a large effect on basic cognitive skills?

One possible answer to this question is that playing video games does *not* actually produce dramatic improvements on largely unrelated tasks. As was the case with the Mozart effect, Green and Bavelier's initial study could turn out to be an outlier—subsequent studies may show that video-game training is not as potent as originally thought. But it is also possible that there really is something about playing a first-person action video game that does release untapped potential with minimal effort. Video games can be more engaging and intense than many other activities that draw on the same cognitive abilities, so they could conceivably provide more productive and efficient training that extends beyond the game itself.

More recently, Bavelier and her colleagues have used much more extensive training, often thirty to fifty hours, to find further cognitive benefits of video games. These studies have shown transfer to several different basic perceptual abilities. One study found that video-game training improved contrast sensitivity, which is essentially the ability to detect a shape that is similar in brightness to the background, like a darkly clad person walking along a poorly lit sidewalk.[62] Another showed that action video-game training improved the ability to identify letters placed close together in the periphery of the visual field, essentially increasing the spatial resolution of attention.[63] Given how basic and fundamental these skills are to all aspects of perception, these findings are even more surprising than the original field-of-view result.[64] Metaphorically, these findings suggest that practicing video games is akin to putting on your glasses—it improves all aspects of visual perception. For example, increased contrast sensitivity should make driving at night easier. Even though these followup studies involved substantially more training, they showed broad transfer to abilities that could affect many real-world skills. That said, none of these articles have reported on transfer to performance on real-world tasks, and given the lack of any direct evidence, the authors are appropriately careful not to claim any impact beyond the lab.

As with the Mozart effect, one worrisome aspect of these video-game findings is that the majority of the evidence comes from a single group of researchers. Unlike with the Mozart effect, the group's studies consistently appear in top-tier, peer-reviewed journals rather than obscure scientific backwaters. A bigger problem, though, is that training studies do not lend themselves to easy replication. Studies of the Mozart effect are easy to conduct—bring people into the lab for an hour, play them some Mozart, and give them a few cognitive tests. All you really need is a CD player and some pens. Studies of video-game training are much grander in scale. Each participant must be trained for many hours under direct supervision of laboratory personnel. That requires full-time research staff, more computers, a lot more money to pay subjects for their time, and the space to accommodate hundreds of subject-hours of testing. Few labs are devoted to doing this sort of research, and those that are not typically don't have the funding or resources available for a quick attempt at replication.

To our knowledge, only one published study from a laboratory un-affiliated with the original researchers has successfully replicated the core result of the original Green and Bavelier article. In that study, Jing Feng, Ian Spence, and Jay Pratt of the University of Toronto showed that playing an action video game for ten hours improved the ability to imagine simple shapes rotating as well as the ability to pay attention to objects that the subjects were not directly looking at. They also found that women, who are on average somewhat worse than men on these spatial tasks, improved more from the training.[65]

A second study, although not a direct replica of the Green and Bave-lier experiment, did show a positive effect of video-game practice using a different game and a different subject population: seniors.[66] This study addresses one of the major motivations for brain training: helping to preserve and improve cognitive functioning in aging. In this ex-periment, cognitive neuroscientist Chandramallika Basak and her col-leagues randomly assigned one group of seniors to play Rise of Nations and another group to a no-training control condition. Rise of Nations is a slow-paced strategy game that requires players to keep track of a lot of information while switching back and forth between different strategic elements. The researchers' hypothesis was that training on this sort of strategy game would improve what's known as "executive func-tioning," which is the ability to allocate cognitive resources effec-tively among multiple tasks and goals. Their study found substantial transfer from the video game to a variety of laboratory measures of ex-ecutive functioning. That makes sense given the demands of the game, but because the study did not include any other games for comparison, it's also possible that the benefits had nothing to do with being trained on this particular kind of video game, or indeed with video-game training at all. Seniors in the training group might simply have been more motivated to improve because they knew they were receiving special treatment as part of a study, and that motivation could have led to the biggest improvements for those tasks where they were already the most impaired.[67]

These questions about the proper interpretation of the original Green-Bavelier study will be moot unless it can be consistently and independently replicated. One large-scale attempt to do just that, led by video-game researcher Walter Boot, did not produce the same results as the earlier experiments.[68] Dan was one of the coauthors of Boot's paper and participated in the design of the study. The original study and the replication by Feng's group were both relatively small in scope: In each case, no more than ten subjects were assigned to each condition, and their training lasted only about ten hours. Boot's study used more than twice as many subjects in each condition and gave the subjects more than twice as much training, over twenty hours on each game. He also used a much larger battery of cognitive tasks, including all of the ones used by Green and Bavelier plus about twenty others. The battery itself took up to two hours to complete, and each participant completed all the tasks before and after the training as well as once about halfway through it. Boot used the same Tetris and Medal of Honor games used in the original study, as well as the Rise of Nations game used in Basak's experiment. Like Basak, he had the idea that training with that sort of strategy game would not enhance attention and perception, but instead would improve performance on measures of problem solving, reasoning, and possibly memory. Boot also included a group that received no training at all in order to provide a clear estimate of how much people might improve just by retaking the cognitive tasks before and after training. So this study was designed to test all of the alternative explanations for the positive findings that the original studies did not address—as well as the possibility that training released untapped potential.

One oddity in all of the previous experiments showing positive evidence of video-game training is that none of the control groups did any better the second time they took the cognitive tests than they did the first time. In the original study by Green and Bavelier, the subjects who played Tetris (a video game, but not a fast-paced, first-person "action" game) showed no improvement when they did the cognitive tasks for a second time, after completing their training. The same was true for the replication by Feng and colleagues: Subjects in the control condition did no better when retaking the cognitive tasks. It also held true for most of the positive effects in the Basak study and for the subsequent studies conducted by Bavelier and her colleagues. Given what we know about practice and learning, this finding is hard to explain; people almost always perform better when they do a task a second time. Such improvements are typical as well for the sorts of tasks used in the Brain Age software and other brain-training products. In fact, these routine practice effects are exactly the "evidence" those programs rely on to back their claims that their users' brains are "improving."

Why does lack of improvement in the control conditions matter? Because the evidence for the positive effects of video-game training is based on a comparison to these control groups. To support the claim that video games improve cognition, an experiment must show that people trained with video games improve more than people receiving other training or no training. It's much easier to show an improvement relative to a control group if the control group shows no improvement at all. Had subjects in the control groups improved as expected, the benefits that could be ascribed to video games would have been reduced.

In Boot's experiment, unlike the others, the control group did show a typical increase in performance from the first to the last testing session. The group that practiced action video games also improved on the cognitive tasks. But it improved by the same amount as the control group, meaning that there was no specific effect of video-game training on cognitive abilities.[69] This failure to replicate is especially significant because Boot doubled the amount of training and used more subjects and control groups—all of which strengthened the design of the study and made it a more definitive test of the broad transfer hypothesis advanced by Green and Bavelier. Their initially promising idea that a small amount of video-game training could have big effects does not seem to be borne out. It's possible that some subtle differences in the methods among the various studies account for the different results, but if the effect is that fragile, it is hard to imagine that video games will turn out to be a panacea for cognitive decline.[70]

Recall that the first four experiments in Green and Bavelier's *Nature* article showed that video-game experts consistently outperformed novices on the same tasks that benefited from training in their experiment. Since the effects of training appear to be somewhat tenuous, you might now wonder why experts should tend to outperform novices. One explanation is that the cognitive differences between experts and novices might require a lot more than ten or even fifty hours of training to develop. The experts in these studies often play more than twenty hours of video games in a single week! If it takes that much effort to transfer skill from video games to general perception, would video-game training really be a worthwhile thing to do (if you didn't already love playing video games)? The benefit of being a little faster on a selective attention task is probably not worth the hundreds of hours you would have to spend to receive it—you would be better off practicing the specific skills you are trying to improve. Given the lack of direct evidence that video-game training would even have consequences for our daily lives—say, by making us safer drivers—the potential benefits of training are even more uncertain.

A more subtle concern is that the experts might not actually be any better at these cognitive tasks even if they do show better performance in the lab. How could that be? Some other factor unrelated to cognitive abilities might enhance performance. In his interview with Dan, Walter Boot raised a possibility rarely discussed in the scientific literature:

> Video-game experts might perform better because they know they have been selected to be in the study based on their expertise.

Participants recruited through advertisements or flyers targeting gamers know they're being selected because they're an expert, because they are special, and they might be more motivated, more attentive, and have expectations that they should perform well. Because of all the media coverage, especially in blogs frequented by gamers, they know that they are expected to do better. And the nonexperts might not even know they are in a video-game study.[71]

In other words, the experts might outperform the novices not because they are inherently better at these tasks or because they have thousands of hours of video-game experience, but because they know that the study is about video-game expertise and that they are expected to do better. This sort of "expectancy effect" is a well-known issue in this kind of experiment. One way to address the problem would be to recruit subjects without any mention of video games and then measure video-game expertise only after subjects are finished with all the cognitive tasks. That way, subjects would have no way of knowing that the study is about video-game expertise. Unfortunately, it's an inefficient way to conduct a study, because you might need to test many additional subjects in order to have enough who meet the criteria for a novice or expert.

Regardless of how the subjects are recruited, it is dangerous to draw any causal conclusions about the role of video games in cognition from studies of differences between expert and novice players—training experiments are essential to draw proper inferences about cause.[72] Watch out for misreporting of such expertise effects in the media—journalists regularly claim that video games cause improvements when the studies they describe show only a difference between expert and novice players. Some writers have promoted the idea that video games have benefits extending far beyond increased attention or perceptual abilities—enhancing general intelligence, social ability, confidence, and logical thinking—with even less actual evidence for these claims.[73]

Give Your Brain a Real Workout

In promoting Brain Age, Nintendo's website makes the following broad claim about how its products enhance brain function:

> Everyone knows you can prevent muscle loss with exercise, and use such activities to improve your body over time. And the same could be said for your brain. The design of Brain Age is based on the premise that cognitive exercise can improve blood flow to the brain. All it takes is as little as a few minutes of play time a day. For everyone who spends all their play time at the gym working out the major muscle groups, don't forget—your brain is like a muscle, too. And it craves exercise.[74]

As it turns out, the final sentence is accurate, but not in the way that Nintendo's marketers intended. They meant to imply that cognitive exercise is necessary to keep your brain functioning well. In reality, aerobic physical exercise is likely far better for your brain.[75] Cognitive neuroscientist Arthur Kramer, a colleague of Dan's at the University of Illinois, led one of the best-known studies of how improving physical fitness can affect cognitive abilities.[76] Their experiment, published in *Nature,* randomly assigned 124 sedentary but otherwise healthy seniors to one of two training conditions for six months: aerobic fitness, in which the subjects spent about three hours each week walking, and an anaerobic exercise condition, in which subjects spent the same amount of time doing stretching and toning exercises. Although both forms of exercise are good for your body and lead to better overall fitness, aerobic exercise more effectively improves the health of your heart and increases blood flow to your brain.

Not surprisingly, both training groups experienced the expected benefits to their physical fitness. The surprising result, though, is that walking for as little as a few hours a week also led to large improvements on *cognitive* tasks, particularly those that rely on executive functions like planning and multitasking. The stretching and toning exercise had no cognitive benefits. Kramer's group also conducted a meta-analysis of all the clinical trials of the effects of aerobic fitness training on cognition through 2001; the results confirmed a sizable benefit of this type of fitness training for cognition.[77]

The benefits of exercise are deeper than improvements in behavior and cognition. With age, most adults start to lose some of the gray matter in their brains. (This could be part of the reason for the accompanying cognitive declines.) In another clinical trial, Kramer's group randomly assigned seniors to the same aerobic and anaerobic six-month training regimens just described, except this time, they first used MRI scanning to acquire a complete picture of each subject's brain before and after the fitness training.[78] The result was astounding: Seniors who had walked for just forty-five minutes a day for three days each week preserved much more gray matter in their frontal brain regions than did those who had done stretching and toning. Aerobic exercise actually did keep their brains healthier and younger.

It might seem counterintuitive, but the best thing you can do to preserve and maintain your mental abilities may have little to do with cognition at all. Training your brain directly might have less impact than exercising your body, particularly if you exercise in a way that maintains your aerobic fitness. The exercise doesn't even need to be particularly strenuous. You don't need to compete in triathlons; just walking at a reasonable clip for thirty minutes or more a few times a week leads to better executive functioning and a healthier brain. Despite Nintendo's claims that you need to exercise your brain, it seems that sitting in a chair and doing cognitive puzzles is far less beneficial than walking around the block a few times. Exercise improves cognition broadly by increasing the fitness of your brain itself. And doing puzzles does nothing for your longevity, your health, or your looks.

conclusion

the myth of intuition

WHAT DO YOU LEARN WHEN you read profiles of corporate CEOs? You expect to find out what makes them tick: how they got to their current position, what inspired them to make the decisions they did, why their management style sets them up for success. And most important, you expect to learn about someone whose approach to business—and perhaps life in general—is worth emulating.

As we discussed in Chapter 4, the only way to be sure that you understand something is to test your knowledge. Let's do that now. Apply what you've learned about everyday illusions to this profile of business leader Larry Taylor. Some of the illusions will shine through, but others will be more subtle. See if you can spot them all.

———

Larry Taylor is on his way to work. A stocky man with a military-style buzz cut and intense blue eyes, he sits ramrod straight behind the steering wheel. Despite being the CEO of Chimera Information Systems, a privately held corporation with more than $900 million in annual sales, he doesn't have a driver. It would be awkward to have a driver when your car is just a Toyota Camry with cloth seats, not a Mercedes or Lexus with full leather and burl-wood interior. Taylor makes the forty-minute commute every day. En route, he talks with several of his top managers by phone, getting updates on software development projects, marketing plans, and sales progress—all before he arrives at the office.

All you need to do is follow Taylor around for a few hours to see why his company's revenues are growing at a rate of 45 percent per year, and why he was voted the most innovative and effective executive in the Midwest last year. According to industry analysts, Taylor's arrival in the corner office in 2003 is *the* reason why Chimera has changed from a dowdy vendor of inventory-management software to an industry-leading developer of "middleware" for Web 2.0—applications that sit between a company's public website and private data warehouses, managing communication between the two. Taylor's next move will be to create software that enables even the smallest Internet retailers—the hundreds of thousands of EdsArgyleSocks.coms and eBay storefronts of the world—to manage their supply chains with the sophistication of an Amazon or a Walmart. According to Taylor, this is a $2 billion market opportunity that is wide open.

Today, Taylor is talking to his chief financial officer, Jane Flynt, about Chimera's quarterly earnings release that's due in a week. Taylor speaks with the slight Texas drawl he acquired growing up in San Antonio. There is a pause in the conversation when Flynt steps away from her phone to ask an assistant to run some new analyses that Taylor suggested. At this moment, Taylor mutes his phone and explains the real reason he hired Flynt, who had never been the head of finance at a large company, over other candidates with Ivy League pedigrees and much more experience.

"It was almost two years ago, but I remember it like it was yesterday," says Taylor. "It was a crazy time . . . we needed to have a new CFO in place for the next board meeting, which was coming up fast, but I was traveling to see customers most days of the week back then. So I had them come in on a Sunday morning." The four candidates on the short list duly showed up at 9:00 a.m., in their Sunday best. As a final "test" in the interview, Taylor handed out laptops with PowerPoint installed and asked each candidate to prepare and deliver a five-minute presentation on why he or she should be chosen as Chimera's new CFO. And he told them that they had to deliver their presentations to him *and* to the other candidates, in the company boardroom. "When I said that, their jaws all dropped at once," Taylor recalled. "They all had to be as nervous as a bunch of cats in a room full of rocking chairs." He gave them just ten minutes with the computers to make their slides. "I picked Flynt to go first, and I thought she would wet herself. But she didn't. She gave one of the best speeches I had ever heard in my life. What I kept thinking about was how self-assured she was under all the pressure of the situation I'd set up. I let the other guys give their talks, but I knew right then that I wanted Jane, and when the interviews were over I hired her on the spot."

Taylor is renowned at Chimera for the quickness with which he grasps complex ideas and information. "I only need to read a document once, and I pretty much completely understand it, and I'll remember all of the details, too," he tells us. A recent profile of Taylor in *Inventory World* reported that "Taylor says that he knows everything about how Chimera's products work, often more than their own developers, whom he sometimes embarrasses with tough questions about software architecture and standards."

He is a voracious reader—not just of company reports, trade journals, and business books, but also the latest science and history, and even an occasional vampire novel to keep up with the current obsession of his teenage daughters. From his business and science reading, he's picked up dozens of ideas that he's implemented at Chimera. To boost the inventiveness and productivity of his software engineers, he ordered their managers to play classical music on the public address system for thirty minutes every day; behind the music, subliminal messages exhort employees to do their best.

Taylor learned how to play poker in high school, and he showed a talent for it in college, quickly becoming the biggest winner at his fraternity's regular game. After graduating, he spent a couple of years as a professional poker player on the tournament and cash-game circuit. Nowadays he finds his high-stakes action in the boardroom rather than the casino, but he still plays poker occasionally on the Internet, using the screen name "royalflushCEO." Does his experience in poker influence his approach to business strategy? Is making a huge bluff to convince an opponent to fold a good hand the equivalent of making a risky but potentially rewarding investment in an unproven technology or market? "It doesn't work like that," Taylor says. "When I'm making a big decision for Chimera I don't think about poker tactics. I think more about the broader lessons I took from the game. There's a saying in poker that goes 'think long, think wrong.' It means that sometimes, the more you think about a decision, the more likely you are to make the wrong choice. I read Malcolm Gladwell's book *Blink,* and it taught me that you have to go with your gut instincts, trust your intuition, when you're faced with a complex, important decision."

Taylor relied on his instincts when he decided to bet his company's future on the new logistics software for mom-and-pop Internet businesses. He'd learned from his reading that he was not using as much of his brainpower as he could be. His left brain was so busy analyzing every option in cost-benefit detail that his more emotional right brain never had a chance to take in the big picture. "I had two warring groups within Chimera on this launch question," he says later in the day after coming out of a meeting with the project team. One group was gung ho for the new product, but the other had a laundry list of objections. Taylor had to referee and make the final call. "This time I told myself from the outset that I wouldn't get bogged down in the specifics of the market, the pricing, the project timelines, and so on. Our marketing folks had prepared a profile of the target customer"—a thirty-five-year-old single mother who runs an eBay business out of a spare bedroom in her house—"and I just thought about that woman, and how important her business was to her family and her future, and I visualized her making more money from that business thanks to our software, and I knew that jumping into this market was the right thing to do."

The product launch is set for the end of the year. On the drive home, Larry Taylor is a bit more relaxed than he was at the office, but he's not completely at rest. He is on the phone again—this time talking to his kids.

———

In case it wasn't obvious, the story you just read was entirely made up—100 percent fictitious. Taylor and Flynt don't exist, and Chimera Information Systems is a chimera. We constructed this fake profile to mimic many similar articles we have seen in the business press.[1] It's full of commonsense notions, assumptions, and beliefs that portray Taylor as a somewhat unconventional, but no doubt successful, business leader. Realizing that the profile must be fake wasn't the real test, though.

We intentionally constructed the Larry Taylor story to spotlight the six everyday illusions we have discussed in this book. Did you catch all of them at work? Let's look back and see where Taylor—and the "writer" of the profile—were led astray by everyday illusions:

- Taylor starts his day by talking nonstop on his cell phone while he drives to work. We saw in Chapter 1 that the illusion of attention insidiously makes us think we can do both of these things at once just as well as we can do either one alone.

- During his "interview," Taylor gives an extremely precise recollection of how he hired his chief financial officer, emphasizing his own cleverness in announcing a surprise challenge. He may think he remembers the episode "like it was yesterday," but as we learned in Chapter 2, our memories of even the most salient events are subject to distortion—even as we remain confident that we are recalling them accurately.

- Confidence was an important signal to Taylor when he decided to hire his CFO: Jane Flynt stood out over more experienced, better-educated candidates precisely because of the confidence she exuded. But as we told you in Chapter 3, that sort of confidence is exactly what Jennifer Thompson exuded on the witness stand when Ronald Cotton was sentenced to life in prison for a crime he didn't commit.

- What makes Taylor such a good manager? According to Taylor himself, it is his broad and deep knowledge of Chimera; others praise his ability to grasp complex information quickly. But as Chapter 4 illustrated, we habitually overestimate our own knowledge (especially of how things work), and we quickly make important decisions that we might profitably stop to reflect on if we realized how little we really do know.

- What's behind Chimera's recent success? The experts think it's Taylor—before he became CEO, the company was an also-ran, but now it's a leader. From Chapter 5, we can recognize the illusion of cause that can result from a chronological sequence of events: By itself, the fact that Chimera did better after Taylor than it did before him doesn't prove that his arrival caused the improvement. Other changes to the company around the same time, or changes outside the company, like a general upswing in its industry, might have been responsible.

- The profile also reports that Taylor plays classical music and subliminal messages to his employees and has been trying to access the unused capacity of his own brain. He seems to be under the sway of the illusion of potential that we covered in Chapter 6.

Earlier we mentioned that everyday illusions have a common characteristic: They all make us think that our mental abilities and capacities are greater than they actually are. There's another common thread that connects all of the illusions. In each case, we confuse how easily our minds can do something with how well they are doing it. In psychological lingo, we take the *fluency* with which we process information as a signal that we are processing a lot of information, that we are processing it deeply, and that we are processing it with great accuracy and skill. But effortless processing is not necessarily illusion-free. For example, retrieving memories almost never feels difficult to us. We experience the ease of retrieval, but we don't experience all the distortions that happened to our memories after they were first stored. These distortions happen beneath the surface of our mental lives, without our awareness. We then mistakenly attribute the perceived fluency of our recall to the accuracy, completeness, and permanence of our memories. Fluency plays a similar role in our understanding of perception, attention, confidence, knowledge, and many other mental processes, and in all of these cases, we have seen that significant illusions result.[2]

We aren't arguing that everyday illusions are inherently bad or that they are simply bugs in the mind's software that could have been avoided with better programming. Although the illusions result from our mental limitations, those limitations usually have a countervailing benefit. As we pointed out in Chapter 1, the inattentional blindness that causes us to miss the gorilla is an inevitable consequence of our generally salutary ability to focus attention on a primary goal—in that case, counting basketball passes. As in many other situations, the ability to focus is useful precisely because it greatly increases our ability to carry out otherwise difficult tasks.

In recent years, psychologists have proposed that most of our thought processes can be divided into two types: those that are fast and automatic and those that are slow and reflective. Both contribute to everyday illusions. The rapid, automatic processes involved in perception, memory, and causal inference have serious limitations, but these limitations become much more consequential when our higher-level, reflective, more abstract reasoning abilities fail to see that we are going astray and make appropriate corrections. In other words, we get into more accidents when we talk on a phone while driving both because our attention is limited and because we don't notice this limitation while it's happening.[3]

It's not only Larry Taylor and the misguided "author" of his profile who labor under these everyday illusions. We all do. When we uncritically consume stories like the one about Taylor, or when we do the things that Taylor does, we too fall prey to these illusions. Everyday illusions are so woven into our habits of mind that we don't even realize that they undergird all of the "common sense" that leads us to accept stories like Larry Taylor's.

This type of common sense has another name: intuition. What we intuitively accept and believe is derived from what we collectively assume and understand, and intuition influences our decisions automatically and without reflection. Intuition tells us that we pay attention to more than we do, that our memories are more detailed and robust than they are, that confident people are competent people, that we know more than we really do, that coincidences and correlations demonstrate causation, and that our brains have vast reserves of power that are easy to unlock. But in all these cases, our intuitions are wrong, and they can cost us our fortunes, our health, and even our lives if we follow them blindly.

That's not a message that has been popular lately. Among the general public and among some psychologists, it has become fashionable to argue that intuitive methods of thinking and making decisions are superior to analytical methods. Intuitive thinking is faster and easier, to be sure. And the idea that it might also be more accurate is seductive, because it flies in the face of society's long-standing celebration of rationality and logic as the purest and most objective forms of thought. Toward the end of the profile, we see that Larry Taylor has absorbed this contrarian message. Citing an adage from his days as a poker pro—"think long, think wrong"—and his reading of Malcolm Gladwell's *Blink,* he ignores all the analysis his staff has done and goes with his gut, which tells him that customers will benefit from the new product. He bets the company on this instinct, but he is at peace—and back on the phone while he drives home.

   Taylor's decision might seem like an appalling way to gamble with the money of his investors and the careers of his employees. But sadly, it's not at all far-fetched to portray a CEO who makes a billion-dollar decision on instinct. Business magazines routinely celebrate this kind of "decisive" leadership. For example, in its profile of Percy Barnevik, the celebrated CEO of the Swedish-Swiss company ABB, the magazine *Long Range Planning* gushed, "To meet him . . . is to become immediately aware of an incisive, original approach to management in which the ability to make swift, confident decisions is paramount."[4]

   To cite just one concrete example of the instinctual risk-taking that businesspeople engage in all the time, the decision by top executives of Motorola to launch the Iridium satellite telephone business was driven largely by an intuitive "vision" of customers being able to use a single portable phone to place calls from anywhere in the world, despite the extensive data that Motorola itself generated showing that this would be an economically unsound business. The phone would have cost $3,000, the service would have cost $3 per minute, and communication would have been impossible indoors or in cities with skyscrapers. The product was ideal for the desert nomad with a few thousand dollars burning a hole in his pocket, but impractical for everyone else. According to one outside analyst, even if Iridium captured the entire worldwide market for international business calls from developing countries, it still could not pay for the equipment its system required, let alone its operating expenses. Iridium failed within a year of launch and ultimately lost almost $5 billion.[5]

When First Impressions Are Wrong Impressions

Thomas J. Wise was a celebrated British collector of rare books and manuscripts in the late nineteenth and early twentieth centuries. The catalog of his private collection, which he named the Ashley Library, filled eleven printed volumes. Around 1885, an author named W. C. Bennett showed Wise several copies of a privately printed edition of *Sonnets from the Portuguese*, a famous series of poems written by

Elizabeth Barrett Browning during her courtship with Robert Browning. ("How do I love thee? Let me count the ways . . .") The sonnets were thought to have been first published in a two-volume collected edition of her poems that appeared in 1850. Bennett's forty-seven-page pamphlet, labeled "not for publication," was dated 1847, making it a previously unknown, earlier printing of the sonnets. Wise realized its value as a rarity and purchased a copy for £10. He also alerted several collector friends, who did the same, exhausting Bennett's stock.

Wise's story of how he came upon the Browning volume was corroborated by detailed accounts from one of his friends, Harry Buxton Forman, and from a writer named Edmund Gosse. Over the ensuing years, Wise found and distributed previously unknown volumes of minor works by other writers, including Alfred Tennyson, Charles Dickens, and Robert Louis Stevenson. Numerous private collectors and libraries snapped them up; Wise's fame and wealth grew commensurately. He eventually became known as the leading book collector and bibliographer in all of England.

By the turn of the century, however, some American book dealers were becoming discomfited by the steady stream of newly discovered, author-printed pamphlets. In 1898, George D. Smith's *Price Current of Books* wrote, "Grave suspicions are entertained that some of these are being manufactured—but that these suspicions are well-grounded, cannot be said . . . Maybe 'The Last Tournament' by Tennyson is worth $300, but it is curious that every Tennyson collector of note has been supplied with one lately!" Despite this and other isolated challenges to their provenance, the pamphlets were broadly respected as genuine for decades.

In the 1930s, two young British dealers, John Carter and Graham Pollard, formed their own suspicions about the authenticity of some of Wise's finds. They began a meticulous program of research in which they gathered and analyzed all of the evidence about the provenance of the Browning *Sonnets* pamphlet. They identified eight separate ways in which the existence of the volume was inconsistent with other facts known about Browning and her work, or with typical experience in rare books. For example, no copies inscribed by the author had ever been found, no copies existed that had been trimmed and bound in the way that was customary at the time of their printing, and the special private printing was not mentioned in any letters, memoirs, or other documents left by the Brownings.

Carter and Pollard next turned to direct scientific analysis. Although the forensic science of the 1930s was not what it is today, it was possible to examine the paper used to print the *Sonnets* under a microscope. All paper manufactured in the United Kingdom before 1861 was made from rags, straw, or a strawlike material called esparto. Wood pulp was not used to make paper until 1874. Carter and Pollard put the Browning pamphlet under their microscope and saw a substantial amount of chemically treated wood pulp in its fibers. From this, and much other carefully gathered evidence, they concluded that the putative 1847 printing of the *Sonnets* had to be a forgery produced after 1874. They performed similar analyses on fifty other pamphlets and found decisive evidence that twenty-one of them were similarly forged.

The two dealers published the results of their research in 1934, in a 412-page book titled *An Enquiry into the Nature of Certain XIXth Century Pamphlets*. They stopped short of explicitly accusing Wise of forgery, but their case left no doubt that he was guilty.[6] He denied the charges until his death three years later. Subsequent investigations revealed that he had also stolen pages out of many rare books in the British Library. He is still celebrated today, but no longer as a great collector or bibliographer; instead, he is universally regarded as one of the greatest literary forgers of all time.

How did Wise pull off this fraud on such a massive scale? In evaluating his individual items for their collections, private buyers and institutional librarians didn't have the opportunity to analyze the full scope of Wise's offerings, or the skill to perform chemical analysis. Individually, the items looked authentic, and each nicely filled a gap in an author's known body of work. Intuition was of no help in discovering the fraud. The deception was only uncovered through the use of deductive logic, based on the overall pattern of newly discovered pamphlets, a careful comparison with other historical sources and facts, and scientific study of the items themselves. The story of Thomas Wise and of the detective work performed by John Carter and Graham Pollard illustrates a triumph of deliberation and analysis over instinct. Gut feelings led professional, expert collectors to spend small fortunes accumulating Wise's pamphlets; rigorous analysis revealed their mistake.[7]

Ironically, one of the best-known cases used to demonstrate the power of intuition also involved the detection of a forgery. In his bestselling book *Blink*, which is subtitled *The Power of Thinking Without Thinking*, Malcolm Gladwell opens his case for "rapid cognition," which is another name for intuition, with the story of art experts who could tell immediately that a purported ancient Greek statue known as a *kouros* was a fake, while scientific experts incorrectly judged it to be authentic.[8] Gladwell's compelling narrative vividly portrays a case in which intuition outdid analysis. And as we've seen repeatedly, a single vivid example that illustrates a causal argument may be taken as proof unless we think carefully about the information we haven't been given—and thinking about what is *missing* from a story does not come naturally. The case of the *kouros* might be an anomaly. After all, how often do art experts intuit that a piece is forged when scientific analysis says it's genuine? Cases like Wise's—in which intuitions are refuted by analysis—might well be more common. Moreover, neither story informs us whether intuition or analysis is more accurate when the artwork actually is genuine.

The story of Thomas J. Wise is just one example of deliberate, scientific analysis overcoming flawed, intuitive judgments; but just as Gladwell's *kouros* story does not prove that intuition trumps analysis, our Wise story does not prove that analysis always trumps intuition. Intuition has its uses, but we don't think it should be exalted above analysis without good evidence that it is truly superior. The key to successful decision-making, we believe, is knowing when to trust your intuition and when to be wary of it and do the hard work of thinking things through.[9]

Picking Preserves and Recognizing Robbers

Are there times when deliberation consistently yields worse judgments than snap decisions and gut intuition? Yes, and here's an example from a classic experiment. Suppose you were asked to participate in a blind taste-test of five different brands of strawberry jam. After tasting all of the jams, but before being asked to rate their quality, you spend a couple of minutes writing down your reasons for liking and disliking each jam. Then you rate each one on a scale from 1 to 9. How accurate would your ratings be, assuming we judged accuracy by comparing your ratings with those given by a panel of experts assembled by *Consumer Reports* magazine?

When psychologists Timothy Wilson and Jonathan Schooler conducted this experiment with college students as their subjects, they found that the ratings the students gave to the jams bore almost no resemblance to those given by the experts. They should have been able to tell which ones were good and which ones were not—the jams varied widely in quality and included those ranked 1st, 11th, 24th, 32nd, and 44th best out of the 45 that *Consumer Reports* had reviewed. Did the students have no taste for jam, or did the popular palate have a different preference from the expert one? Not at all. In a separate condition of the experiment, rather than writing the reasons they liked and disliked each jam, each subject wrote about something entirely unrelated: their reasons for choosing their college major. The subjects then rated the jams, and despite not having thought about them at all after tasting them, they made ratings that were much closer to those of the experts.[10]

Why does thinking about jams make our decisions about them worse? There are two reasons. First, thinking about the jams doesn't give us any more information about them—once we taste them, we have all the information we are going to get. Second, and we think more important, is the fact that jam preferences result mainly from emotional responses, not logical analysis. Emotional responses tend to happen automatically and rapidly, in contrast to the slower, deliberative processing underlying analytic reasoning. A decision about how something tastes is a visceral judgment that can't be improved by cogitating about it. Thinking about it only generates irrelevant information that essentially jams up our intuitive, emotional reaction.

Although taste preferences rely more on emotion than logic, deciding whether to launch a major new product seems to be a good occasion for setting emotion aside and spending some time on analysis. But the distinction isn't always so obvious. In general, when there are few objective grounds for determining whether a decision is right or wrong, intuition can't be beat. But even when there are objective criteria, gut responses sometimes outperform analytical ones. Recall again the case from Chapter 3 of Jennifer Thompson, who confidently and repeatedly identified the innocent man Ronald Cotton as her rapist. One reason she was so confident was that she focused all her conscious attention on memorizing his appearance, in part to distract herself from the trauma and in part to help the police catch him if she survived. She caught glimpses of his face and body, and she wrote later of trying to store details, "to record information" in her mind—his height, the shape of his nose, his skin tone. It's no wonder she was so confident—she had worked hard to memorize his features during the most stressful moment of her life.

Unfortunately, thinking in words about a person's appearance can actually *impair* your ability to recognize that person later. Although this possibility was known in the 1950s, interest in it was revived by a series of experiments conducted in 1990, when it was given the new name "verbal overshadowing."[11] In one experiment, subjects watched a thirty-second video of a bank robbery that included a view of the robber's face. One group of subjects then spent five minutes writing a description of the face "in as much detail as possible." A control group spent five minutes doing something unrelated. Afterward, the subjects tried to pick the robber out of a set of photographs of eight similar-looking individuals, and then indicated how confident they were in their choices.

The protocol used in this procedure mimics what happens in criminal cases (like Thompson's). The police routinely ask witnesses to give detailed descriptions of suspects, and those same witnesses later try to identify a suspect in a photographic lineup. In the experiment, those subjects who did an unrelated task successfully identified the suspect 64 percent of the time. But what about those who wrote detailed notes about the suspect? They picked the right suspect only 38 percent of the time! The verbal information in the written notes overshadowed the nonverbal information captured by the initial visual perception of the face, and the verbal information turned out to be less accurate. Ironically, our intuition tells us that analyzing a face will help us remember it better, but in this case at least, it is better for analysis to step back and let more automatic, pattern recognition processes take over. This experiment did not involve an emotional evaluation, only an objective test of memory, but reflective deliberation did not help.[12]

Deliberation will outperform intuition when you have conscious access to all the necessary data. In such cases, analysis *can* generate new information that will help you make a better decision. Let's return for one last time to the game of chess. In Chapter 6, we presented the remarkable finding that chess grandmasters can play the game just as well blindfolded as they can with normal sight of the board. Grandmasters and masters also can play an extremely competent game with just five minutes—or less—in which to make all of their moves. Chris used to lose regularly to a grandmaster who played the entire game using a total of less than one minute to make all his moves, while giving Chris five minutes to make his. How is this possible?

The leading theory is that expert players recognize familiar patterns in the clusters of pieces they see on the board, and these patterns are connected in their minds to potential strategies, tactics, and even specific moves that are likely to work in those situations. In extreme cases, their pattern recognition may be so good, and their opponents so weak, that grandmasters can win games without doing much analysis at all. In essence, they can rely entirely on intuition and still play well.

Recall the study in which Chris and his colleague Eliot Hearst used a computer program to find the mistakes grandmasters made in blindfold chess. In another part of that study, they compared games under ordinary tournament conditions, in which each game lasts up to five hours, to games under "rapid" conditions, in which the game is over in about one hour. (Neither of these conditions involved blindfold play.) If chess expertise resides exclusively in fast, intuitive pattern recognition, then the grandmasters should have made just as many mistakes when they had five hours as when they had just one hour. But under rapid conditions, the number of mistakes went up by 36 percent, a highly significant increase.[13] In chess, having more time to think enables you to make better-quality moves—whether you are the world champion, a grandmaster, or an amateur—so there must be more to making good decisions in chess than just intuitive pattern recognition. The same is true for most of the important decisions we make in our lives.

Technology to the Rescue?

It's easier to point out the nature of everyday illusions and their potentially dire consequences than it is to find solutions to the problems they pose. But we see three broad approaches that might lessen the impact of these illusions in our lives.

First, simply learning how everyday illusions work—for example, by reading this book—will help you notice and avoid being victimized by them in the future. However, your ability to consciously supervise everything your mind is up to is limited. We have told you our best ideas for anticipating and avoiding everyday illusions, but this kind of knowledge alone will not completely solve the problem.

Second, you could try to enhance your cognitive abilities through training. However, as we have seen, cognitive training is unlikely to improve performance enough to dispel everyday illusions, for two reasons: (1) increasing overall brainpower is not as simple as doing mental exercise, playing video games, or listening to classical music; and (2) the cognitive abilities you *can* improve through training will probably not help you override everyday illusions. Mental exercise may be good for you in some ways, and may even be its own reward, but it won't lead to an illusion-free life.

Technology holds promise as a helpful tool to avoid everyday illusions. Indeed, there are already many mundane examples of technologies that have helped us overcome mental limitations. Writing, for example, helped humans preserve historical information more precisely and in larger quantity than would have been possible through memory and oral tradition. Similarly, the invention of calculating machines reduced the number of costly errors resulting from our limited ability to manipulate numbers in our heads.

Innovations like these have been critical to improving our productivity and quality of life. But they address only the limitations of our cognitive systems, not the illusions that beset them. Illusions result from mistaken judgments about our limitations, and it is these judgments that we must adjust. Technology can help us, but we must first be willing to acknowledge that automated judgments may sometimes be better than our own judgments—a difficult and controversial step.

Still, we don't think that technological innovation can entirely solve the problem. A complementary approach to replacing human judgment might be to change our environment so that our limitations become irrelevant. In other words, if we know the limits of our cognition, we can redesign our surroundings to avoid the consequences of mistaken intuitions. For example, now that you have read about the illusion of attention, we hope that you have been dissuaded from talking on a phone while driving. But the temptation to distract yourself while driving has only increased as phones have morphed into Internet access points and video-game machines. The best approach to overcoming the illusion of attention would be to reduce the temptation: Remove the power adapter from your car or keep the phone out of reach in a purse or briefcase in the backseat.

No amount of training will enable people to notice everything around them, and despite our best intentions, we cannot readily dismiss our intuitive (and incorrect) beliefs about what captures our attention. But with knowledge of the illusion of attention, we can proactively restructure our lives so that we are less likely to be misled by the illusion. We think the same is true of the other everyday illusions, and we hope that people more inventive than we are will take up the challenge of designing solutions that help us overcome not just the limitations of our minds but our everyday illusions about them as well.

Look for Invisible Gorillas

You have reached the end of our book. As Woody Allen said when he reached the end of his legendary stand-up comedy routine, "I wish I had some kind of affirmative message to leave you with. I don't. Would you take two negative messages?"[14]

One of our messages in this book is indeed negative: Be wary of your intuitions, especially intuitions about how your own mind works. Our mental systems for rapid cognition excel at solving the problems they evolved to solve, but our cultures, societies, and technologies today are much more complex than those of our ancestors. In many cases, intuition is poorly adapted to solving problems in the modern world. Think twice before you decide to trust intuition over rational analysis, especially in important matters, and watch out for people who tell you intuition can be a panacea for decision-making ills. And if anyone ever asks you to watch a video and count the passes of a basketball . . .

But we also have an affirmative message to leave you with. You can make better decisions, and maybe even live a better life, if you do your best to look for the invisible gorillas in the world around you. We were just trying to be clever when we titled our original article on the gorilla experiment "Gorillas in Our Midst," but in a metaphorical sense, there *are* gorillas in our midst. There may be important things right in front of you that you aren't noticing due to the illusion of attention. Now that you know about this illusion, you'll be less apt to assume you're seeing everything there is to see. You may think you remember some things much better than you really do, because of the illusion of memory. Now that you understand this illusion, you'll trust your own memory, and that of others, a bit less, and you'll try to corroborate your memory in important situations. You'll recognize that the confidence people express often reflects their personalities rather than their knowledge, memory, or abilities. You'll be wary of thinking you know more about a topic than you really do, and you will test your own understanding before mistaking familiarity for knowledge. You won't think you know the cause of something when all you really know is what happened before it or what tended to accompany it. You'll be skeptical of claims that simple tricks can unleash the untapped potential in your mind, but you'll be aware that you can develop phenomenal levels of expertise if you study and practice the right way.

Chris once gave his seminar students the assignment of finding an interesting story from history or current events in which everyday illusions played an important role. The list they generated was fascinating in its scope: a controversial shooting by police in Brooklyn, the epic Ponzi scheme of Bernard Madoff, a living person pronounced dead who woke up in the morgue, and even the causes of the Vietnam War and the explosion of the space shuttle *Challenger*.

You can do this too. Take any opportunity you find to pause and observe human behavior through the lenses we've given you. Try to track your own thoughts and actions as well, to make sure your intuitions and gut-level decisions are justified. Try your best to slow down, relax, and examine your assumptions before you jump to conclusions.

When you think about the world with an awareness of everyday illusions, you won't be as sure of yourself as you used to be, but you will have new insights into how your mind works, and new ways of understanding why people act the way they do. Often, it's not because of stupidity, arrogance, ignorance, or lack of focus. It's because of the everyday illusions that affect us all. Our final hope is that you will always consider this possibility before you jump to a harsher conclusion.

ACKNOWLEDGMENTS

On September 30, 2004, in Cambridge, Massachusetts, we received the Ig Nobel Prize for psychology. The prize was awarded "for demonstrating that when people pay close attention to something, it's all too easy to overlook anything else—even a woman in a gorilla suit." Two days later, we were walking to a lecture hall at MIT to give a brief talk about the gorilla experiment when our conversation turned to the growing visibility of the gorilla video outside our home territory of cognitive psychology. More and more people were telling us that the video didn't just point out a quirk of vision, it gave them new and broader insights into how their minds worked—or failed to work. Before then, our thinking about the gorilla video had been limited to its implications for visual perception and attention, but we began to realize that, metaphorically, it might help people to think about cognitive limitations more generally. Over the course of that walk, we laid the foundation for this book, an exploration of the significance of cognitive limitations and our (un) awareness of them. So our first duty is to thank Marc Abrahams, creator and impresario of the Ig Nobel Prizes, for giving us the "honor" that sparked this project. And we might not have gotten the prize were it not for Malcolm Gladwell, whose description of our gorilla study in the *New Yorker* in 2001 helped bring it to broader attention.

We owe an even greater debt to Ulric Neisser, whose groundbreaking work on selective looking inspired the gorilla study. During Dan's final year of graduate school, Neisser returned to the faculty at Cornell, giving Dan the invaluable opportunity to talk to, argue with, and learn from his intellectual idol. Those conversations inspired Dan to try to replicate Neisser's studies at Harvard. Without Neisser's inspiration, the gorilla experiment never would have happened.

Several people provided advice while our ideas for this book were still germinating. These early contributors include Michael Boylan, Bill Brewer, Neal Cohen, Marc Hauser, Stephen Kosslyn, and Susan Rabiner. While writing the book, we received valuable information on specific topics from Adrian Bangerter, George Bizer, David Baker, Walter Boot, David Dunning, Larry Fenson, Kathleen Galotti, Art Kramer, Justin Kruger, Dick Lehr, Jose Mestre, Michelle Meyer, Stephen Mitroff, Jay Pratt, Fred Rothenberg, Alan Schwartz, John Settlage, Kenneth Steele, Richard Thaler, and Frederick Zimmerman.

Several people subjected themselves to extended interviews as part of our research for the book. Although a few of them do not appear in the final version of the book, all contributed substantially to our thinking about everyday illusions. For giving their time and agreeing to be interviewed, we thank Walter Boot, Bill Brewer, Daniel Chabris, Steven Franconeri, Jim Keating, Ed Kieser, Leslie Meltzer, Stephen Mitroff, Steven Most, Tyce Palmaffy, Trudy Ramirez, Leon Rozenblit, Melissa Sanchez, and Michael Silverman.

Many people gave us feedback on our writing, some reading drafts of several chapters and others reading the entire manuscript more than once. First and foremost, our editor at Crown, Rick Horgan, and his assistant, Nathan Roberson, helped us organize our prose in a way that balanced the need to keep the book moving swiftly from one port of call to the next while remaining anchored to the underlying science. The following people provided insightful commentary on specific chapters and sections, often correcting our misconceptions: Walter Boot, Nancy Boyce, Daniel Chabris, Jack Chen, Nicholas Christakis, Diana Goodman, Jamie Hamilton, Art Kramer, James Levine, Allie Litt, Steve McGaughey, Lisa McManus, Michael Meyer, Michelle Meyer, Steven Most, Kathy Richards, Leon Rozenblit, Robyn Schneiderman, Rachel Scott, Michael Silverman, David Simons, Paul Simons, Kenneth Steele, Courtnie Swearingen, and Richard Thaler. We would like to give special thanks to Steve

McGaughey, Michelle Meyer, Kathy Richards, David Simons, and Pat Simons for carefully reading and giving us extensive feedback on the entire book.

Several people gave input on our national survey of beliefs about how the mind works, including Diane Beck, Aaron Benjamin, Daniel Benjamin, George Bizer, Neal Cohen, Gary Dell, Jeremy Gray, Jamie Hamilton, Daniel Levin, Alejandro Lleras, Michelle Meyer, Neal Roese, Jennifer Shephard, Lisa Shin, and Annette Taylor. Kristen Pechtol collaborated with Chris on a preliminary version of the survey that was tested with students at Union College. Jay Leve of SurveyUSA provided thoughtful feedback about the wording of our survey and additional statistical information we needed for data analysis.

Our literary agent, Jim Levine, was instrumental in helping us craft a proposal for our book that brought all of the everyday illusions together into a coherent narrative. He also deserves the credit for coining the phrase "everyday illusions." Our thanks also go to Dan Ariely for introducing us to Jim. Steven Pinker and Daniel Gilbert graciously helped with our proposal. Elizabeth Fisher at Levine-Greenberg was tremendously helpful in coordinating international-rights sales and in guiding us through the complicated process of negotiations with international agents and publishers.

We could not have completed this project without the flexibility and support provided by our academic institutions, the psychology departments at Union College (Chris) and the University of Illinois (Dan). Dan would also like to acknowledge the Center for Advanced Study at the University of Illinois for sabbatical support when we were beginning our research for the book.

Since we have tried to explain everyday illusions by appealing to scientific research, our success depends on the work of many other scientists. Although we describe much of our own research in this book, that research did not occur in a vacuum, and we were not alone in doing it. We would like to thank all of our research collaborators and coauthors, without whom much of that work could not have been done. More broadly, we would like to thank all of our colleagues whose work we cited and discussed throughout this book, mostly without their knowledge. Although they might not always agree with our interpretations of their ideas and results, we hope that we have done justice to their important scientific contributions. Chris would like to acknowledge the lifelong influence of Stephen Kosslyn, his mentor before, during, and after graduate school, who taught him much about scientific thinking and generously supported him in the pursuit of his own independent research directions. Dan would particularly like to thank his long-term collaborator, Daniel Levin, whose ideas and writing about metacognition helped motivate many of the arguments we put forward throughout this book.

Finally, we would each like to thank our families. Chris thanks his wife, Michelle Meyer; their son, Caleb; and his own parents, Daniel and Lois Chabris, for all their love and support, and for putting up with him and the whole project. Dan thanks his wife, Kathy Richards, and their children, Jordan and Ella, for tolerating far too many long days and working weekends. He would also like to thank his parents, Pat and Paul Simons, and his brother, David Simons, for helping him to think clearly and for arguing with him when he didn't.

We hope that we haven't overlooked anyone whom we should have thanked, but if we have, please consider attributing our omission to an everyday illusion rather than an intentional slight.

Chapter 1: "I Think I Would Have Seen That"

1. Details of this case are drawn from a variety of sources, including several excellent, in-depth investigative articles written by award-winning journalist Dick Lehr for the *Boston Globe*. Lehr has written a book, *The Fence* (New York: HarperCollins, 2009), that discusses the case and the larger issues surrounding it. Our sources also include the following articles by Dick Lehr in the *Globe*: "Boston Police Turn on One of Their Own," December 8, 1997, p. A1; "Truth or Consequences," September 23, 2001; "Free and Clear," January 22, 2006; "Witness in '95 Brutality Case Offers New Account," September 17, 2006. Other sources included the opinions of the U.S. district and circuit courts in the case, especially *United States v. Kenneth M. Conley*, 186 F.3d 7 (1st Cir. 1999); and *Kenneth M. Conley v. United States*, 415 F.3d 183 (1st Cir. 2005); as well as a brief filed by Conley in U.S. District Court for the District of Massachusetts (*Kenneth M. Conley v. United States*, No. 01-10853-WGY, No. 01-97-cr-10213-WGY, June 26, 2003). When any sources provided discrepant details, we have regarded *The Fence* as definitive because it was written most recently and incorporated the most research.

2. Biographical information about Michael Cox is from a profile prepared for his participation in a conference on "Race, Police, and the Community" at Harvard Law School, December 7–9, 2000, law.harvard.edu/academics/clinical/cji/rpcconf/coxm.htm (accessed May 18, 2009).

3. S. Murphy, "A Settlement Is Reached in Beating of Police Officer," *The Boston Globe,* March 4, 2006, p. B3.

4. Lehr, "Boston Police Turn on One of Their Own."

5. The juror quotes are from Lehr, "Truth or Consequences." The widespread belief that police officers are superior to civilians at observing and remembering relevant information appears to be inconsistent with the scientific evidence; e.g., P. B. Ainsworth, "Incident Perception by British Police Officers," *Law and Human Behavior* 5 (1981): 231–236.

6. Perjury is the crime of making a false statement while under oath in a legal proceeding. Each individual false statement can lead to a separate charge of perjury. Conley was accused of perjuring himself by claiming (1) that he did not see Cox (or any other police officer) chase Brown to the fence, and (2) that he did not see the attack on Cox. He was

acquitted of the second charge but convicted of the first. His conviction for obstruction of justice, which is the more general crime of interfering with law enforcement, in essence flowed automatically from the jury's finding that he had committed perjury, and it did not reflect any additional malfeasance.

7. All four suspects from the gold Lexus were arrested that night. The victim at the hamburger restaurant had been shot multiple times in the chest, allegedly because he'd witnessed another shooting at a nearby bar earlier that same night. He died several days later. The next year, two of the suspects were convicted of first-degree murder; Smut Brown, who wasn't accused of pulling the trigger himself, was acquitted. Michael Cox eventually recovered from his physical injuries and returned to work after a six-month absence. He went on to become a deputy superintendent of police in Boston. Two of those accused by Cox of being involved in the beating were later found civilly liable and lost their jobs when Cox sued the Boston Police Department.

8. Our study was reported in the following article: D. J. Simons and C. F. Chabris, "Gorillas in Our Midst: Sustained Inattentional Blindness for Dynamic Events," *Perception* 28 (1999): 1059–1074. Dan first learned about Neisser's 1970s experiments when he was a college student. Neisser's experiments used a complicated mirror apparatus to create ghostlike images of people who appeared to walk through one another. He designed those videos to test whether subjects could pay attention to one set of people while ignoring others who occupied exactly the same areas. That is, he asked whether people focus their visual attention on individual objects rather than on individual regions of space, and when they focus on objects, how selectively they focus. The most detailed description of Neisser's earlier studies that inspired our experiment is in U. Neisser, "The Control of Information Pickup in Selective Looking," in *Perception and Its Development: A Tribute to Eleanor J. Gibson,* ed. A. D. Pick, 201–219 (Hillsdale, NJ: Erlbaum, 1979).

9. The term *inattentional blindness* comes from the title of a 1998 MIT Press book by Arien Mack of the New School for Social Research in New York and the late Irvin Rock of the University of California at Berkeley, two psychologists who did pioneering work in this area. In their original experiments, subjects stared at a point on a computer screen until a large cross appeared. One arm of the cross—either the horizontal or the vertical—was always longer than the other, and subjects tried to judge which was longer. The cross was visible for only a fraction of a second before it disappeared, so this was not an easy judgment to make accurately. After a few trials of this task, an additional, unexpected object appeared along with the cross. The object could be a geometric figure like a small square, or a simple picture, or even a word. In most cases about one-quarter of subjects claimed not to have seen the unexpected object. Neisser's original selective-looking studies and our gorilla experiment provide a somewhat more dramatic demonstration of inattentional blindness because they presented a large, central, moving object for several seconds, rather than a briefly flashed static image, but the conclusion is consistent: It is surprisingly easy to not notice what is in plain view.

10. We hired SurveyUSA to ask a nationally representative sample of fifteen hundred adults a series of questions designed to probe how people think about the workings of their own minds. The respondents matched the entire U.S. population in gender, age, and regional distribution. SurveyUSA used a prerecorded voice to read a set of sixteen statements, and after each one, respondents used their telephone keypad to indicate whether they

strongly agreed, mostly agreed, mostly disagreed, strongly disagreed, or weren't sure. We also collected demographic information about each person's age, sex, income level, and race. Finally, we asked people how many psychology classes they had taken and how many books about psychology they had read over the past three years. This sort of prerecorded survey provides a level of control that is ideal for scientific research because each person hears exactly the same questions, in the same order, and in the same voice. SurveyUSA has been one of the most accurate political polling firms over the past few election cycles. The entire poll was completed over the course of one week in early June 2009. The percentages of agreement we give represent the sum of respondents who answered "strongly agree" or "mostly agree" to the question. If 75 percent either strongly or mostly agree with a statement, this means that the other 25 percent either strongly or mostly disagree, or are not sure. However, it is important to keep in mind that all of the statements we presented are almost certainly false, so the rate of agreement in a world without everyday illusions should be close to 0 percent!

11. Our colleague Daniel Levin, a psychology professor at Vanderbilt University, along with Bonnie Angelone of Rowan University, described the gorilla experiment to over one hundred undergraduate students, but without actually showing them the video or asking them to perform the task. After hearing about the experiment, including the appearance of the gorilla—but not hearing about the results—they were asked whether they would have noticed the gorilla if they had participated in the experiment themselves. Fully 90 percent of them predicted that they would have seen it. When we originally conducted the study, though, only 50 percent actually did. See D. T. Levin and B. L. Angelone, "The Visual Metacognition Questionnaire: A Measure of Intuitions About Vision," *American Journal of Psychology* 121 (2008): 451–472.

12. Simons and Chabris, "Gorillas in Our Midst."

13. *CSI: Crime Scene Investigation,* Season 2, Episode 9, "And Then There Were None" (originally broadcast on CBS, November 22, 2001).

14. Lehr, *The Fence,* 270.

15. O. Johnson, "Fed Court: Convicted Hub Cop's Trial Unfair," *The Boston Herald,* July 21, 2005, p. 28. Ironically, the witness, Officer Robert Walker, had initially claimed that he saw Conley at the fence. Later he recanted, saying that he had not actually seen Conley but said that he had because he was at the scene and *should have seen him.* Another victim of the illusion of attention! The appeals court found that the problem was not Walker's faulty intuition about how the mind works, but the fact that the defense was never told about an FBI memo that documented his later requests for hypnosis and a polygraph (lie detector) test, information that would tend to cast further doubt on the credibility of his memories.

One more interesting twist in the case of Kenny Conley deserves mention. In 2006, months after Conley rejoined the police force, Smut Brown was interviewed by Dick Lehr while Brown was in jail in Maine for a drug conviction ("Witness in '95 Brutality Case Offers New Account"). Brown told Lehr about a crucial misrepresentation in the original trial eight years earlier. Brown had testified that he had seen a white cop on the other side of the fence, and he identified Conley as the white cop who had eventually caught him. The way this information was presented in court gave the impression that Conley was the white cop Brown had seen standing next to the beating. But Brown did not specifically identify Conley as the cop he had seen next to the beating. The prosecution never asked him to, and the defense did not cross-examine him on this specific point. Brown later said that he had gotten a good look at the officer on the other side of the fence, but not at the one who caught him, and he had just assumed they were the same person. Speaking of Conley, Brown told Lehr, "When I seen him sitting at the defense table I didn't have no clue, like, why they were using me for that—because I didn't recognize him." In fact, Brown claimed that just before he testified, he spotted the cop he had seen at the site of the beating standing in the courthouse hallway and that he told this to the FBI agent in charge of the case. If true, Brown's jailhouse claim would further undermine the legal case against Conley, by subtracting one witness who placed him at the scene of the attack on Cox. But as we will discuss in Chapter 2 of this book, this sort of sudden recollection is easily distorted, and trusting a memory like this can be dangerous, even when the person doing the remembering does not have self-serving motives for changing his previous story.

16. C. Ross, "2 Embattled Cops Welcomed Back to Force," *The Boston Herald,* May 20, 2006, p. 6; Lehr, "Free and Clear."

17. D. Wedge, "Two Officers Cleared in '95 Beating Get Back $$$," *The Boston Herald,* November 20, 2007, p. 4.

18. Lehr, *The Fence,* 328.

19. This quote is from p. 100 of R. Pirsig, *Zen and the Art of Motorcycle Maintenance* (New York: William Morrow, 1974).

20. Except as noted, all of the quotes and facts about this incident are drawn from the wonderfully detailed and illustrated National Transportation Safety Board (NTSB) Marine Accident Brief for Accident # DCA-01-MM-022 (www.ntsb.gov/publictn/2005/MAB0501.htm). Other sources include M. Thompson, "Driving Blind," *Time,* February 18, 2001 (www.time.com/time/magazine/article/0,9171,99833,00.html); T. McCarthy and J. McCabe, "Bitter Passage," *Time,* April 15, 2001 (www.time.com/time/magazine/article/0,9171,106402-1,00.html); and S. Waddle, *The Right Thing* (Nashville, TN: Integrity Publishers, 2003).

21. This quote is used by permission from the transcript of a portion of an interview of Scott Waddle by Stone Phillips for *Dateline NBC.*

22. For a recent analysis of "looked but failed to see" accidents, see A. Koustanaï, E. Boloix, P. Van Elslande, and C. Bastien, "Statistical Analysis of 'Looked-But-Failed-to-See' Accidents: Highlighting the Involvement of Two Distinct Mechanisms," *Accident Analysis and Prevention* 40 (2008): 461–469.

23. D. Memmert, "The Effects of Eye Movements, Age, and Expertise on Inattentional Blindness," *Consciousness and Cognition* 15 (2006): 620–627. Memmert's subjects were children with an average age of about eight years, but the rate of noticing the gorilla was virtually the same as in our studies of college students: 8 out of 20, or 40 percent. Psychologists use many different devices for tracking a subject's eye movements. A typical design involves a small, lightweight helmet with one or two cameras directed at the subject's eyes. Harmless infrared light is bounced off the subject's eyes and detected by the cameras. Because the cameras are in a fixed position relative to the subject's head (they're attached firmly to the helmet, which is attached firmly to their head), experimenters can use these reflections to determine which way subjects are looking. Many systems use a

second camera to determine where the subject's head is relative to the scene being viewed, providing the necessary additional information to calculate exactly where in an image the subject is fixating their eyes. Current eye-tracking systems can measure the focus of gaze with exceptionally high spatial and temporal precision.

24. Details about this accident and its consequences were reported in an article on ESPN.com entitled "Big Ben in Serious Condition After Motorcycle Accident" on June 12 and June 13, 2006 (sports.espn.go.com/nfl/news/story?id=2480830). Other details and some quotes come from the following stories: M. A. Fuoco, "Multiple Injuries, Few Answers for Roethlisberger," *The Pittsburgh Post Gazette,* June 13, 2006 (www.post-ga zette.com/pg/06164/697828-66.stm); J. Silver, "Roethlisberger, Car Driver Are Both Charged," *The Pittsburgh Post Gazette,* June 20, 2006 (www.post-gazette.com/pg/06171/ 699570-66.stm); D. Hench, "Steelers' QB Hurt in Crash," *Portland Press Herald,* June 13, 2006.

25. Statistics and quotes are drawn from the Hurt report: H. H. Hurt Jr., J. V. Ouel-let, and D. R. Thom, *Motorcycle Accident Cause Factors and Identification of Countermeasures,* Volume 1: Technical report. Traffic Safety Center, University of Southern California, 1981.

26. Hurt et al., *Motorcycle Accident Cause Factors,* 46. The larger study discussed in this report conducted on-site accident evaluations for 900 motorcycle accidents in the Los Angeles area, and it also examined 3,600 accident reports. The criteria used to select these 62 cases for additional analysis were not described in the report.

27. S. B. Most, D. J. Simons, B. J. Scholl, R. Jimenez, E. Clifford, and C. F. Chabris, "How Not to Be Seen: The Contribution of Similarity and Selective Ignoring to Sustained Inattentional Blindness," *Psychological Science* 12 (2000): 9–17.

28. P. L. Jacobsen, "Safety in Numbers: More Walkers and Bicyclists, Safer Walking and Bicycling," *Injury Prevention* 9 (2003): 205–209. These results have been corroborated in other countries and other time periods; for similar analyses in Australia, see D. L. Robinson, "Safety in Numbers in Australia: More Walkers and Bicyclists, Safer Walking and Bicycling," *Health Promotion Journal of Australia* 16, no. 1 (2005): 47–51. See also Tom Vanderbilt's excellent book *Traffic* (New York: Knopf, 2008), which discusses this issue and a number of related issues involving expectations and accidents. This book was an informative resource for the material in this chapter on driving.

29. S. B. Most and R. S. Astur, "Feature-Based Attentional Set as a Cause of Traffic Accidents," *Visual Cognition* 15 (2007): 125–132.

30. Fuoco, "Multiple Injuries, Few Answers for Roethlisberger."

31. E. Fischer, R. F. Haines, and T. A. Price, "Cognitive Issues in Head-Up Displays," NASA Technical Paper 1711, 1980. See also R. F. Haines, "A Breakdown in Simultaneous Information Processing," in *Presbyopia Research,* ed. G. Obrecht and L. W. Stark (New York: Plenum Press, 1991).

32. Statistics and some of the analyses in this section are drawn from "Runway Safety Report: Trends and Initiatives at Towered Airports in the United States, FY 2004 through FY 2007," Federal Aviation Administration, June 2008. You could encounter a runway incursion much sooner or much later than our estimate of three thousand years of daily round-trip flying, but in any case it is highly unlikely that you will in your lifetime. Details of the Tenerife crash are taken from ". . . What's He Doing? He's Going to Kill Us

All!" *Time,* April 11, 1977 (www.time.com/time/magazine/article/0,9171,918815,00. html) and from the Wikipedia entry on the Tenerife disaster, en.wikipedia.org/wiki/ Tenerife_disaster (accessed January 19, 2009).

33. Fischer et al., "Cognitive Issues in Head-Up Displays," 15.

34. I. Larish and C. D. Wickens, *Divided Attention with Superimposed and Separated Imagery: Implications for Head-up Displays,* Aviation Research Laboratory Technical Report ARL-91-04/NASA-HUD-91-1, 1991.

35. Evidence for driving impairment while talking on a cell phone comes from D. A. Redelmeier and R. J. Tibshirani, "Association Between Cellular-Telephone Calls and Motor Vehicle Collisions," *New England Journal of Medicine* 336 (1997): 453–458; and D. L. Strayer, F. A. Drews, and D. J. Crouch, "Comparing the Cell-Phone Driver and the Drunk Driver," *Human Factors* 48 (2006): 381–391. Evidence linking alcohol consumption to increased inattentional blindness comes from S. L. Clifasefi, M. K. T. Takarangi, and J. S. Bergman, "Blind Drunk: The Effects of Alcohol on Inattentional Blindness," *Applied Cognitive Psychology* 20 (2005): 697–704. In this study, subjects were less likely to notice the unexpected gorilla after having had an alcoholic beverage. Alcohol could have its effect by directly altering the ability to detect unexpected objects or by making the primary counting task more difficult.

36. E. Goodman, "We Love, Hate Our Cell Phones," *The Boston Globe,* July 6, 2001. Consistent with Goodman's claim, a survey found that cell phone users agreed more strongly with the statement "I can use a cellular phone safely when driving" than with "People, in general, can use a cellular phone safely when driving." M. S. Wogalter and C. B. Mayhorn, "Perceptions of Driver Distraction by Cellular Phone Users and Nonusers," *Human Factors* 47 (2005): 455–467.

The New York legislation that took effect on December 1, 2001, involved adding Section 1225-c to the New York vehicle and traffic law. Part of the law stated, "The court shall waive any fine for which a person who violates the provisions of section 1225-c of the vehicle and traffic law . . . supplies the court with proof that, between the date on which he or she is charged with having violated such section and the appearance date for such violation, he or she possesses a hands-free mobile telephone." This "get out of jail" provision was in effect until March 2002. The effect of this law essentially meant that rather than paying a fine, people caught using a handheld phone could pay a cell-phone vendor for a hands-free headset. Consequently, it's not surprising that the major telecommunication companies supported the legislation.

Nokia's recommendation to use hands-free phones was titled "Safety Is the Most Important Call You Will Ever Make: A Guide to Safe and Responsible Wireless Phone Use" and its top safety tip was to "Get to know your wireless phone and its features such as speed dial and redial." AT&T's flier was headed "A special offer just for you" and provided a coupon for a free hands-free earpiece. The statistic that 77 percent of people believe that talking on a hands-free phone is safer comes from the SurveyUSA representative national poll we commissioned, conducted June 1–8, 2009.

37. W. J. Horrey and C. D. Wickens, "Examining the Impact of Cell Phone Conversations on Driving Using Meta-Analytic Techniques," *Human Factors* 48 (2006): 196–205.

38. In most variants of the "gorilla" experiment, the gorilla did not stop to thump its

chest. Instead, it just walked through the scene, remaining visible for five seconds. We created the "chest thump" version that we described earlier for a separate test to explore how dramatic we could make the event and still provoke inattentional blindness.

39. B. J. Scholl, N. S. Noles, V. Pasheva, and R. Sussman, "Talking on a Cellular Telephone Dramatically Increases 'sustained inattentional blindness'" [Abstract], *Journal of Vision* 3 (2003): 156 (journalofvision.org/3/9/156/). More recent observational studies show that people are often oblivious to their surroundings when talking on a phone. For example, people walking across a college campus while talking on a phone were less likely than undistracted pedestrians to notice a unicycling clown nearby: I. E. Hyman Jr., S. M. Boss, B. M. Wise, K. E. McKenzie, and J. M. Caggiano, "Did You See the Unicycling Clown? Inattentional Blindness While Walking and Talking on a Cell Phone," *Applied Cognitive Psychology.*

40. This finding and the explanations in the next paragraph are based on F. A. Drews, M. Pasupathi, and D. L. Strayer, "Passenger and Cell Phone Conversations in Simulated Driving," *Journal of Experimental Psychology: Applied* 14 (2008): 392–400.

41. The phenomenon of inattentional deafness can be traced to studies from the 1950s and 1960s on the ability to attend selectively to information presented to one ear while ignoring sounds in the other ear. Under those conditions, people often fail to notice unexpected messages in the ignored ear. The term "inattentional deafness" was first used by Mack and Rock in their 1998 book *Inattentional Blindness.* For examples of early work on selective listening, see E. C. Cherry, "Some Experiments upon the Recognition of Speech, with One and with Two Ears," *Journal of the Acoustical Society of America* 25 (1953): 975–979; and A. Treisman, "Monitoring and Storage of Irrelevant Messages in Selective Attention," *Journal of Verbal Learning and Verbal Behavior* 3 (1964): 449–459.

42. G. Weingarten, "Pearls Before Breakfast," *The Washington Post,* April 8, 2007, p. W10 (www.washingtonpost.com/wp-dyn/content/article/2007/04/04/AR2007040401721.html). Biographical information about Bell comes from Weingarten's article and the Wikipedia entry on Joshua Bell (en.wikipedia.org/wiki/Joshua_Bell). The biographical quote about Bell is from his official biography, www.joshuabell.com/biography (accessed January 16, 2009).

43. Later, Joshua Bell had a different memory of his feelings. In the revised edition of *Predictably Irrational* (New York: HarperCollins, 2009), Dan Ariely writes of meeting Bell and asking about his day as a busker: "I wanted to know how he felt about being overlooked and ignored by so many people. He responded that he was really not all that surprised, and admitted that expectation is an important part of the way we experience music" (p. 272).

44. Nokia Corporation, "Survey Results Confirm It: Women Are Better Multi-taskers Than Men," press release, November 22, 2007, www.nokia.com/press/press-releases/showpressrelease?newsid=1170280 (accessed January 28, 2009). Despite the title of this press release, it reports no actual test of multitasking abilities, just a nonrepresentative survey of popular beliefs about multitasking abilities. A typical study of the inefficiency of multitasking is J. S. Rubinstein, D. E. Meyer, and J. E. Evans, "Executive Control of Cognitive Processes in Task Switching," *Journal of Experimental Psychology: Human Perception and Performance* 27 (2001): 763–797. There is frequent discussion of differences in brain

anatomy between men and women that could explain a difference in multitasking ability, but we have been unable to find experiments that offer unequivocal evidence for a general superiority of women in dividing attention between multiple tasks or goals.

45. These findings are reported in D. Memmert, "The Effects of Eye Movements, Age, and Expertise on Inattentional Blindness," *Consciousness and Cognition* 15 (2006): 620–627; and D. Memmert, D. J. Simons, and T. Grimme, "The Relationship Between Visual Attention and Expertise in Sports," *Psychology of Sport and Exercise* 10 (2009): 146–151.

46. T. E. Lum, R. J. Fairbanks, E. C. Pennington, and F. L. Zwemer, "Profiles in Patient Safety: Misplaced Femoral Line Guidewire and Multiple Failures to Detect the Foreign Body on Chest Radiography," *Academic Emergency Medicine* 12 (2005): 658–662.

47. Omitting a final step in a process (e.g., removing a guidewire) once the main objective of the process has been achieved (e.g., placing the central line correctly) is a common sort of mistake known as a *post-completion error.* This is the type of error you are making when you walk away with your stack of copies while the original document is still sitting on the glass, or when you type out an e-mail saying "as shown in the document I have attached" but hit "send" before you attach the document.

48. D. B. Spring and D. J. Tennenhouse, "Radiology Malpractice Lawsuits: California Jury Verdicts," *Radiology* 159 (1986): 811–814.

49. W. James, *The Principles of Psychology* (New York: Henry Holt, 1890). For a discussion of how people search for rare items, see J. M. Wolfe, T. S. Horowitz, and N. M. Kenner, "Rare Items Often Missed in Visual Searches," *Nature* 435 (2005): 439–440.

50. The examples of uses of the gorilla video are from several sources. The first is from an e-mail sent to Dan's company, Viscog Productions, Inc., on August 5, 2004, about the usefulness of its DVD that includes the gorilla video. Mahzarin Banaji, a Harvard psychology professor, used inattentional blindness in an analysis of discrimination; see the story entitled "Tenure and Gender" in *Harvard Magazine,* January 2005 (harvardmaga zine.com/2005/01/tenure-and-gender.html). The parallels between inattentional blindness and the failure to detect terrorists was discussed in "Background Briefing," ABC Radio National (Australia) with Gerald Tooth, December 8, 2002. Links to diet were discussed in "Awareness, Fat Loss, & Moonwalking Bears," December 31, 2008, www .bellyfatreport.com/?s=bear (accessed June 9, 2009). Dean Radin's views are presented in D. Radin, *Entangled Minds: Extrasensory Experiences in a Quantum Reality* (New York: Paraview Pocket Books, 2006). (Later in this book we discuss one of the main reasons why people come to believe in psychic phenomena despite the absence of scientific evidence to support their existence.) Discussion of bullying was from an e-mail received by Viscog Productions on September 1, 2008. The link to religion is from a March 2008 sermon by Reverend Daniel Conklin of the Epiphany Parish in Seattle, www.epiphany seattle.org/sermons/Lent4-2008.html (accessed June 28, 2009).

51. Wolfe et al., "Rare Items Often Missed."

52. For a brief discussion, see T. Griffiths and C. Moore, "A Matter of Perception," *Aquatics International,* November/December 2004 (www.aquaticsintl.com/2004/nov/ 0411_rm.html).

53. Examples of GPS-induced accidents come from the following sources: "Driver Follows GPS into Sand," Reuters, October 10, 2006 (www.news.com.au/story/0,23599,

20555319-13762,00.html); "Train Hits Car, and a G.P.S. Is Blamed," Associated Press, October 1, 2008 (www.nytimes.com/2008/10/01/nyregion/01gps.html); T. Carey, "SatNav Danger Revealed: Navigation Device Blamed for Causing 300,000 Crashes," July 21, 2008 (www.mirror.co.uk/news/top-stories/2008/07/21/satnav-danger-revealed-navigation -device-blamed-for-causing-300-000-crashes-89520-20656554/); "Lorry Driver Had to Sleep in Cab for Three Nights After Sat-Nav Blunder Left Him Wedged in Country Lane," *Daily Mail,* November 1, 2007 (www.dailymail.co.uk/news/article-491073/Lorry-driver -sleep-cab-nights-sat-nav-blunder-left-wedged-country-lane.html); "Sat-Nav Dunks Dozy Drivers in Deep Water," *The Times (London) Online,* April 20, 2006 (www.timesonline .co.uk/tol/news/article707216.ece). The ford in this last example is normally about two feet deep.

Chapter 2: The Coach Who Choked

1. Many of the details and quotes for the Bobby Knight/Neil Reed story are taken from an article entitled "A Dark Side of Knight," first published on the CNN/Sports Il- lustrated website on March 18, 2000, updated September 10, 2000. The article was intended to expose some of the vulgar and abusive antics Knight exhibited during prac- tices, with the implication that his behavior had caused the players to leave. However, the story acknowledged that Knight's program had no more departures than other top college basketball programs. Some students who left the program, like Richard Mandeville, re- gretted not doing so sooner. Other players, like Alan Henderson—who stayed in the pro- gram, graduated, and became a top shooting guard in the NBA—spoke more fondly of Knight's motivational techniques. Henderson admitted that Knight had been a tough coach who "got on me sometimes like he got on everybody," but praised him for his desire to improve his players and his generosity and willingness to help. Other quotes were taken from the following CNN/Sports Illustrated articles: "Defending 'The General,'" April 12, 2000; and "The Knight Tape," September 9, 2000. Biographical details on Bobby Knight are drawn from the National Basketball Association Hoopedia blog, hoopedia. nba.com/index.php?title=Bob_Knight, and from Wikipedia, en.wikipedia.org/wiki/ Bob_Knight (both accessed June 29, 2009). Many of the incidents from Knight's career are documented in "Bob Knight's Outburst Timeline," *USA Today,* November 14, 2006.

2. As we mentioned in a note to Chapter 1, our items were designed to present beliefs that the scientific consensus regards as false, so an ideal rate of agreement would be 0 percent. We also found that 83 percent of people believe that amnesia, or sudden memory loss, results in the inability to recall one's name and identity. This belief may reflect the way amnesia is usually portrayed in movies, television, and literature. For example, when we meet Matt Damon's character in the movie *The Bourne Identity,* we learn that he has no memory for who he is, why he has the skills he does, or where he is from. He spends much of the movie trying to answer these questions. But the inability to remember your name and identity is exceedingly rare in reality. Amnesia most often results from a brain injury that leaves the victim unable to form *new* memories, but with most memories of the past intact. (Some movies do accurately portray this more common syndrome, known as "anterograde" amnesia; our favorite is *Memento.*)

3. This pattern of recall is known as the *serial position curve.* This "U-shaped" curve

(better recall of items from the beginning and end of a list than from the middle of the list, hence the U-shaped function) is one of the best-established findings in the literature on memory function; see H. Ebbinghaus, *Memory: A Contribution to Experimental Psychology*, trans. H. A. Ruger and C. E. Bussenius (New York: Columbia University, 1885/1913). For evidence of a serial position curve with this particular type and length of list, see H. L. Roediger III and K. B. McDermott, "Creating False Memories: Remembering Words Not Presented in Lists," *Journal of Experimental Psychology: Learning, Memory, and Cognition* 21 (1995): 803–814.

4. Evidence for a seven-item limit on short-term memory comes from G. A. Miller, "The Magical Number Seven, Plus or Minus Two: Some Limits on Our Capacity for Processing Information," *Psychological Review* 63 (1956): 81–97. Evidence that children lack adult memorization skills comes from J. H. Flavell, A. G. Friedrichs, and J. D. Hoyt, "Developmental Changes in Memorization Processes," *Cognitive Psychology* 1 (1970): 324–340. This study shows that preschool children also think they will remember more than they actually do. Primary school students also overestimate their memory abilities, but not nearly as much as preschoolers.

5. J. Deese, "On the Prediction of Occurrence of Particular Verbal Intrusions in Immediate Recall," *Journal of Experimental Psychology* 58 (1959): 17–22; Roediger and McDermott, "Creating False Memories."

6. The study was described in the following article: W. F. Brewer and J. C. Treyens, "Role of Schemata in Memory for Places," *Cognitive Psychology* 13 (1981): 207–230. Some of the earliest demonstrations that memory encodes meaning in the form of associations with what we already know come from this classic: F. C. Bartlett, *Remembering: A Study in Experimental and Social Psychology* (Cambridge: Cambridge University Press, 1932).

7. "The Knight Tape," CNN/Sports Illustrated, September 9, 2000.

8. This quote is also from CNN/Sports Illustrated's report "The Knight Tape."

9. Increased wait times have become more common with increased use of cell phones and decreased numbers of operators. For example, in Las Vegas in 2002, only 65 percent of calls were answered within the national standard of ten seconds (A. Packer, "Metro 911 Calls Often Put on Hold," *Las Vegas Sun*, October 23, 2004). At the two largest call centers in Los Angeles and San Francisco, average wait times are more than fifty seconds, and in some extreme cases, callers had to wait more than ten *minutes* for an operator (R. Lopez and R. Connell, "Cell Phones Swamping 911 System," *The Los Angeles Times*, August 26, 2007).

10. Chris learned of the incident in a conversation with the witnesses on May 30, 2008. He asked them not to talk about it further before he could interview each of them separately. The interview with Leslie Meltzer took place by telephone on August 5, 2008; the interview with Tyce Palmaffy took place by telephone on December 30, 2008.

11. Different people have different roles on a movie set, and each may notice elements related to his or her area of focus. Costumers might notice changes to clothing, cinematographers focus on lighting changes, etc. The script supervisor is the one person responsible for trying to make sure all the important details match across shots. See A. Rowlands, *The Continuity Supervisor*, 4th ed. (Boston: Focal Press, 2000); P. P. Miller, *Script Supervising and Film Continuity*, 3rd ed. (Boston: Focal Press, 1999).

12. At the time of this writing, a Google search for "film flubs" turns up more than thirty-five hundred hits.

13. "Film Flubs: Mistakes Made and Left in Popular Movies," *Dateline NBC*, March 22, 1999. *Saving Private Ryan* won the Academy Award for editing in 1998 and *Shakespeare in Love* was nominated that same year (see awardsdatabase.oscars.org). Mankiewicz also assumed that the filmmakers were unaware of the errors. Script supervisor Trudy Ramirez told Dan in an interview on June 6, 2009, "The amount of handling and viewing and the numbers of people that are involved in the post-production process and in the editing is so extensive, that for something to literally get through with every one of those people being unaware is highly unlikely. I don't know how many times it's happened, if ever. A number of people would have discussed the merits of utilizing the shot with an error prior to it ending up in the film." In other words, they might have needed a shot of soldiers walking across a field, but they didn't have one with seven soldiers, so they decided to use the one with eight soldiers despite the error. The facts about *The Godfather* and *Spartacus* come from the Internet Movie Database, www.imdb.com/title/tt0068646/goofs; www.imdb.com/title/tt0054331/goofs (both accessed November 14, 2009).

14. D. T. Levin and D. J. Simons, "Failure to Detect Changes to Attended Objects in Motion Pictures," *Psychonomic Bulletin and Review* 4 (1997): 501–506. You can view the film at www.theinvisiblegorilla.com.

15. Subjects answering yes were then asked to describe the changes they noticed. Only one subject reported noticing anything, and that person's description was sufficiently vague that it was not clear whether the individual had actually noticed a change.

16. The term "change blindness" was coined in this article: R. A. Rensink, J. K. O'Regan, and J. J. Clark, "To See or Not to See: The Need for Attention to Perceive Changes in Scenes," *Psychological Science* 8 (1997): 368–373.

17. The term "change blindness blindness" and the data described in this paragraph come from: D. T. Levin, N. Momen, S. B. Drivdahl, and D. J. Simons, "Change Blindness Blindness: The Metacognitive Error of Overestimating Change-Detection Ability," *Visual Cognition* 7 (2000): 397–412. Of 300 subjects, 76 percent predicted they would notice the change to the plates, and 90 percent of 297 subjects predicted they would notice the change to the scarf.

18. These quoted responses are taken from an unpublished replication of the earlier studies (which were done at Cornell by the two Dans) that Dan conducted while he was at Harvard. They are typical of responses written by subjects in all of these change blindness experiments. Levin and Simons ("Failure to Detect Changes to Attended Objects") found that across four different pairs of actors performing two different simple actions, approximately two-thirds of the subjects failed to report any change. For the particular video described in the text, none of the subjects in the original experiment reported the change.

19. See Levin and Simons, "Failure to Detect Changes to Attended Objects." A video of a subject participating in this study can be viewed at www.theinvisiblegorilla.com.

20. Script supervisors have many responsibilities on set, including keeping track of all the details of each take (e.g., the cameras used, what actors said, how the action progressed, how long the shot was, etc.). Their extensive notes guide the entire postproduction process.

21. Quotes from Trudy Ramirez are from an e-mail correspondence on June 2–6, 2009, and a telephone interview with Dan on June 6, 2009. Dan also corresponded with a second script supervisor, Melissa Sanchez (on November 14, 2004, and June 2–3, 2009), who was tremendously helpful in guiding our writing of this section.

22. Two of the best-known training manuals for script supervisors, *Script Supervising and Film Continuity* by Pat Miller and *The Continuity Supervisor* by Avril Rowlands, give advice that is entirely consistent with what Trudy Ramirez said: Don't count on your ability to remember visual details. Miller, who advises readers to take photographs and copious notes, recognizes the limits of memory: "It is humanly impossible and patently unnecessary for you to simultaneously watch and note every detail in a scene. The mark of a competent continuity supervisor is not so much the possession of extraordinary powers of observation . . . but your confidence in knowing what is important to observe" (p. 177). Rowlands agrees: ". . . it is *what* you notice that is important. You will never notice everything that is happening within a shot and it is not necessary that you should, providing the things you *do* notice and write down are those which are important in order to preserve continuity" (p. 68).

23. Of 108 undergraduates, 98 percent predicted they would notice the person change (Levin et al., "Change Blindness Blindness").

24. D. J. Simons and D. T. Levin, "Failure to Detect Changes to People During a Real-World Interaction," *Psychonomic Bulletin and Review* 5 (1998): 644–649.

25. This experiment is described in D. T. Levin, D. J. Simons, B. L. Angelone, and C. F. Chabris, "Memory for Centrally Attended Changing Objects in an Incidental Real-World Change Detection Paradigm," *British Journal of Psychology* 93 (2002): 289–302. A demonstration of the experiment was broadcast on the BBC program *Brain Story* and was also re-created on *Dateline NBC* in 2003.

26. For an overview of the evidence for change blindness, see D. J. Simons and M. Ambinder, "Change Blindness: Theory and Consequences," *Current Directions in Psychological Science,* 14 (2005): 44–48.

27. Simons and Levin, "Failure to Detect Changes to People." The studies in which we changed the race or sex of the actor have not yet been published. We conducted one study in which we replaced a male actor with a female actor in the counter paradigm mentioned earlier, and nobody missed the change. Dan and his former graduate student Stephen Mitroff also conducted a series of video-based change detection experiments in which the race or sex of an actor was changed. Again, nobody missed these changes.

28. Of people who noticed the change, 81 percent correctly selected the first actor from the lineup, and 73 percent correctly picked the second. Those missing the change selected the correct first actor 37 percent of the time and the correct second actor 32 percent of the time. See Levin et al., "Memory for Centrally Attended Changing Objects."

29. Details of this case and quotes are taken from a story by M. Rich: "Christmas Essay Was Not His, Author Admits," *The New York Times,* January 9, 2009.

30. K. A. Wade, M. Garry, J. D. Read, and S. Lindsay, "A Picture Is Worth a Thousand Lies: Using False Photographs to Create False Childhood Memories," *Psychonomic Bulletin and Review* 9 (2002): 597–603.

31. D. L. M. Sacchi, F. Agnoli, and E. F. Loftus, "Changing History: Doctored Photographs Affect Memory for Past Public Events," *Applied Cognitive Psychology* 21 (2007):

1005–1022. The story of this famous photograph, which was really four different photographs shot by four separate photographers, is discussed in the *New York Times* "Lens" blog (lens.blogs.nytimes.com/2009/06/03/behind-the-scenes-tank-man-of-tiananmen/).

32. S. J. Sharman, M. Garry, J. A. Jacobson, E. F. Loftus, and P. H. Ditto, "False Memories for End-of-Life Decisions," *Health Psychology* 27 (2008): 291–296. The *Seinfeld* quote is from "The Comeback," Episode 147, broadcast January 30, 1997. A transcript of the dialog can be found online at www.seinfeldscripts.com/TheComeback.html (accessed July 24, 2009).

33. K. Frankovic, "To Tell the Truth to Pollsters," cbsnews.com, August 15, 2007 (www.cbsnews.com/stories/2007/08/15/opinion/pollpositions/main3169223.shtml).

34. F. W. Colgrove, "Individual Memories," *American Journal of Psychology* 10 (1899): 228–255. The quote is from pages 247–248.

35. R. Brown and J. Kulik, "Flashbulb Memories," *Cognition* 5 (1977): 73–99.

36. Bush's false memory was documented in D. L. Greenberg, "President Bush's False 'Flashbulb' Memory of 9/11/01," *Applied Cognitive Psychology* 18 (2004): 363–370. The video footage of the first plane hitting the World Trade Center came from a French film crew that had been following a New York City firefighter and his comrades for a documentary. They happened to be filming firefighters investigating a gas leak near the World Trade Center when they heard a loud noise overhead. They turned their camera up just in time to catch the first plane hitting the first building. CBS broadcast its documentary in March 2002, six months after the attack. Clips of the relevant portion can be found on YouTube. See also J. Kiesewetter, "Brothers Filming Documentary Caught '9/11' on Tape," Gannett News Service, March 10, 2002.

37. At the time of this writing, there are many websites that promote the idea that President Bush knew about the attacks in advance, citing his comments about seeing the first plane as evidence. A Google search with the terms "Bush," "first," "plane," and "9/11" turns up many of them. Incidentally, if Bush had been so diabolically clever as to plan the 9/11 attacks, feign surprise, and cover everything up from Congress, the courts, and the media, why would he then reveal his involvement to a child? Conspiracy theories tend to fail spectacularly another test of cognitive plausibility by depending on the notion that a select few individuals have near-superhuman abilities to control and coordinate events and information.

38. U. Neisser and N. Harsch, "Phantom Flashbulbs: False Recollections of Hearing the News About Challenger," in *Affect and Accuracy in Recall: Studies of "Flashbulb" Memories*, ed. E. Winograd and U. Neisser (Cambridge: Cambridge University Press, 1992).

39. "The Knight Tape," CNN/Sports Illustrated, September 9, 2000.

40. From a conversation on November 27, 2008, and a letter from Daniel D. Chabris to Christopher F. Chabris (dated December 2, 2008).

41. Interviews and conversation with Leslie Meltzer and Tyce Palmaffy.

42. J. M. Talarico and D. C. Rubin, "Confidence, Not Consistency, Characterizes Flashbulb Memories," *Psychological Science* 14 (2003): 455–461.

43. Details about the case of Hillary Clinton's Bosnia memory are drawn from a fact-checking story published as "Hillary's Balkan Adventure, Part II," washingtonpost.com, March 21, 2008. The Peggy Noonan quote is from her column "Getting Mrs. Clinton," *The Wall Street Journal,* March 28, 2008. The satirical cover image was published by *The*

New Republic, May 7, 2008; the image can be seen at meaningfuldistractions.files.word press.com/2008/05/newrepubhill.jpg (accessed August 30, 2009). Bill Clinton's comments came in a speech in a high school gymnasium in Indiana. He was quoted as saying, in reference to the people attacking his wife's statements, "and some of them when they're 60 they'll forget something when they're tired at 11 at night, too." These comments were reported by Mike Memoli and posted to the MSNBC website by Domenico Montanaro in "Bill's Back on the Trail," MSNBC First Read, April 10, 2008. Hillary Clinton did later joke about the claims when appearing on the NBC *Tonight Show with Jay Leno* (April 3, 2008): "I was worried I wasn't going to make it . . . I was pinned down by sniper fire at the Burbank airport."

44. In this experiment, 41 percent of the 59 subjects thought they could recall ten or more digits. The maximum number of random digits a person can hear and recall successfully is known as their "digit span." Given reasonable assumptions of a population mean digit span of 6.6 digits and standard deviation of 1.1 digits, only about 0.5 percent of people (1 in 200) should have a digit span of ten or greater. These results and analyses are presented in Experiment 2 of Levin et al., "Change Blindness Blindness."

45. For a discussion of how intuitions about the accuracy of memory interact with the nature of the recollective experience, see W. F. Brewer and C. Sampaio, "Processes Leading to Confidence and Accuracy in Sentence Recognition: A Metamemory Approach," *Memory* 14 (2006): 540–552.

46. T. Sharot, M. R. Delgado, and E. A. Phelps (2004), "How Emotion Enhances the Feeling of Remembering," *Nature Neuroscience* 7 (2004): 1376–1380.

Chapter 3: What Smart Chess Players and Stupid Criminals Have in Common

1. For information about Lyme disease, see G. P. Wormser et al., "The Clinical Assessment, Treatment, and Prevention of Lyme Disease, Human Granulocytic Anaplasmosis, and Babesiosis: Clinical Practice Guidelines by the Infectious Diseases Society of America," *IDSA Guidelines* 43 (2006): 1089–1134.

2. We surveyed 103 players in all; 31 in Parsippany and 72 in Philadelphia.

3. Our follow-up examination of ratings from years after the original survey necessarily included only those players who kept playing tournament chess through that period. Others became inactive, perhaps because their ratings were not improving as they had hoped. When those players are added to the analysis, using the last ratings they had before they dropped out, the level of overconfidence is 71 points at five years (as opposed to 54 points without those players).

4. C. Darwin, *The Descent of Man* (London: John Murray, 1871), 3.

5. A transcript of the dialogue from *Take the Money and Run* (which was released in 1969) can be found online, www.script-o-rama.com/movie_scripts/t/take-the-money -and-run-script.html (accessed April 24, 2009).

6. D. Lehr, *The Fence* (New York: HarperCollins, 2009), 39–40.

7. Evidence that criminals tend to be less intelligent comes from pp. 247–249 of R. J. Herrnstein and C. Murray, *The Bell Curve: Intelligence and Class Structure in American Life* (New York: Free Press, 1994). Examples of inept criminals are drawn from "Daft Burglar Writes Name on Wall," BBC News, September 6, 2007 (news.bbc.co.uk/2/hi/ uk_news/england/manchester/6981558.stm); and "Man Jailed After Trying to Pass $1

Million Bill at Pittsburgh Giant Eagle," WTAE-TV4, October 9, 2007 (www.thepitts
burghchannel.com/news/14300133/detail.html?rss=pit&psp=news). The largest bill in
circulation is the $100 bill. Apparently a set of fake $1 million notes was distributed by a
church in Texas; Porter was not the only person who tried to pass one. It is not clear
whether the people who tried to spend them actually thought they were legal tender.

8. The experiments described in this section are reported in J. Kruger and D. Dunning, "Unskilled and Unaware of It: How Difficulties in Recognizing One's Own Incompetence Lead to Inflated Self-Assessments," *Journal of Personality and Social Psychology* 77
(1999): 1121–1134. The finding that the less competent are more prone to overestimate
their ability than the highly competent has been called the "Dunning-Kruger Effect,"
presumably because Dunning was a professor and Kruger was a graduate student at the
time. It earned its discoverers the Ig Nobel Prize for psychology in 2000 (improbable
.com/ig/ig-pastwinners.html). Kruger is now a professor at New York University's business school.

9. Kruger and Dunning, "Unskilled and Unaware of It," 1121. In Little Rock, Arkansas, in 2007 a man named Langston Robbins entered a bank, walked right past an
off-duty cop working as a security guard, and placed a holdup note in front of the teller.
The cop arrested him after a struggle and a short chase. Lieutenant Terry Hastings of the
Little Rock police told the Associated Press, "I just don't know why he didn't see a uniformed police officer standing basically right in front of him. . . . My guess is he's just not
the brightest of people." As we have seen, not noticing something right in front of you (or
along your path, as in this case or the Kenny Conley incident) is a common occurrence
that has nothing to do with an individual's intelligence, or lack thereof. Hastings's reaction, though, has everything to do with the illusion of attention. What *was* perhaps unin-
telligent about Robbins's plan—like McArthur Wheeler's—was attempting the robbery
with no disguise in front of a surveillance camera. See "Foiled Robbery Attempt Leads to
Police Chase," KATV-7, September 6, 2007 (www.katv.com/news/stories/0907/453127.
html); the security video is available at "Police Say Tape Shows Attempted Bank Robbery
in Front of Uniformed Cop," USA Today On Deadline blog, September 7, 2007 (blogs.usa
today.com/ondeadline/2007/09/police-say-tape.html). Several of the examples of stupid
crimes that we have mentioned in this section come from "The Top Ten Stupid Criminals
of 2007," Neatorama blog (www.neatorama.com/2007/12/18/the-top-ten-stupid-criminals-
of-2007/), which has links to original news sources.

10. Research about judgments of beauty is reviewed in N. Etcoff, *Survival of the Pret-
tiest: The Science of Beauty* (New York: Doubleday, 1999).

11. These percentages were constructed from additional information provided by Justin Kruger (personal communication, January 24, 2009). For the top quartile of subjects
on the sense of humor test, the correlation between subject ratings of funniness and come-
dian ratings was $r=.57$; for the bottom quartile it was $r=-.13$ (in each case the correlation
is across jokes).

12. Here and in similar contexts in this book, when we refer to the "average" person
or someone performing better than "average," we are using the term *average* in an informal rather than a statistical sense. Although average in a statistical sense refers to the
mean value, we are referring to the median. The median student has a better sense of
humor than 50 percent of the other students and a worse sense of humor than the other 50
percent. If sense of humor is symmetrically distributed about a mean value—and we have

no reason to suspect otherwise—then the mean student is the median student as well. When the distribution is biased in one direction or the other, the mean and median may differ, but in the examples we discuss, they typically will be close to each other.

13. We also used regression analysis to show that a player's chess rating is the single best predictor of chess overconfidence, beating out age, education level, years playing the game, years playing competitively, and the number of months since the player's last tournament (i.e., how "in practice" the player was at the time of our survey). For example, rating explains 23 percent of the variance in overconfidence, while sex, age, and years of education together only explain an additional 10 percent.

14. They chose reasoning as a skill to improve because it's harder to improve a person's sense of humor (especially if that person didn't laugh at the joke about the child making God cry). Educational psychologist Diane Horgan raises the intriguing alternative that a better understanding of one's skill level is not necessarily the result of greater skill. Instead, the causation can also run in the other direction: Realistically understanding your skill level might help you improve by enabling you to adjust your expectations, properly gauge feedback, identify your strengths and weaknesses, and so on. If you are overconfident in your ability, you may also be less motivated to improve it. After all, you "know" that you are already good, so you don't need to practice more. These considerations should give pause to advocates of increasing children's self-esteem as a salve for educational underachievement. See D. Horgan, "Children and Chess Expertise: The Role of Calibration," *Psychological Research* 54 (1992): 44–50.

15. Seventy-one percent of men and 66 percent of women believe they have above-average intelligence (M. Campbell, "100% Canadian," *The Globe and Mail,* December 30, 2000). Evidence that drivers think they are better than average is from O. Svenson, "Are We All Less Risky and More Skillful Than Our Fellow Drivers?" *Acta Psychologica* 47 (1981): 143–148. This study also included a group of American students, who were slightly more confident in their abilities than their Swedish counterparts: 93 percent thought they were more skillful than 50 percent of their peers, and 88 percent thought they were safer. Evidence about self-judged attractiveness comes from a study of college students in which men judged themselves to be about 15 percent more attractive than they actually were. Women viewed themselves as slightly less attractive than they actually were, although both men and women viewed themselves as above average in attractiveness (the women in the study were judged to be a little more above average in attractiveness). See M. T. Gabriel, J. W. Critelli, and J. S. Ee, "Narcissistic Illusions in Self-Evaluations of Intelligence and Attractiveness," *Journal of Personality* 62 (1994): 143–155. Interestingly, a meta-analysis of a number of studies that measured the relationship between self-rated attractiveness and actual attractiveness (as rated by others) showed only a small relationship. In other words, how attractive you judge yourself to be is only slightly related to how attractive others think you are. See A. Feingold, "Good-Looking People Are Not What We Think," *Psychological Bulletin* 111 (1992): 304–311.

16. This belief in one's own incompetence, despite all external evidence to the contrary, is sometimes known as the "Impostor Syndrome." See M. E. Silverman, *Unleash Your Dreams: Tame Your Hidden Fears and Live the Life You Were Meant to Live* (New York: Wiley, 2007), 73–75; M. F. K. R. de Vries, "The Danger of Feeling Like a Fake," *Harvard Business Review* (2005).

17. In the Kruger and Dunning study, the top 25 percent of subjects in sense of humor were, on average, funnier than 87.5 percent of the study participants (because the subjects occupied the 75–100th percentiles of the sense of humor distribution, and the midpoint of that range is 87.5). However, these subjects estimated, on average, that they were funnier than just 70 percent of their peers, indicating an average underconfidence of 17.5 percent.

18. D. Baird, *A Thousand Paths to Confidence* (London: Octopus, 2007), 10.

19. R. M. Kanter, *Confidence: How Winning Streaks and Losing Streaks Begin and End* (New York: Crown Business, 2004), 6.

20. A. Tugend, "Secrets of Confident Kids," *Parents,* May 2008, pp. 118–122.

21. A transcript and video recording of the so-called malaise speech can be found at the Miller Center of Public Affairs website (millercenter.org/scripps/archive/speeches/detail/3402).

22. The story of Carter's speech, its political context, and the response to it is told in K. Mattson, *"What the Heck Are You Thinking, Mr. President?" Jimmy Carter, America's "Malaise," and the Speech That Should Have Changed the Country* (New York: Bloomsbury, 2009).

23. J. B. Stewart, *Den of Thieves* (New York: Simon & Schuster 1991), 117, 206; J. Kornbluth, *Highly Confident: The Crime and Punishment of Michael Milken* (New York: Morrow, 1992).

24. The conversation between Tenet and Bush was reported in B. Woodward, *Plan of Attack* (New York: Simon & Schuster, 2004), 249. Fleischer's quote is from a White House press conference, April 10, 2003, www.whitehouse.gov/news/releases/2003/04/20030410-6.html (accessed July 2006). Evidence about the absence of WMDs comes from *Comprehensive Report of the Special Advisor to the DCI on Iraq's WMD* (also known as the "Duelfer Report") (https://www.cia.gov/library/reports/general-reports-1/iraq_wmd_2004/index.html).

25. This is not as unusual a decision process as you might think. The U.S. Supreme Court uses it during the conferences that follow oral arguments in its cases: The Chief Justice states his views on the case, followed by the other justices, from the most to least senior. An advantage of this process is that it ensures that everyone gets to speak, and in the case of tough-minded federal judges who are appointed for life, it probably does more good than harm. When some group members are clearly subordinate to others, though, it is a recipe for bad outcomes. The Supreme Court's decision-making process is described in W. H. Rehnquist, *The Supreme Court: How It Was, How It Is* (New York: William Morrow, 1987).

26. In his book *The Wisdom of Crowds* (New York: Doubleday, 2004), James Surowiecki reviews over a century of work, dating back to Sir Francis Galton, showing that the average of independent guesses comes closer to the actual total than the vast majority of the individual estimates that make up the average.

27. From a discussion Chris had with Richard Hackman on April 27, 2009.

28. C. Anderson and G. J. Kilduff, "Why Do Dominant Personalities Attain Influence in Face-to-Face Groups? The Competence-Signaling Effects of Trait Dominance," *Journal of Personality and Social Psychology* 96 (2009): 491–503. In a second experiment, similar results were obtained with a more realistic, open-ended group task that involved simulated business decision-making.

29. Information on William Thompson comes from Wikipedia, en.wikipedia.org/

wiki/William_Thompson_(confidence_man) (accessed May 2, 2009); and from the article "Arrest of the Confidence Man," *New-York Herald,* July 8, 1849, chnm.gmu.edu/lostmuseum/lm/328/ (accessed May 2, 2009).

30. The story of Frank Abagnale is based on Wikipedia, en.wikipedia.org/wiki/Frank_Abagnale (accessed May 2, 2009); and on his memoir: F. W. Abagnale and S. Redding, *Catch Me If You Can* (New York: Grosset & Dunlap, 1980).

31. The experiments described here are reported in C. F. Chabris, J. Schuldt, and A. W. Woolley, "Individual Differences in Confidence Affect Judgments Made Collectively by Groups" (poster presented at the annual convention of the Association for Psychological Science, New York, May 25–28, 2006).

32. In an experiment with 61 subjects, confidence levels between the two test versions were correlated ($r=.80$) but accuracy was not ($r=-.05$). In another experiment with 72 subjects, confidence correlated only $r=.12$ with scores on a twelve-item version of Raven's Advanced Progressive Matrices, a nonverbal "gold standard" measure of general cognitive ability. Earlier research by others indicated that confidence is a domain-general trait: G. Schraw, "The Effect of Generalized Metacognitive Knowledge on Test Performance and Confidence Judgments," *Journal of Experimental Education* 65 (1997): 135–146; A-R. Blais, M. M. Thompson, and J. V. Baranski, "Individual Differences in Decision Processing and Confidence Judgments in Comparative Judgment Tasks: The Role of Cognitive Styles," *Personality and Individual Differences* 38 (2005): 1707–1713.

33. Cesarini and colleagues found that genetic differences explain 16–34 percent of the differences among individuals in overconfidence. They studied 460 pairs of twins from the Swedish Twin Registry and asked them to estimate their cognitive abilities relative to the other subjects in the study. The difference between their estimated ranks and their actual ranks on a cognitive test was taken as a measure of overconfidence. D. Cesarini, M. Johannesson, P. Lichtenstein, and B. Wallace, "Heritability of Overconfidence," *Journal of the European Economic Association* 7 (2009), 617–627.

34. Quotes and information in this section are from H. Cooper, C. J. Chivers, and C. J. Levy, "U.S. Watched as a Squabble Turned into a Showdown," *The New York Times,* August 17, 2008, p. A1 (www.nytimes.com/2008/08/18/washington/18diplo.html). A detailed summary of the Russia–Georgia War is available on Wikipedia (en.wikipedia.org/wiki/2008_South_Ossetia_war).

35. D. D. P. Johnson, *Overconfidence and War: The Havoc and Glory of Positive Illusions* (Cambridge, MA: Harvard University Press, 2004).

36. A similar collective overconfidence might have contributed to the decision to invade Iraq in 2003. Richard Pearle, then chairman of the Defense Policy Board, when interviewed later on PBS *WideAngle,* noted the strong consensus within the Bush administration on the need to overthrow Saddam Hussein: "It's not quite the case that the president has the only vote that counts, but his thumb on the scale is not insignificant. And I don't think he's meeting a lot of resistance, frankly. I think the other senior officials of the administration have come to the same conclusion he has."

37. The average confidence of the individual subjects was 70 percent, and the average confidence of the groups was 74 percent, a small but statistically significant increase; 36 groups of two people each participated in this experiment, 12 each in the three conditions (Chabris et al., "Individual Differences in Confidence").

38. See "The Case of the Missing Evidence" (www.blog.sethroberts.net/2008/09/13/the-case-of-the-missing-evidence/).

39. C. G. Johnson, J. C. Levenkron, A. L. Sackman, and R. Manchester, "Does Physician Uncertainty Affect Patient Satisfaction?" *Journal of General Internal Medicine* 3 (1988): 144–149.

40. B. McKinstry and J. Wang, "Putting on the Style: What Patients Think of the Way Their Doctor Dresses," *British Journal of General Practice* 41 (1991): 275–278; S. U. Rehman, P. J. Nietert, D. W. Cope, and A. O. Kilpatrick, "What to Wear Today? Effect of Doctor's Attire on the Trust and Confidence of Patients," *The American Journal of Medicine* 118 (2005): 1279–1286; and A. Cha, B. R. Hecht, K. Nelson, and M. P. Hopkins, "Resident Physician Attire: Does It Make a Difference to Our Patients?" *American Journal of Obstetrics and Gynecology* 190 (2004): 1484–1488. White lab coats also appear to be a source of infection: A. Treakle, K. Thom, J. Furuno, S. Strauss, A. Harris, and E. Perencevich, "Bacterial Contamination of Health Care Workers' White Coats," *American Journal of Infection Control* 37 (2009): 101–105.

41. Information on the Jennifer Thompson rape case is based primarily on judicial opinions in the case and on the following sources: J. M. Doyle, *True Witness: Cops, Courts, Science, and the Battle Against Misidentification* (New York: Palgrave Macmillan, 2005); an episode of the PBS series *Frontline*, "What Jennifer Saw," broadcast February 25, 1997; a joint memoir, J. Thompson-Cannino, R. Cotton, and E. Torneo, *Picking Cotton: Our Memoir of Injustice and Redemption* (New York: St. Martin's Press, 2009); and an article by Jennifer Thompson, "I Was Certain, But I Was Dead Wrong," *Houston Chronicle,* June 20, 2000, www.commondreams.org/views/062500-103.htm (accessed May 3, 2009). Direct quotes are also drawn from these sources.

42. *Neil v. Biggers,* 409 U.S. 188 (1972).

43. Kassin and colleagues surveyed 63 expert-witness psychologists and found that 46 said the evidence for this statement was either "very" or "generally" reliable: S. M. Kassin, P. C. Ellsworth, and V. L. Smith, "The 'General Acceptance' of Psychological Research on Eyewitness Testimony: A Survey of the Experts," *American Psychologist* 44 (1989): 1089–1098.

44. Innocence Project website, www.innocenceproject.org/understand/Eyewitness-Misidentification.php (accessed February 21, 2009).

45. R. C. L. Lindsay, G. L. Wells, and C. M. Rumpel, "Can People Detect Eyewitness-Identification Accuracy Within and Across Situations?" *Journal of Applied Psychology* 66 (1981): 79–89.

46. S. Sporer, S. Penrod, D. Read, and B. L. Cutler, "Choosing, Confidence, and Accuracy: A Meta-analysis of the Confidence-Accuracy Relation in Eyewitness Identification Studies," *Psychological Bulletin* 118 (1995): 315–327. They report an average correlation across studies of $r = .41$ between witness confidence and accuracy in simulated lineup tasks (when the "witness" chooses someone from the lineup, which Jennifer Thompson did in the Ronald Cotton investigation, as opposed to choosing no one; i.e., claiming the perpetrator is not in the lineup).

47. G. L. Wells, E. A. Olson, and S. D. Charman, "The Confidence of Eyewitnesses in Their Identifications from Lineups," *Current Directions in Psychological Science* 11 (2002): 151–154.

48. We are not claiming that physical evidence is always infallible. It can be relied on only to the extent that it is produced by honest, careful technicians applying valid science. That said, the forensic science behind such common techniques as hair and fiber analysis and fingerprint matching is surprisingly primitive (e.g., see National Research Council, *Strengthening Forensic Science in the United States: A Path Forward* [Washington, DC: National Academies Press, 2009]). Circumstantial evidence, which is often derided as being lower in value than direct evidence from eyewitnesses, can in fact be more reliable than any other kind of evidence—even a sworn confession—because it does not stand or fall based on a single disputable fact (e.g., whether a witness has good memory, or whether a confession was coerced). A good circumstantial case can be compelling because it involves a large number of circumstances that would be unlikely to all occur together by chance.

Chapter 4: Should You Be More Like a Weather Forecaster or a Hedge Fund Manager?

1. Basic facts about the Human Genome Project, which involved researchers in several countries, can be found at the U.S. Department of Energy (DOE) website devoted to the project (www.ornl.gov/sci/techresources/Human_Genome/home.shtml). The DOE was involved in biomedical research because of the recognition that radiation from nuclear weapons and other sources could affect human genes. The majority of the project's funding, however, came from the budget of the National Institutes of Health (NIH).

2. The story of the gene count betting pool is based on a series of articles in *Science* magazine: E. Pennisi, "And the Gene Number Is . . . ?" *Science* 288 (2000): 1146–1147; E. Pennisi, "A Low Number Wins the GeneSweep Pool," *Science* 300 (2003): 1484; and E. Pennisi, "Working the (Gene Count) Numbers: Finally, a Firm Answer?" *Science* 316 (2007): 1113. Other sources include an Associated Press article from October 20, 2004 (reprinted at www.thescienceforum.com/Scientists-slash-estimated-number-of-human-genes-5t.php), and an article by Cold Spring Harbor Laboratory's David Stewart, who maintained the official handwritten ledger in which all bets were recorded, www.cshl.edu/public/HT/ss03-sweep.pdf (accessed August 27, 2009). The pool's defunct website has been archived at web.archive.org/web/20030424100755/www.ensembl.org/Genesweep/ (accessed August 27, 2009).

3. The prediction was made in a talk given by Herbert Simon on behalf of himself and Allen Newell at the National Meeting of the Operations Research Society of America on November 14, 1957: H. A. Simon and A. Newell, "Heuristic Problem Solving: The Next Advance in Operations Research," *Operations Research* 6 (1958): 1–10. They also predicted that within ten years, computers would be proving important mathematical theorems and composing high-quality original music, and that most theories in psychology would be expressed in the form of computer programs designed to simulate the human mind. None of these things fully came to pass, though some progress was made on each of them.

4. Nowadays even laptop computers are the equal of the world's top players. The history of the bets is described by D. Levy and M. Newborn, *How Computers Play Chess* (New York: Computer Science Press, 1991). The match between Kasparov and Deep Blue is recounted in the following works: M. Newborn, *Deep Blue: An Artificial Intelligence Milestone* (New York: Springer, 2003); F-H. Hsu, *Behind Deep Blue: Building the Com-*

puter That Defeated the World Chess Champion (Princeton, NJ: Princeton University Press, 2002); and D. Goodman and R. Keene, *Man Versus Machine: Kasparov Versus Deep Blue* (Cambridge, MA: H3 Publications, 1997).

5. P. Ehrlich, *The Population Bomb* (New York: Ballantine, 1968).

6. Quoted by J. Tierney, "Science Adviser's Unsustainable Bet (and Mine)," Tierney-Lab blog, December 23, 2008 (tierneylab.blogs.nytimes.com/2008/12/23/science-advisors-unsustainable-bet-and-mine/). Other information on the Ehrlich-Simon wager is drawn from the following sources: J. Tierney, "Betting on the Planet," *The New York Times,* December 2, 1990; J. Tierney, "Flawed Science Advisor for Obama?" TierneyLab blog, December 19, 2008 (tierneylab.blogs.nytimes.com/2008/12/19/flawed-science-advice-for-obama/); and E. Regis, "The Doomslayer," *Wired,* February 1997.

7. J. L. Simon, "Resources, Population, Environment: An Oversupply of False Bad News," *Science* 208 (1980): 1431–1437.

8. We could have gone on and on with examples of scientific overconfidence; for example, even physicists have been found to be overconfident when historical data was examined to see how accurately they had measured well-known physical constants, like the speed of light: M. Henrion and B. Fischhoff, "Assessing Uncertainty in Physical Constants," *American Journal of Physics* 54 (1986): 791–797.

9. R. Lawson, "The Science of Cycology: Failures to Understand How Everyday Objects Work," *Memory and Cognition* 34 (2006): 1667–1775.

10. L. G. Rozenblit, "Systematic Bias in Knowledge Assessment: An Illusion of Explanatory Depth," PhD dissertation, Yale University, 2003.

11. From an interview Dan conducted with Leon Rozenblit on August 14, 2008.

12. B. Worthen, "Keeping It Simple Pays Off for Winning Programmer," *The Wall Street Journal,* May 20, 2008, p. B6 (online.wsj.com/article/SB121124841362205967.html).

13. Information on the Big Dig drawn primarily from the project's official website (masspike.com/bigdig/index.html).

14. Information on the Brooklyn Bridge and Sydney Opera House is from B. Flyvbjerg, "Design by Deception: The Politics of Megaproject Approval," *Harvard Design Magazine,* Spring/Summer 2005, pp. 50–59. Information on the Sagrada Familia is from R. Zerbst, *Gaudi: The Complete Buildings* (Hong Kong: Taschen, 2005) and from Wikipedia (en.wikipedia.org/wiki/Sagrada_Família). The entire history of public architecture can be seen as one of cost overruns and delays. Bent Flyvbjerg, an expert on urban planning at the University of Aalborg in Denmark, has coauthored a study of three hundred such projects in twenty countries. He argues persuasively that all parties involved have learned to deliberately lowball the estimates, because if legislators and their constituents appreciated the true costs and uncertainties involved in these projects, they would never support them. In other words, those who do understand the complex systems—or at least understand the limits of their own knowledge—are exploiting the very lack of that understanding among the general public. See B. Flyvbjerg, N. Bruzelius, and W. Rothengatter, *Megaprojects and Risk: An Anatomy of Ambition* (Cambridge: Cambridge University Press, 2003).

15. The first quote is from Robert Burns, the second is from Helmuth Graf von Moltke, and the third is from Douglas Hofstadter.

16. This quip is usually attributed to Yogi Berra, whose sayings often had this sort of twisted logic, but a version of it was apparently said earlier by the physicist Neils Bohr.

17. This study is described on p. 142 of P. B. Carroll and C. Mui, *Billion Dollar Lessons: What You Can Learn from the Most Inexcusable Business Failures of the Last 25 Years* (New York: Portfolio, 2008).

18. The classic volume on the positive nature of most self-deception is S. E. Taylor, *Positive Illusions: Creative Self-Deception and the Healthy Mind* (New York: Basic Books, 1989). The idea that depressed people are less subject to everyday illusions is speculative; there is a controversial line of research suggesting that depressed people have a more realistic understanding of how much they can control events (e.g., L. B. Alloy and L. Y. Abramson, "Judgment of Contingency in Depressed and Nondepressed Students: Sadder but Wiser?" *Journal of Experimental Psychology: General* 108 [1979]: 441–485).

19. The idea of the "outside view" is described in detail in D. Lovallo and D. Kahneman, "Delusions of Success: How Optimism Undermines Executive Decisions," *Harvard Business Review* (July 2003): 56–63. The tendency to underestimate the time to complete a task is often called the "planning fallacy," and the formal name for the technique of comparing a project to similar ones to estimate completion time is called "reference class forecasting." This method has been endorsed by the American Planning Association. See B. Flyvbjerg, "From Nobel Prize to Project Management: Getting Risks Right," *Project Management Journal* (August 2006): 5–15. Another way to use the disinterested knowledge of other people to help in forecasting project durations (and other future events) is to set up a prediction market, a sort of artificial financial futures market in which individuals invest or gamble money on making the most accurate prediction. The aggregation of multiple, independent predictions, each from someone motivated by financial gain and not personally involved in carrying out the plan, can yield much more accurate forecasts than those made by even expert individuals. For discussion, see C. R. Sunstein, *Infotopia: How Many Minds Produce Knowledge* (Oxford: Oxford University Press, 2006); and R. W. Hahn and P. C. Tetlock, *Information Markets: A New Way of Making Decisions* (Washington, DC: AEI Press, 2006).

20. Techniques like these were studied experimentally in R. Buehler, D. Griffin, and M. Ross, "Exploring the 'Planning Fallacy': Why People Underestimate Their Task Completion Times," *Journal of Personality and Social Psychology* 67 (1994): 366–381.

21. Information on Brian Hunter and Amaranth Advisors comes from: A. Davis, "Blue Flameout: How Giant Bets on Natural Gas Sank Brash Hedge-Fund Trader," *The Wall Street Journal,* September 19, 2006, p. A1 (online.wsj.com/article/SB115861715980366723. html); and H. Till, "The Amaranth Collapse: What Happened and What Have We Learned Thus Far?" EDHEC Business School, Lille, France, 2007. The comparison between Amaranth and other debacles is based on "List of Trading Losses" in Wikipedia, en.wikipedia.org/wiki/List_of_trading_losses (accessed March 27, 2009).

22. Information on various investment strategies comes from the following sources: "Dow Theory" in Wikipedia, en.wikipedia.org/wiki/Dow_theory (accessed March 25, 2009); discussion of the Nifty Fifty in Chapter 8, "The Amazing Two-Tier Market," in D. N. Dreman, *Psychology and the Stock Market: Investment Strategy Beyond Random Walk* (New York: Amacom, 1977). "Dogs of the Dow" is a nickname for a strategy proposed by Michael O'Higgins in his book *Beating the Dow: A High-Return, Low-Risk Method for*

Investing in the Dow Jones Industrial Stocks with as Little as $5000 (New York: HarperCollins, 1991). The "Foolish Four" strategy, a derivative of one of O'Higgins's ideas, is described by Robert Sheard in *The Unemotional Investor: Simple Systems for Beating the Market* (New York: Simon & Schuster, 1998). Both of the latter two books were bestsellers.

23. It is arguably wrong to view a house as an investment. A typical asset bought for investment purposes is not usable while you own it; there's nothing you can physically *do* with your Google stock or your municipal bonds or your money-market funds. (You can't even frame your pretty stock certificates anymore, unless you make a special request for them from your broker.) The right way to think of a house is as a hybrid of a consumable product that must be repaired and upgraded over time, like a car or a computer, and an underlying investment (which is based partly on the value of the land where it stands).

People make mistakes when thinking about housing prices for a variety of reasons, one of which is failing to make this distinction. For example, many homeowners mistakenly believe that improving their homes will increase the home's value by a greater amount than the cost of the improvement; in fact, every one of twenty-nine common home improvements yields an average increase in resale value less than 100 percent of its cost (see "Remodeling 2007 Cost Versus Value Report" [www.remodeling.hw.net/costvsvalue/index .html]; and D. Crook, *The Wall Street Journal Complete Homeowner's Guidebook* [New York: Three Rivers Press, 2008]). Remodeling a home office costs $27,193 on average, but increases the home's value by only $15,498, or 57 percent of the original expenditure, not counting any interest paid if the remodeling was financed. Even remodeling a kitchen, one of the classic value centers of a house, returns only 74 percent of the money spent. Look at it this way: If your house would sell for $500,000 today, but you decide to "invest" $40,000 in a new kitchen before you put the house on the market, you should expect to get about $530,000 for it. Putting the same money in the bank would be a much better investment: You wouldn't earn much in interest, but at least you wouldn't lose the $10,000!

When told these facts, people often become incredulous and even angry—precisely because they contradict a foundational piece of "knowledge" homeowners have about their "investments." We will return to this subject later in this chapter when we discuss the necessary conditions for financial bubbles and panics. There are, of course, other reasons to remodel a house besides any expected "investment" gain: A recent study showed that additional full or half bathrooms in a house were more strongly associated with owner satisfaction than any other feature measured, including additional bedrooms, air conditioning, and a garage. See R. N. James III, "Investing in Housing Characteristics That Count: A Cross-Sectional and Longitudinal Analysis of Bathrooms, Bathroom Additions, and Residential Satisfaction," *Housing and Society* 35 (2008): 67–82.

24. M. Piazzesi and M. Schneider, "Momentum Traders in the Housing Market: Survey Evidence and a Search Model," Stanford University manuscript, 2009, www.stanford .edu/~piazzesi/momentum%20in%20housing%20search.pdf (accessed August 17, 2009).

25. Alberto Ramirez's mortgage story is from C. Lloyd, "Minorities Are the Emerging Face of the Subprime Crisis," SF Gate, April 13, 2007 (www.sfgate.com/cgi-bin/article .cgi?f=/g/a/2007/04/13/carollloyd.DTL). Ninja loans, and other bad home-finance ideas, are mentioned in S. Pearlstein, " 'No Money Down' Falls Flat," *The Washington Post*, March 14, 2007, p. D1 (www.washingtonpost.com/wp-dyn/content/article/2007/ 03/13/AR2007031301733_pf.html). Ed Glaeser's quote comes from E. Glaeser, "In

Housing, Even Hindsight Isn't 20-20," *The New York Times* Economix blog, July 7, 2009 (economix.blogs.nytimes.com/2009/07/07/in-housing-even-hindsight-isnt-20-20/?hp).

26. R. Lowenstein, "Triple-A Failure," *The New York Times Magazine,* April 27, 2008 (www.nytimes.com/2008/04/27/magazine/27Credit-t.html). Similar problems beset so-called "quant" funds, which were hedge funds that made trading decisions entirely or mostly based on the predictions of computer models that were calibrated with historical data that didn't include market conditions like the increasingly risky environment of 2007. See H. Sender and K. Kelly, "Blind to Trend, 'Quant' Funds Pay Heavy Price," *The Wall Street Journal,* August 9, 2007.

27. R. H. Thaler, A. Tversky, D. Kahneman, and A. Schwartz, "The Effect of Myopia and Loss Aversion on Risk Taking: An Experimental Test," *Quarterly Journal of Economics* 112 (1997): 647–661.

28. Interestingly, the most active traders also tended to have smaller portfolios at the beginning of the study than did the least active ones; obviously this difference would tend to magnify over time since their net returns would be lower as well. See B. Barber and T. Odean, "Trading Is Hazardous to Your Wealth: The Common Stock Investment Performance of Individual Investors," *Journal of Finance* 55 (2000): 773–806. Men, especially single men, also trade much more frequently than women, and earn correspondingly lower returns on their investments. See also B. Barber and T. Odean, "Boys Will Be Boys: Gender, Overconfidence, and Common Stock Investment," *Quarterly Journal of Economics* 116 (2001): 261–292.

29. Unless you are a coin collector, you don't know enough to distinguish a counterfeit penny from a real one. Even coin collectors might fail to recognize subtle changes unless they're actively looking for them. As a child, Dan collected coins, and he did spot one obvious fake. He was at a coin show, and a vendor was selling a really old coin that he claimed was from ancient Greece. The coin was well worn, with few details still visible. It certainly looked like it could be more than two thousand years old, and the figure on the front looked like a Greek hero. Dan didn't buy it, though—it had a date of "300BC" partially visible below the figure! (Some counterfeiters apparently are not terribly bright.)

30. The idea that the mind works like a Web browser comes from R. A. Rensink, "The Dynamic Representation of Scenes," *Visual Cognition* 7 (2000): 17–42. In philosophy and psychology, metaphors for the workings of the mind often draw on the latest and greatest in technology. Early models of the mind appealed to the notions of hydraulics, with the flows of fluids causing different thoughts and actions. Such models were gradually replaced by the notion of the mind as a mechanical device, with metaphorical gears. In the 1960s, the dominant model of the mind was as an information-processing device. Essentially, the mind was treated as a powerful computer. The computer metaphor continues to hold sway in psychology, with some adjustments corresponding to further changes in technology: an emphasis on the parallel nature of processing, off-loading of some types of processing to specialized modules (just as computer graphics are often handled by a special chip set), and so on. For an interesting discussion of the effects of technological developments on the nature of scientific theories, see G. Gigerenzer, "From Tools to Theories: A Heuristic of Discovery in Cognitive Psychology," *Psychological Review* 98 (1991): 254–267.

31. B. Popken, "Do Coat Hangers Sound as Good as Monster Cables?" *The Consumerist* blog, March 3, 2008, consumerist.com/362926/do-coat-hangers-sound-as-good-monster-cables (accessed June 29, 2009).

32. If you want some snarky entertainment, read the user reviews of the Denon cable at Amazon.com. Just search the site for "Denon Ethernet cable." As of August 2009, one Amazon user was even offering one of these cables "used" for sale at $2,500!

33. D. S. Weisberg, F. C. Keil, J. Goodstein, E. Rawson, and J. R. Gray, "The Seductive Allure of Neuroscience Explanations," *Journal of Cognitive Neuroscience* 20 (2008): 470–477. The "curse of knowledge" described in the example we gave from this experiment has implications for the illusion of knowledge. If we assume that other people know what we know, and we think we know more than we do, then we must think other people know more than they do as well!

34. These results are from Experiment 1 of D. P. McCabe and A. D. Castel, "Seeing Is Believing: The Effect of Brain Images on Judgments of Scientific Reasoning," *Cognition* 107 (2008): 343–352.

35. The Allstate ad is on the company's website, www.allstate.com/content/refresh-attachments/Brain-Ad.pdf (accessed November 15, 2009).

36. Agricultural facts taken from Wikipedia, en.wikipedia.org/wiki/Illinois (accessed February 27, 2009).

37. Details about Illinois weather forecasting and WILL are from an interview with Ed Kieser conducted by Dan on February 27, 2009.

38. P. Hughes, "The Great Leap Forward: On the 125th Anniversary of the Weather Service, A Look at the Invention That Got It Started," *Weatherwise* 47, no. 5 (1994): 22–27.

39. J. P. Charba and W. H. Klein, "Skill in Precipitation Forecasting in the National Weather Service," *Bulletin of the American Meteorological Society* 61 (1980): 1546–1555. There has been much discussion of "chaos" in physical systems like the earth's climate, and the now-clichéd idea that a butterfly can flap its wings on one side of the world and influence the weather weeks later on the opposite side of the world. None of this makes it impossible to predict whether it will rain tomorrow.

40. This demonstration was suggested by one of Dan's teaching assistants, Richard Yao, who experienced it in a class as an undergraduate at Northwestern University.

41. R. A. Price and S. G. Vandenberg, "Matching for Physical Attractiveness in Married Couples," *Personality and Social Psychology Bulletin* 5 (1979): 398–400.

42. The meteorologist preference question was asked of the 72 chess players in Philadelphia who participated in the study of overconfidence in chess ability that we discussed in Chapter 3. The question was first used in G. Keren, "On the Calibration of Probability Judgments: Some Critical Comments and Alternative Perspectives," *Journal of Behavioral Decision Making* 10 (1997): 269–278. See also G. Keren and K. H. Teigen, "Why Is $p = .90$ Better Than $p = .70$? Preference for Definitive Predictions by Lay Consumers of Probability Judgments," *Psychonomic Bulletin and Review* 8 (2001): 191–202. The popular preference for certainty in weather reports was noted anecdotally over a century ago. When William Ernest Cooke introduced estimates of uncertainty to weather forecasting in 1906, he predicted that the public would prefer his new method, but immediately below his first article, a note by one Professor E. B. Garriott appeared, giving no fewer

than five specific arguments why Cooke's "scheme" was impractical, concluding with "because our public insist upon having our forecasts expressed concisely and in unequivo-cal terms." W. E. Cooke, "Forecasts and Verifications in Western Australia," *Monthly Weather Review* 34 (1906): 23–24.

43. P. E. Tetlock, *Expert Political Judgment: How Good Is It? How Can We Know?* (Princeton, NJ: Princeton University Press, 2005). In weather forecasting, meteorologists understand the need to show that over time their methods outperform a simple model that assumes that tomorrow's weather will be the same as today's weather. And they are easily able to make enough verifiable predictions to show that they can beat such models. People in many other disciplines lack that ready source of feedback and they often do not check whether their models can outperform such simple heuristics. Even when they do have access to such data (e.g., public financial data can be used to determine whether a money manager's method of actively picking stocks outperforms the returns of a passive index fund), they often do not bother to check. If they did, perhaps they would not ex-press quite as much confidence as they do.

44. We thank our editor, Rick Horgan, for suggesting these two examples.

45. Citation for Herbert Simon from Nobel Prize website (nobelprize.org/nobel_ prizes/economics/laureates/1978/index.html).

46. In August 2009, Amaranth agreed to a settlement with the U.S. government over the charges, but Brian Hunter did not. As of earlier that year, he was an adviser to Peak Ridge Capital Group, where his "Commodity Volatility Fund" was up 138 per-cent in its first six months. "To have lost that amount of money and get back into the market with a similar-type trade takes a lot of confidence, if not arrogance," said one industry analyst. See S. Kishan, "Ex-Amaranth Trader Hunter Helps Deliver 17% Gain for Peak Ridge," Bloomberg.com, May 19, 2009 (www.bloomberg.com/apps/news?pid= 20601087&sid=aUlBVaEHAk04&refer=home); "Ex-Amaranth Trader Makes Good, Possibly," the *New York Times* DealBook blog, April 11, 2008 (dealbook.blogs.nytimes. com/2008/04/11/ex-amaranth-trader-makes-good-possibly/); A. Davis, "Amaranth Case Shows Trading's Dark Side," *The Wall Street Journal,* July 26, 2007, p. C3; C. Kahn, "Fed-eral Judge Orders Amaranth Advisors to Pay $7.5M for Price Manipulation," Associated Press, August 12, 2009 (ca.news.finance.yahoo.com/s/12082009/2/biz-finance-federal-judge-orders-amaranth-advisors-pay-7-5m.html); J. Strasburg, "A Decade Later, Meri-wether Must Scramble Again," *The Wall Street Journal,* March 27, 2008, p. C1 (online. wsj.com/article/SB120658664128767911.html); and G. Zuckerman and C. Karmin, "Re-bounds by Hedge-Fund Stars Prove 'It's a Mulligan Industry,'" *The Wall Street Journal,* May 12, 2008, p. C1 (online.wsj.com/article/SB121055428158584071.html).

Chapter 5: Jumping to Conclusions

1. Details from this case and the subsequent outbreak of measles in Indiana were taken from the CDC report "Import-Associated Measles Outbreak—Indiana, May–June 2005," *Morbidity and Mortality Weekly Report* (MMWR) 54 (October 27, 2005): 1073–1075. Other details came from A. A. Parker, W. Staggs, G. H. Dayan, I. R. Ortega-Sánchez, P. A. Rota, L. Lowe, P. Boardman, R. Teclaw, C. Graves, and C. W. LeBaron, "Implications of a 2005 Measles Outbreak in Indiana for Sustained Elimination of Mea-

sles in the United States," *New England Journal of Medicine* 355 (2006): 447–455. Other information about measles discussed in this section comes from the preceding sources as well as the following additional sources: World Health Organization Measles Fact Sheet, www.who.int/mediacentre/factsheets/fs286/en/ (accessed March 24, 2009); CDC report "Outbreak of Measles—San Diego, California, January–February 2008," *Morbidity and Mortality Weekly Report* (MMWR) 57 (February 22, 2008): 203–206; "Confirmed Measles Cases in England and Wales: An Update to End–May 2008," 2008, Health Protection Report 2, no. 25 (2008); S. B. Omar, W. K. Y. Pan, N. A. Halsey, L. H. Moulton, A. M. Navar, M. Pierce, and D. A. Salmon, "Nonmedical Exemptions to School Immunization Requirements: Secular Trends and Association of State Policies with Pertussis Incidence," *Journal of the American Medical Association* 296 (2006): 1757–1763; CDC report "Measles—United States, January 1–April 25, 2008," *Morbidity and Mortality Weekly Report* (MMWR) 57 (May 1, 2008): 494–498; CDC report "Update: Measles—United States, January–July 2008," *Morbidity and Mortality Weekly Report* (MMWR) 57 (May 1, 2008): 893–896. Information about the measles outbreak in Romania from: Associated Press, "Measles Outbreak Sickens 4000 in Romania," December 5, 2005. After we wrote this chapter, an excellent article reporting on this case and its implications was published in *Wired*: A. Wallace, "An Epidemic of Fear: How Panicked Parents Skipping Shots Endangers Us All," *Wired*, November 2009, www.wired.com/magazine/2009/10/ff_waron science/.

2. In Romania, more than four thousand people contracted measles and ten people died during the outbreak that was the source of the missionary girl's infection.

3. Evidence that people can recognize their friends by their gait alone comes from J. E. Cutting and L. T. Kozlowski, "Recognizing Friends by Their Walk: Gait Perception Without Familiarity Cues," *Bulletin of the Psychonomic Society* 9 (1977): 353–356. Evidence that people can judge teachers from a brief glimpse comes from N. Ambady and R. Rosenthal, "Half a Minute: Predicting Teacher Evaluations from Thin Slices of Nonverbal Behavior and Physical Attractiveness," *Journal of Personality and Social Psychology* 64 (1993): 431–441.

4. Examples of pareidolia discussed in this section come from the following sources: Associated Press, " 'Virgin Mary Grilled Cheese' Sells for $28,000," November 23, 2004 (www.msnbc.msn.com/id/6511148/); "Jesus Seen in Cheese Snack," CNN.com, May 18, 2009 (www.cnn.com/video/#/video/living/2009/05/18/pkg.tx.cheese.snack.jesus.KTXA); "Message from Allah 'in Tomato,' " BBC News, September 9, 1999 (news.bbc.co.uk/2/hi/uk_news/443173.stm). Other religious pareidolia examples are summarized by Wikipedia, en.wikipedia.org/wiki/Perceptions_of_religious_imagery_in_natural_phenomena (accessed May 28, 2009).

5. This experiment is reported in N. Hadjikhani, K. Kveraga, P. Naik, and S. Ahlfors, "Early (M170) Activation of Face-Specific Cortex by Face-like Objects," *Neuroreport* 20 (2009): 403–407. The researchers showed their subjects pictures from an entertaining book that contains nothing but "found" images of faces in other common objects: F. Robert and J. Robert, *Faces* (San Francisco: Chronicle Books, 2000).

6. K. Stollznow, "Merchandising God: The Pope Tart," *The Skeptic* (Autumn 2000): 28–34. The winning bid turned out to be a hoax, so Stollznow donated the Pope Tart to the second-highest bidder, a radio station DJ in Texas.

7. The experiments are reported in D. A. Redelmeier and A. Tversky, "On the Belief That Arthritis Pain Is Related to the Weather," *Proceedings of the National Academy of Sciences* 93 (1996): 2895–2896. According to these authors, modern medical textbooks downplay any relationship between the weather and arthritis pain. More recent studies have agreed in finding little to no connection, e.g., F. V. Wilder, B. J. Hall, and J. P. Barrett, "Osteoarthritis Pain and Weather," *Rheumatology* 42 (2003): 955–958. The 1972 survey of arthritis patients is from D. F. Hill, "Climate and Arthritis in Arthritis and Allied Conditions," in *A Textbook of Rheumatology* (8th ed.), ed. J. L. Hollander and D. C. McCarty, 256–263 (Philadelphia: Lea and Feringer, 1972) (as described by M.S. Shutty Jr., G. Cundiff, and D.E. DeGood, "Pain Complaint and the Weather: Weather Sensitivity and Symptom Complaints in Chronic Pain Patients," *Pain* 49 [1992]: 199–204). This tendency to see patterns we expect even when they aren't present has been known for more than forty years. It can even interfere with our ability to see patterns that actually are present but are unexpected. The seminal research on the effects of expectations on pattern perception involved the use of the Rohrshach "ink blot" test to categorize psychiatric patients as homosexual; see L. J. Chapman and J. P. Chapman, "Illusory Correlation as an Obstacle to the Use of Valid Psychodiagnostic Signs," *Journal of Abnormal Psychology* 74 (1969): 21–28.

8. Examples of correlations like this one, with a clear noncausal interpretation that makes much more sense than any causal one, can be found in almost every introductory psychology textbook (we use *Psychology* by Scott Lilienfeld and three coauthors). However, we have not been able to find a study in which this particular correlation was actually measured!

9. BBC News, "Sex Keeps You Young," March 10, 1999 (news.bbc.co.uk/2/hi/ health/294119.stm). For details of the original study, see D. Weeks and J. James, *Secrets of the Superyoung* (New York: Villard Books, 1998).

10. The headlines cited in this section and the research underlying them included the following sources: Headline from CNN.com, "Drop That BlackBerry! Multitasking May Be Harmful," August 25, 2009 (www.cnn.com/2009/HEALTH/08/25/multitasking. harmful/index.html). For the original study, see E. Ophir, C. Hass, and A. D. Wagner, "Cognitive Control in Media Multitaskers," *Proceedings of the National Academy of Sciences*, 2009. Headline from Reuters Health, "Bullying Harms Kids' Mental Health: Study," February 6, 2008 (www.reuters.com/article/healthNews/idUSCOL67503120080206). For the original study, see L. Arseneault, B. J. Milne, A. Taylor, F. Adams, K. Delgado, A. Caspi, and T. E. Moffitt, "Being Bullied as an Environmentally Mediated Contributing Factor to Children's Internalizing Problems: A Study of Twins Discordant for Victimization," *Archives of Pediatrics and Adolescent Medicine* 162 (2008): 145–150. The article compared twins at age ten, of whom one had been bullied between ages seven and nine and one had not been bullied. Headline from MindHacks blog, "Does Your Neighborhood Cause Schizophrenia?" by Vaughn Bell, July 5, 2007, www.mindhacks.com/blog/ 2007/07/does_your_neighbourh.html (accessed June 1, 2009). The blog post and subsequent comments discuss various models in which environmental factors might contribute in a causal way to rates of schizophrenia, although the study itself was not a random-assignment experiment and does not permit that conclusion. For the original study, see J. B. Kirkbride, P. Fearon, C. Morgan, P. Dazzan, K. Morgan, R. M. Murray, and

P. B. Jones, "Neighborhood Variation in the Incidence of Psychotic Disorders in South-east London," *Social Psychiatry and Psychiatric Epidemiology* 42 (2007): 438–445. Head-line from BBC News Online, "Housework Cuts Breast Cancer Risk," December 29, 2006 (news.bbc.co.uk/2/hi/health/6214655.stm). For the original study, see P. H. Lahmann et al., "Physical Activity and Breast Cancer Risk: The European Prospective Investigation into Cancer and Nutrition," *Cancer Epidemiology Biomarkers and Prevention* 16 (2007): 36–42. Headline from Associated Press, "Sexual Lyrics Prompt Teens to Have Sex," by L. Tanner, August 6, 2006 (www.sfgate.com/cgi-bin/article.cgi?f=/n/a/2006/08/06/national/a215010D94.DTL). For details of the original study, see S. C. Martino, R. L. Collins, M. N. Elliott, A. Strachman, D. E. Kanouse, and S. H. Berry, "Exposure to Degrading Versus Nondegrading Music Lyrics and Sexual Behavior Among Youth," *Pediatrics* 118 (2006): 430–441.

11. D. T. Max, "The Unfinished: David Foster Wallace's Struggle to Surpass 'Infinite Jest,'" *The New Yorker*, March 9, 2009, pp. 48–61 (www.newyorker.com/reporting/2009/03/09/090309fa_fact_max). For a discussion of some methods of inferring causation without conducting experiments, see: S. G. West, "Alternatives to Randomized Experiments," *Current Directions in Psychological Science* 18 (2009): 299–304.

12. J. M. Keenan, S. D. Baillet, and P. Brown, "The Effects of Causal Cohesion on Comprehension and Memory," *Journal of Verbal Learning and Verbal Behavior* 23 (1984): 115–126. Reading sentences that require a causal inference also produces increased brain activity in a range of regions that differs from those activated by reading pairs of sentences that do not require an inference. See G. R. Kuperberg, B. M. Lakshmanan, D. N. Caplan, and P. J. Holcomb, "Making Sense of Discourse: An fMRI Study of Causal Inferencing Across Sentences," *Neuroimage* 33 (2006): 343–361.

13. R. B. Cialdini, "What's the Best Secret Device for Engaging Student Interest? The Answer Is in the Title," *Journal of Social and Clinical Psychology* 24 (2005): 22–29; C. Heath and D. Heath, *Made to Stick: Why Some Ideas Survive and Others Die* (New York: Random House, 2007). Heath and Heath discuss this idea extensively in the course of giving advice on how to create and communicate memorable messages.

14. From *The Simpsons*, Episode 723, "Much Apu about Nothing," first aired May 5, 1996 (www.thesimpsons.com/episode_guide/0723.htm).

15. From U.S. Supreme Court oral arguments on April 29, 2009, in *Northwest Austin Municipal Utility District No. 1 v. Holder* (No. 08-322). Official transcript available from www.supremecourtus.gov/oral_arguments/argument_transcripts.html (accessed June 22, 2009).

16. Although randomized experiments are occasionally conducted in the area of public policy, often to test the presumed effects of financial incentives, they are the exception to the rule that most laws and regulations are passed based on assumptions that they will change behavior, rather than on evidence that they will. For discussion, see Chapter 3 of I. Ayres, *Super Crunchers: Why Thinking-by-Numbers Is the New Way to Be Smart* (New York: Bantam Books, 2007).

17. For a keen analysis of this problem in the business literature, see P. Rozenweig, *The Halo Effect . . . and the Eight Other Business Delusions That Deceive Managers* (New York: Free Press, 2007). The problems of the Hush Puppies story are discussed in

C. Thompson, "Is the Tipping Point Toast?" *Fast Company*, January 28, 2008 (www
.fastcompany.com/magazine/122/is-the-tipping-point-toast.html).

18. All Chris Matthews quotes come from transcripts of *Hardball*, retrieved from
Lexis/Nexis.

19. The story of Sherry Lansing is discussed in L. Mlodinow, "Meet Hollywood's Latest Genius," *The Los Angeles Times*, July 2, 2006. See also C. Eller, "Paramount CEO Brad
Grey Signs on for Five More Years," *The Los Angeles Times*, January 8, 2009 (articles.la
times.com/2009/jan/08/business/fi-grey8).

20. Statistics from the Centers for Disease Control: www.cdc.gov/ncbddd/Autism/
faq_prevalence.htm (accessed June 20, 2009) and www.cdc.gov/mmwr/preview/
mmwrhtml/ss5810a1.htm (accessed December 23, 2009).

21. Details about Andrew Wakefield and the subsequent media attention to the alleged link between the MMR vaccine and autism are drawn from a comprehensive book
by Paul Offit published in 2008 by Columbia University Press: *Autism's False Prophets:
Bad Science, Risky Medicine, and the Search for a Cure*. The book documents the history of
alleged cures and causes of autism, pointing out how false causes have been promulgated
by the media. It is essential reading for anyone whose child has been diagnosed with autism and anyone who has questions about the risks of vaccines.

22. A. J. Wakefield et al., "Ileal-Lymphoid-Nodular Hyperplasia, Non-specific Coli-
tis, and Pervasive Developmental Disorder In Children," *Lancet* 351 (1998): 637–641.

23. Wakefield's quote is from Offit (*Autism's False Prophets*, p. 20).

24. Offit (*Autism's False Prophets*, p. 55; emphasis in original).

25. Use of the MMR vaccine ceased in Japan in 1993 (for reasons unrelated to autism), but there was no decrease in autism diagnoses afterward. See H. Honda, Y. Shi-
mizu, and M. Rutter, "No Effect of MMR Withdrawal on the Incidence of Autism: A
Total Population Study," *Journal of Child Psychology and Psychiatry* 46 (2005): 572–579.
One epidemiological study examined all children born in Denmark between 1991 and
1998 (over 500,000 children) and found no difference in the rates of autism for those who
had received the MMR vaccine and those who had not: K. M. Madsen, A. Hviid, M.
Vestergard, D. Schendel, J. Wohlfahrt, P. Thorsen, J. Olsen, and M. Melbye, "A Population-
Based Study of Measles, Mumps, and Rubella Vaccination and Autism," *New England
Journal of Medicine* 347 (2002): 1477–1482. Other epidemiological studies find the same
result, with no association between vaccination and autism or between the timing of
vaccinations and autism. For details, see L. Dales, S. J. Hammer, and N. J. Smith, "Time
Trends in Autism and in MMR Immunization Coverage in California," *Journal of
the American Medical Association* 285 (2001): 1183–1185; B. Taylor, E. Miller, C. P. Farrington, M.-C. Petropoulos, I. Favot-Mayaud, J. Li, and P. A. Waight, "Autism and Measles,
Mumps, and Rubella Vaccine: No Epidemiological Evidence for a Causal Association,"
Lancet 353 (1999): 2026–2029; C. P. Farrington, E. Miller, and B. Taylor, "MMR and
Autism: Further Evidence Against a Causal Association," *Vaccine* 19 (2001): 3632–3635;
and E. Fombonne, R. Zakarian, A. Bennett, L. Meng, and D. McLean-Heywood, "Pervasive Developmental Disorders in Montreal, Quebec, Canada: Prevalence and Links
with Immunizations," *Pediatrics* 118 (2006): e139–e150. Andrew Wakefield's claims of
an association between MMR and autism later became embroiled in controversy over
such issues as how the initial study was funded and how the patients were selected; see

Brian Deer, "Focus: MMR—The Truth Behind the Crisis," *The Sunday Times (London),* February 22, 2004. That year, most of the original paper's twelve coauthors, but not Wakefield, published a retraction of the suggestion that their findings could support a causal connection between MMR vaccination and autism. See S. H. Murch et. al., "Retraction of an Interpretation," *Lancet* 363 (2004), 750.

26. Heath and Heath, *Made to Stick.*

27. D. Ansen, "Pulp Friction," *Newsweek,* October 13, 2003.

28. V. S. Ramachandran and S. Blakeslee, *Phantoms in the Brain: Probing the Mysteries of the Human Mind* (New York: Harper Perennial, 1999), xiii.

29. Jenny McCarthy quotes are from an interview on CNN *Larry King Live,* September 26, 2007. Describing her initial research process, McCarthy said she "went online, researched, I typed in Google and then autism."

30. Paul Offit quotes are from National Public Radio *Morning Edition,* December 11, 2008.

31. Quotes in this paragraph are from an essay by Jenny McCarthy and Jim Carey: "Jenny McCarthy: My Son's Recovery from Autism," CNN.com, April 4, 2008 (www.cnn.com/2008/US/04/02/mccarthy.autismtreatment).

32. For a detailed history of purported cures for autism that have proven to be nothing but snake oil, see Offitt (*Autism's False Prophets*). For evidence on the genetic bases of autism, see R. Muhle, S. V. Trentacoste, and I. Rapin, "The Genetics of Autism," *Pediatrics* 113 (2004): e472–e486. For evidence on the differential brain development of children with autism, see E. DiCicco-Bloom, C. Lord, L. Zwaigenbaum, E. Courchesne, S. R. Dager, C. Schmitz, R. T. Schultz, J. Crawley, and L. J. Young, "The Developmental Neurobiology of Autism Spectrum Disorder," *Journal of Neuroscience* 26 (2006): 6897–6906. For a compilation of many studies examining the effectiveness of behavioral interventions, see J. M. Campbell, "Efficacy of Behavioral Interventions for Reducing Problem Behaviors in Autism: A Quantitative Synthesis of Single-Subject Research," *Research in Developmental Disabilities* 24 (2003): 120–138. See also the following report from the American Academy of Pediatrics: S. M. Myers, C. P. Johnson, and Council on Children with Disabilities, "Management of Children with Autism Spectrum Disorders," *Pediatrics* 120 (2007): 1162–1182. The possibility that McCarthy's son Evan was misdiagnosed and never actually had autism was suggested by Dr. Daniel Rubin in a letter to the editor of *Neurology Today,* a publication of the American Academy of Neurology: D. B. Rubin, "Fanning the Vaccine-Autism Link," *Neurology Today* 8 (2008): 3, www.neurotodayonline.com/pt/re/neurotoday/pdfhandler.00132985-200808070-00005.pdf (accessed June 20, 2009). Rubin argues that Evan might have had a seizure disorder known as Landau-Kleffner syndrome, which is often misdiagnosed as autism. The disorder is described on the website of the National Institute of Neurological Disorders and Stroke, www.ninds.nih.gov/disorders/landaukleffnersyndrome/landaukleffnersyndrome.htm (accessed June 20, 2009).

More generally, autism is a descriptive term for a set of symptoms that can have many different causes. The spectrum of children diagnosed with autism is broad, ranging from kids who are completely nonverbal and unable to interact with others to people who successfully integrate themselves into society and have highly productive careers and relationships. Moreover, the range of behaviors exhibited in autism varies widely, with some people with the diagnosis showing aggressive antisocial behavior and others exhibiting extreme shyness and passivity. Behavioral therapies can be effective in treating the symptoms of autism for many children, helping them learn to interpret and understand the social behaviors of others or eliminating undesirable behaviors. Yet, like cancer, autism is not a single thing. There can be no single cure for cancer because cancer is not a single disease, and there can be no single cure for autism because autism represents a constellation of neurological and behavioral atypicalities that can manifest themselves in a wide assortment of ways.

33. Evidence about secretin comes from the following sources: D. Armstrong, "Autism Drug Secretin Fails in Trial," *The Wall Street Journal,* January 6, 2004 (online.wsj.com/article/SB107331800361143000.html?); A. D. Sandler, K. A. Sutton, J. DeWeese, M. A. Girardi, V. Sheppard, and J. W. Bodfish, "Lack of Benefit of a Single Dose of Synthetic Human Secretin in the Treatment of Autism and Pervasive Developmental Disorder," *New England Journal of Medicine* 341 (1999): 1801–1806; and J. Coplan, M. C. Souders, A. E. Mulberg, J. K. Belchic, J. Wray, A. F. Jawad, P. R. Gallagher, R. Mitchell, M. Gerdes, and S. E. Levy, "Children with Autistic Spectrum Disorders. II: Parents Are Unable to Distinguish Secretin from Placebo Under Double-Blind Conditions," *Archives of Disease in Childhood* 88 (2003): 737–739. The subject is also discussed extensively by Paul Offit in *Autism's False Prophets.*

34. Recall our example of the perceived link between arthritis pain and the weather. In that case, even when people had all of the necessary numbers to properly calculate the correlation, they did not do so. Instead, they judged the strength of a relationship primarily from the number of cases where the putative cause and the putative effect were both present. In the weather/arthritis case, those were the times when the weather was cold and rainy and pain was higher. In the autism example, those were the cases in which kids were vaccinated and later developed autism. In both cases, people ignored all of the other critical numbers. This reasoning error was discovered nearly fifty years ago: J. Smedslund, "The Concept of Correlation in Adults," *Scandinavian Journal of Psychology* 4 (1963): 165–173.

35. A recent "cure" for autism, promoted by believers in the vaccine theory, involves large doses of the drug Lupron, which suppresses testosterone. Lupron is occasionally used to chemically castrate violent sex offenders. It might well lead to more docile behavior, but so would a frontal lobotomy. Unlike changing a child's diet, administering Lupron could have substantial negative side effects, such as delayed puberty and heart and bone problems, not to mention regular, painful injections. The prime promoters of the drug as an autism therapy have conducted no clinical trials and have no special training in the medical subfields related to autism, and no scientific studies have ever been conducted on the use of the drug in autism. For some details on this "therapy" and its promoters, see T. Tsouderos, "Miracle Drug Called Junk Science," *Chicago Tribune,* May 21, 2009 (www.chicagotribune.com/health/chi-autism-lupron-may21,0,242705.story).

36. Retrieved from Amazon.com on July 27, 2009.

37. From the representative national poll conducted by SurveyUSA on our behalf in June 2009 (see notes to Chapter 1 for details).

38. For a discussion of such differences, see D. C. Penn, K. J. Holyoak, and D. J. Povi-

nelli, "Darwin's Mistake: Explaining the Discontinuity Between Human and Nonhuman Minds," *Behavioral and Brain Sciences* 31 (2008): 109–178.

Chapter 6: Get Smart Quick!

1. R. Cimini, "Mangini Gets Players Tuned In," *New York Daily News,* July 31, 2007 (www.nydailynews.com/sports/football/jets/2007/07/31/2007-07-31_mangini_gets_players_tuned_in.html).

2. S. Yun, "Music a Sound Contribution to Healing: Good Samaritan Taking Cacophony Out of Hospital Care," *Rocky Mountain News,* May 31, 2005, www.mozarteffect.com/RandR/Doc_adds/RMNews.htm (accessed June 24, 2009).

3. Zell Miller gave his speech on June 22, 1998, and requested $105,000 of public funds, according to "Random Samples," *Science,* January 30, 1998 (www.scienceonline.org/cgi/content/summary/279/5351/663d).

4. "Slovak Hospital Plays Mozart to Babies to Ease Birth Trauma," Agence France-Presse, September 10, 2005, www.andante.com/article/article.cfm?id=25923 (accessed May 29, 2009).

5. F. H. Rauscher, G. L. Shaw, and K. N. Ky, "Music and Spatial Task Performance," *Nature* 365 (1993): 611.

6. Shaw described this idea as a "bold prediction" in the report on the Mozart effect done by the Fox Family Channel on their program "Exploring the Unknown" (broadcast in 1999).

7. G. L. Shaw, *Keeping Mozart in Mind*, 2nd ed. (San Diego, CA: Academic Press, 2004), 160. You may be reminded of our comments in Chapter 4 on "neurobabble" as you read these claims about a special relationship between Mozart's music and the workings of the brain.

8. Mozart biographer Alfred Einstein, quoted by Shaw (*Keeping Mozart in Mind,* 162).

9. R. A. Knox, "Mozart Makes You Smarter, Calif. Researchers Suggest," *The Boston Globe,* October 14, 1993.

10. According to a report on *NBC Nightly News*, August 1999.

11. No studies have ever tested infants, a fact noted by Rauscher herself in a quote here: "Random Samples," *Science,* January 30, 1998 (www.scienceonline.org/cgi/content/summary/279/5351/663d).

12. Followup studies by Rauscher and her colleagues included the following (among others): F. H. Rauscher, G. L. Shaw, and K. N. Ky, "Listening to Mozart Enhances Spatial-Temporal Reasoning: Towards a Neurophysiological Basis," *Neuroscience Letters* 185 (1995): 44–47; and F. H. Rauscher, K. D. Robinson, and J. J. Jens, "Improved Maze Learning Through Early Music Exposure in Rats," *Neurological Research* 20 (1998): 427–432.

13. C. Stough, B. Kerkin, T. Bates, and G. Mangan, "Music and Spatial IQ," *Personality and Individual Differences* 17 (1994): 695.

14. All studies of the Mozart effect conducted up to the summer of 1999 are summarized in C. F. Chabris, "Prelude or Requiem for the 'Mozart Effect'?" *Nature* 400 (1999): 826–827.

15. K. M. Steele, K. E. Bass, and M. D. Crook, "The Mystery of the Mozart Effect: Failure to Replicate," *Psychological Science* 10 (1999): 366–369.

16. According to a personal communication between Chris and Kenneth Steele, June 13, 2009.

17. K. M. Steele, "The 'Mozart Effect': An Example of the Scientific Method in Operation," *Psychology Teacher Network,* November–December 2001, pp. 2–3, 5.

18. Mentioned in Kevin Kwong's review of upcoming music and theater events in the *South China Morning Post* entitled "Just the Ticket," August 25, 2000.

19. A. Bangerter and C. Heath, "The Mozart Effect: Tracking the Evolution of a Scientific Legend," *British Journal of Social Psychology* 43 (2004): 605–623. This paper argues that coverage of the Mozart effect supports the theory that rumors and legends spread because they "address the needs or concerns of social groups." We agree, and we argue further that the particular need involved here is the need to believe that all of us have untapped mental potential that can easily be released. Adrian Bangerter published an expanded version in French as *La diffusion des croyances populaires: Le cas de l'effet Mozart* (Grenoble: Presses Universitaires de Grenoble, 2008).

20. The most famous exposition of this argument appears in S. J. Gould, *The Mismeasure of Man* (New York: Norton, 1981).

21. Sir Francis Galton performed this experiment at a country fair in England and reported it in this article: F. Galton, "Vox Populi," *Nature* 75 (1907): 450–451. For more on this topic, see J. Surowiecki, *The Wisdom of Crowds* (New York: Doubleday, 2004); and C. Sunstein, *Infotopia: How Many Minds Produce Knowledge* (New York: Oxford University Press, 2006).

22. E. G. Schellenberg and S. Hallam, "Music Listening and Cognitive Abilities in 10 and 11 Year Olds: The Blur Effect," *Annals of the New York Academy of Sciences* 1060 (2005): 202–209.

23. K. M. Nantais and E. G. Schellenberg, "The Mozart Effect: An Artifact of Preference," *Psychological Science* 10 (1999): 370–373.

24. In addition to the "Blur Effect" study mentioned earlier, two other published studies have failed to find a Mozart effect in school-age children: P. McKelvie and J. Low, "Listening to Mozart Does Not Improve Children's Spatial Ability: Final Curtains for the Mozart Effect," *British Journal of Developmental Psychology* 20 (2002): 241–258; and R. Crncec, S. J. Wilson, and M. Prior, "No Evidence for the Mozart Effect in Children," *Music Perception* 23 (2006): 305–317. The mistaken impression that the Mozart effect works best with fetuses, which led some parents to play classical music to their unborn children by wrapping headphones around the mothers' bellies, might have arisen from publicity given to another finding by Rauscher, published in another obscure journal. She reported exposing rats to the magical Mozart sonata for 60 days in utero, plus several days after they were born, and comparing these animals with a control group for maze-running ability. The Mozart-exposed rats did better (Rauscher, Robinson, and Jens, "Improved Maze Learning"). Rauscher's bête noire, Kenneth Steele, later pointed out that limitations on the auditory perception abilities of rats *prevent them from hearing* many of the notes in the sonata. See K. M. Steele, "Do Rats Show a Mozart Effect?" *Music Perception* 21 (2003): 251–265. However, Rauscher continued to trumpet her rat studies, claiming that gene expression was different in the brains of Mozart-exposed rats compared with control

rats. See F. H. Rauscher, "The Mozart Effect in Rats: Response to Steele," *Music Perception* 23 (2006): 447–453. This is not surprising, of course: The brain processes music—it doesn't go in one ear and out the other—so one would expect to find *some* difference between brains exposed to even just a few notes of music and brains exposed to something else. Finding such a difference, whether in gene expression, blood flow, electrical activity, or whatever, is irrelevant to the debate over the Mozart effect unless the difference is linked to a change in performance that is specific to Mozart's music, and not just a consequence of changes in mood or arousal that could result from many different kinds of stimulation.

25. B. Mook, "In a 'Tot'-anic Size '01 Deal, Disney Buys Baby Einstein," *Denver Business Journal,* March 1, 2002 (www.bizjournals.com/denver/stories/2002/03/04/focus9. html).

26. V. C. Strasburger, "First Do No Harm: Why Have Parents and Pediatricians Missed the Boat on Children and the Media?" *Journal of Pediatrics* 151 (2007): 334–336.

27. F. J. Zimmerman, D. A. Christakis, and A. N. Meltzoff, "Associations Between Media Viewing and Language Development in Children Under Age 2 years," *Journal of Pediatrics* 151 (2007): 364–368. The CDI gives a percentile score for a child based on how many of the ninety words he or she knows and says; the estimate of 8 percent reduction per hour of viewing is based on a drop of seventeen percentile points. That is, consider Jane and Tanya, two children from similar families and with similar experiences, differing only in that Jane never watches baby DVDs but Tanya watches them for an hour per day. If Jane has an average vocabulary for her age (i.e., she is at the 50th percentile), then Tanya would be expected to be at the 33rd percentile, and to use 8 percent fewer words than Jane. Smaller-scale studies have found similar negative effects for some educational TV programming; e.g., see D. L. Linebarger and D. Walker, "Infants' and Toddlers' Television Viewing and Language Outcomes," *American Behavioral Scientist* 48 (2005): 624–645.

28. R. Monastersky, "Disney Throws Tantrum Over University Study Debunking Baby DVDs and Videos," *Chronicle of Higher Education* News Blog, August 14, 2007 (chronicle.com/news/article/2854/disney-throws-tantrum-over-university-study-debunking-baby-dvds-and-videos).

29. Disney spokesman Gary Foster was quoted in H. Pankratz, "Retraction Demanded on 'Baby Einstein,'" *The Denver Post,* August 14, 2007 (www.denverpost.com/news/ci_6617051). In September 2009, Disney announced that it would offer refunds to purchasers of Baby Einstein DVDs during the previous five years. See T. Lewin, "No Einstein in Your Crib? Get a Refund," *The New York Times,* October 23, 2009, p. A1.

30. Information about Eric Mangini's coaching career from Wikipedia, en.wikipedia. org/wiki/Eric_Mangini (accessed June 16, 2009). Of course, it would be wrong to conclude that adding Mozart caused his team's decline—beware the illusion of cause! Most likely it had no effect whatsoever.

31. For a discussion of the effects of hypnosis on memory accuracy (and confidence), see J. F. Kihlstrom, "Hypnosis, Memory and Amnesia," *Philosophical Transactions of the Royal Society of London B* 352 (1997): 1727–1732.

32. Even though people aren't well-informed about the reality of hypnosis and memory, the legal system does look askance at witnesses whose memory has been hypnotically

enhanced, or who request hypnosis to help them remember. Recall Kenny Conley, the Boston cop who was convicted of perjury and obstruction of justice for his testimony that he never saw Michael Cox at the fence. A witness's request to be hypnotized to improve his memory was at the core of the technicality that got his conviction reversed—the request undermined the witness's credibility, and the prosecution failed to disclose it to the defense.

33. After an exhaustive search, Barry Beyerstein of Simon Fraser University wrote, "I confess that I have been frustrated in my attempts to unearth the ultimate source of the 10% myth . . . there is little doubt that the primary disseminators (not to mention beneficiaries) of the 10% myth have been the touts and boosters in the ranks of the self-improvement industry, past and present." See B. L. Beyerstein, "Whence Cometh the Myth That We Only Use 10% of Our Brains?" in *Mind Myths: Exploring Popular Assumptions About the Mind and Brain*, ed. S. Della Salla, 3–24 (Chichester, UK: Wiley, 1999).

34. E. B. Titchener, "The 'Feeling of Being Stared At,'" *Science* 8 (1898): 895–897.

35. See J. E. Coover, "The Feeling of Being Stared At," *The American Journal of Psychology* 24 (1913): 570–575. Our survey result replicates laboratory studies conducted by Jane Cottrell and Gerald Winer showing that college students as well as children believe that they can feel the stares of unseen others. See J. E. Cottrell, G. A. Winer, and M. C. Smith, "Beliefs of Children and Adults About Feeling Stares of Unseen Others," *Developmental Psychology* 32 (1996): 50–61.

36. Some promoters of paranormal phenomena still argue in favor of the idea that people can perceive the stares of others, typically attributing the effect to mysterious effects in quantum mechanics. The methods are often suspect, and none of the studies have been published in mainstream scientific journals. As was the case for the Mozart effect, proponents of the idea that people can feel the stares of others often appeal to other studies replicating the effect, but those other results are not published in mainstream journals. For a discussion by a proponent of these effects, see D. Radin, *Entangled Minds* (New York: Paraview Press, 2006), 125–130. For critiques of their evidence, see M. Shermer, "Rupert's Resonance," *Scientific American*, November 2005 (www.scientificamerican. com/article.cfm?id=ruperts-resonance); D. F. Marks and J. Colwell, "The Psychic Staring Effect: An Artifact of Pseudo Randomization," *Skeptical Inquirer*, September/October 2000 (www.csicop.org/si/show/psychic_staring_effect_an_artifact_of_pseudo_randomization/). Note that we are not saying that what is published in reputable scientific journals is always correct, or that what gets shut out of those journals must be false. There are fads, fashions, and judgment calls in science, and our own papers are not always published in the most prestigious venues (even if they should be!). But for any given phenomenon, if no mainstream scientific journals will publish it, there's an excellent chance it is not based on solid, replicable scientific evidence.

37. W. B. Key, *Subliminal Seduction* (New York: Prentice Hall, 1973). The Vicary experiment is described on pages 22–23, and the "man" experiment is described on pages 29–30.

38. On page 30 of Key's book, the raw data from this experiment are presented in table form. We used his data to calculate that the size of the difference between the control and the subliminal message conditions was large: approximately one standard deviation. The probability that this difference could have arisen just due to chance was an

astonishingly small .0000000001—in other words, it likely was too good to be true. The scientific evidence for subliminal perception, to the extent that it meets rigorous standards and can be reproduced reliably, typically shows small effects, mostly in the speed with which people can respond. And the effects tend to be short-lived. There is still debate in the scientific literature on whether this sort of perception in the absence of awareness even exists at all. For a discussion of some of the challenges involved in demonstrating subliminal perception, see D. Hannula, D. J. Simons, and N. Cohen, "Imaging Implicit Perception: Promise and Pitfalls," *Nature Reviews Neuroscience* 6 (2005): 247–255.

39. The best account of the truth behind Vicary's "experiment" is found in this article: A. R. Pratkanis, "Myths of Subliminal Persuasion: The Cargo-Cult Science of Subliminal Persuasion," *Skeptical Inquirer* 16 (1992): 260–72.

40. See Hannula et al., "Imaging Implicit Perception." The debate is over what it means to say that something was not consciously perceived, and the methods used to assess precisely how much people are aware of. Most scientists, even those who are proponents of the idea that subliminal perception is a robust phenomenon, agree that any effects of the meaning of an unseen stimulus on cognition will tend to be fairly small, and most doubt that subliminal stimuli can persuade us to do something we wouldn't otherwise do.

41. A recent article has made an even stronger claim than the original one made by Vicary. This study showed that subliminally flashing the Israeli flag led Israeli subjects to substantially change their strongly held views on Palestinian statehood and settlements in Gaza. Both those who strongly opposed statehood and those who favored it moderated their views, becoming indistinguishable from each other. Even more amazing, the subliminal flags changed whom the subjects voted for, again in the direction of moderation, this time weeks after the study! To us, this study illustrates how readily people will accept what are fantastical claims when they involve the release of untapped potential to change our minds. The mechanism proposed in the paper, that seeing a flag would implicitly lead to more centrist views, fits only one explanation, generated after seeing the results. It seems more plausible to us that seeing a flag, if it has any effect at all, should make people's views more extreme. Most people believe themselves to be patriotic, and seeing a flag should only strengthen their existing views; it should not cause them to become more centrist. Although the result might be legitimate and replicable, given the ease with which we can succumb to the illusion of untapped potential, we think skepticism is warranted in the face of such a startling finding. It is hard to imagine such a minimal experience changing someone's sincere views so radically, especially considering that they are exposed to so many more direct attempts at persuasion. The original study is R. R. Hassin, M. J. Ferguson, D. Shidlovski, and T. Gross, "Subliminal Exposure to National Flags Affects Political Thought and Behavior," *Proceedings of the National Academy of Sciences* 104 (2007): 19757–19761.

42. A. G. Greenwald, E. R. Spangenberg, A. R. Pratkanis, and J. Eskenazi, "Double-Blind Tests of Subliminal Self-Help Audiotapes," *Psychological Science* 2 (1991): 119–122. According to this rigorous study by four research psychologists, these recordings do appear to induce nonspecific placebo effects, because their listeners use them desiring and expecting to improve their mental function. They also leave some of their users with an illusion of having received the specific benefits sought, even when they haven't.

43. B. Mullen et al., "Newscasters' Facial Expressions and Voting Behavior: Can a Smile Elect a President?" *Journal of Personality and Social Psychology* 51 (1986): 291–295.

44. See M. Gladwell, *The Tipping Point* (New York: Little, Brown, 2000), 74–80. It's also worth mentioning that the evidence in the original study supporting the existence of an association between television news viewing and voting was fairly minimal. The percentages were based on data from fewer than forty people per town, and in some cases, only a handful of people watched ABC. If only five people watched ABC, then a shift of 20 percent represents just one viewer. In a reanalysis of the data from the original study using a standard statistical test known as a chi-square, we found that none of the differences in voting patterns were statistically significant. In other words, there might not even have been a reliable association between viewing preferences and voting patterns, making the causal claim that Peter Jennings influenced voting just by smiling even less likely. In the modern era of polling, sample sizes to make claims like those in the paper would need to be at least an order of magnitude larger.

45. Transcribed from a Flash version of the advertisement on Nintendo's *Brain Age* website, www.brainage.com/launch/ontv.jsp?video=tvspot (accessed June 12, 2009).

46. From Nintendo's consolidated financial statements dated May 7, 2009, www.nintendo.com/corp/report/3QEnglishFinancial.pdf (accessed June 12, 2009).

47. www.focusmm.co.uk/shop/Brain-Trainer-pr-1190.html (accessed June 15, 2009). Immediately after this claim, the website includes a footnote disclaimer that states, "Focus Multimedia and Mindscape are not qualified to offer medical advice. These exercises have been designed for recreational purposes only. No medical claims are made for these exercises, express or implied." Essentially, the site disclaims what it just claimed. This tactic is not at all unusual for materials promoting brain-training software. British consumer organization Which? recently reviewed a number of brain-training programs and evaluated their claims, www.which.co.uk/advice/brain-training/index.jsp (accessed June 15, 2009).

48. As one example, the Real Age website claims that it is possible to quantify someone's brain age and that with the right activities, you can turn back the clock by a measurable number of years, www.realage.com/ralong/entry4.aspx?cbr=GGLE806&gclid=CNGY5MG1qJsCFQJvswodCF-YDA (accessed June 26, 2009). Neither claim is even testable.

49. For example, see T. A. Salthouse, "The Processing-Speed Theory of Adult Age Differences in Cognition," *Psychological Review* 103 (1996): 403–428.

50. Statistics are from the official International Chess Federation (FIDE) records, ratings.fide.com/top.phtml?list=men (accessed June 17, 2009).

51. For a recent review of cognitive-training interventions and other correlational studies, see C. Hertzog, A. F. Kramer, R. S. Wilson, and U. Lindenberger, "Enrichment Effects on Adult Cognitive Development: Can the Functional Capacity of Older Adults Be Preserved and Enhanced?" *Psychological Science in the Public Interest* 9 (2009): 1–65.

52. The results of this study and later follow-up analyses and longitudinal studies are reported in the following articles: K. Ball et al., "Effects of Cognitive Training Interventions with Older Adults: A Randomized Controlled Trial," *JAMA* 288 (2002): 2271–2281; S. L. Willis et al., "Long-Term Effects of Cognitive Training on Everyday Functional Outcomes in Older Adults," *JAMA* 296 (2006): 2805–2814; and F. D. Wolinsky, F. W. Unverzagt, D. M. Smith, R. Jones, A. Stoddard, and S. L. Tennstedt, "The ACTIVE Cognitive Training Trial and Health-Related Quality of Life: Protection That Lasts for 5 Years," *Journal of Gerontology* 61A (2006): 1324–1329.

53. One exception to this limited transfer comes from a specific training technique known as variable priority training. In essence, variable priority training focuses less on enhancing the individual components of a task than on improving your ability to allocate resources to each of them efficiently—it trains your ability to multitask. Although transfer is still limited, in most cases, to other laboratory tasks, the trained abilities are more general than the specific task learned. For a discussion of this and other training methods, see Hertzog et al., "Enrichment Effects on Adult Cognitive Development." See also A. F. Kramer, J. Larish, T. Weber, and L. Bardell, "Training for Executive Control: Task Coordination Strategies and Aging," in *Attention and Performance XVII*, ed. D. Gopher and A. Koriet, 617–652 (Cambridge, MA: MIT Press, 1999).

54. T. A. Salthouse, "Mental Exercise and Mental Aging: Evaluating the Validity of the 'Use It or Lose It' Hypothesis," *Perspectives on Psychological Science* 1 (2006): 68–87.

55. The student trained for more than two hundred hours over the course of twenty months. His initial digit span was the more typical seven items. See K. A. Ericsson, W. G. Chase, and S. Faloon, "Acquisition of a Memory Skill," *Science* 208 (1980): 1181–1182.

56. A. D. de Groot, *Thought and Choice in Chess* (The Hague: Mouton, 1965); W. G. Chase and H. A. Simon, "Perception in Chess," *Cognitive Psychology* 4 (1973): 55–81; W. G. Chase and H. A. Simon, "The Mind's Eye in Chess," in *Visual Information Processing*, ed. W. G. Chase, 215–281 (New York: Academic Press, 1973). Herbert Simon was a political scientist by training, but he became known as one of the most influential computer scientists and cognitive psychologists.

57. Ericsson et al., "Acquisition of a Memory Skill."

58. C. F. Chabris and E. S. Hearst, "Visualization, Pattern Recognition, and Forward Search: Effects of Playing Speed and Sight of the Position on Grandmaster Chess Errors," *Cognitive Science* 27 (2003): 637–648. Eliot Hearst has written, with John Knott, the definitive book on all aspects of blindfold chess: *Blindfold Chess: History, Psychology, Techniques, Champions, World Records, and Important Games* (Jefferson, NC: McFarland, 2009).

59. There are some correlational studies showing that children who play chess do better academically than children who do not, but they do not demonstrate that learning chess causes you to improve in other areas. (Perhaps smarter kids are more likely to be interested in chess.) For example, see K. van Delft, "Chess as a Subject in Elementary School," unpublished report, University of Amsterdam, 1992. No experimental studies on this question have been published in quality journals; the best of these may be "Chess and Cognitive Development," an unpublished 1976 doctoral dissertation by Johan Christiaen of Rijksuniversiteit Gent, Belgium. Christiaen randomly assigned twenty fifth-graders to chess instruction and twenty to a control group and found that the chess group did better on some tests of cognitive development.

60. C. S. Green and D. Bavelier, "Action Video Game Modifies Visual Selective Attention," *Nature* 423 (2003): 534–537. The name "Useful Field of View" is a trademark of Visual Awareness Research Group, Inc.

61. From an interview Dan conducted with Walter Boot on May 14, 2009.

62. See R. Li, U. Polat, W. Makous, and D. Bavelier, "Enhancing the Contrast Sensitivity Function Through Action Video Game Training," *Nature Neuroscience* 12 (2009): 549–551. As in the original study, the control group in this experiment (this time, practicing

a Sims game) showed no improvements the second time it was tested. In this case, that's not terribly surprising, because the task measures a basic aspect of visual processing. It is impressive that the contrast sensitivity advantages persisted even months after training. Where the original studies focused on higher-level cognitive benefits, some of which might be attributable to learned strategies rather than changes in basic abilities, these newer studies focus on basic properties of the visual system. It's harder to see how strategies could influence these measures.

63. See C. S. Green and D. Bavelier, "Action-Video-Game Experience Alters the Spatial Resolution of Attention," *Psychological Science* 18 (2007): 88–94. Again, the control group showed no improvements at all upon retesting.

64. A potential danger any time a study is conducted using a large battery of cognitive tasks is that some performance differences are likely to prove statistically significant by chance. These additional studies report only one or two outcome measures tested before and after thirty or more hours of training. It's not clear whether other measures were tried but showed no differences, so additional replications are needed.

65. J. Feng, I. Spence, and J. Pratt, "Playing an Action Video Game Reduces Gender Differences in Spatial Cognition," *Psychological Science* 18 (2007): 850–855. The sex differences were based on just seven women and three men in each training group, so it will be important to replicate this finding with a larger sample.

66. C. Basak, W. R. Boot, M. W. Voss, and A. F. Kramer, "Can Training in a Real-Time Strategy Video Game Attenuate Cognitive Decline in Older Adults?" *Psychology and Aging* 23 (2008): 765–777.

67. Interestingly, in Boot's study with college students as subjects, training on Rise of Nations did not lead to differential improvements.

68. W. R. Boot, A. F. Kramer, D. J. Simons, M. Fabiani, and G. Gratton, "The Effects of Video Game Playing on Attention, Memory, and Executive Control," *Acta Psychologica* 129 (2008): 387–398.

69. Boot's study showed a comparable amount of improvement to that shown by Green and Bavelier for two of the transfer tasks (the attentional blink and the functional field of view), but Boot's found no significant improvement for any of the groups in the enumeration task, whereas Green and Bavelier showed improvements just for the video-game training group.

70. At least one other recent study has failed to replicate part of the original result as well, although not the training component. The following paper did not find differences between expert and novice video-game players: K. Murphy and A. Spencer, "Playing Video Games Does Not Make for Better Visual Attention Skills," *Journal of Articles in Support of the Null Hypothesis* 6, no. 1 (2009).

71. Quotes are from an interview Dan conducted with Walter Boot on May 11, 2009.

72. The same caveat applies to studies about a topic related to the Mozart effect: the idea that musicians have better cognitive skills (such as better verbal memory) than nonmusicians. This difference is often attributed to their music training, but it could be a so-called "Hawthorne effect"—the simple consequence of knowing you are being singled out and expected to have better performance. Or it could result from some difference between the musicians and nonmusicians that was present before the music training started.

73. For an engrossing presentation of this claim, see Steven Johnson's *Everything Bad*

Is Good for You (New York: Riverhead, 2005). Johnson's book argues convincingly that current television programs and video games are much more complex, and require greater levels of mental effort to process, than the most popular shows and games of the 1970s and 1980s. But it offers no decisive evidence for its provocative thesis that the greater complexity of TV and games is *causing* an increase in intelligence or social ability. For support, Johnson does cite the Flynn effect, a large worldwide increase in measured general cognitive ability during the twentieth century, but this upward trend began long before video games were even invented, and in any case—we are sorry for sounding like a broken record on this point—a correlation or chronological connection does not prove causation. Many other things about society and daily life have changed in the last several decades besides the invention of HBO dramas, reality TV, and massively multiplayer online video games. Johnson grapples with these issues but cannot wrestle them down—because no one can.

74. From the Nintendo Brain Age website, www.brainage.com/launch/training.jsp (accessed June 12, 2009).

75. See Hertzog et al., "Enrichment Effects on Adult Cognitive Development."

76. A. F. Kramer et al., "Ageing, Fitness and Neurocognitive Function," *Nature* 400 (1999): 418–419.

77. S. Colcombe and A. F. Kramer, "Fitness Effects on the Cognitive Function of Older Adults: A Meta-Analytic Study," *Psychological Science* 14 (2003): 125–130. See also A. F. Kramer and K. I. Erickson, "Capitalizing on Cortical Plasticity: Influence of Physical Activity on Cognition and Brain Function," *Trends in Cognitive Sciences* 11 (2007): 342–348.

78. S. J. Colcombe, K. I. Erickson, P. E. Scalf, J. S. Kim, R. Prakash, E. McAuley, S. Elavsky, D. X. Marquez, L. Hu, and A. F. Kramer, "Aerobic Exercise Training Increases Brain Volume in Aging Humans," *Journal of Gerontology: Medical Sciences* 61 (2006): 1166–1170.

Conclusion: The Myth of Intuition

1. Actual leadership profiles like this one are dissected by Phil Rosenzweig in his excellent book *The Halo Effect . . . and the Eight Other Business Delusions That Deceive Managers* (New York: Free Press, 2007); see especially pp. 18–49. Although we have picked on business journalists in this example, we are not intentionally singling them out as subject to these illusions. To be crystal clear: Everyone is subject to everyday illusions, including ourselves.

2. For more on the role of fluency and mistaken attributions about our own thoughts, see D. M. Oppenheimer, "The Secret Life of Fluency," *Trends in Cognitive Sciences* 12 (2008): 237–241; N. Schwartz, "Metacognitive Experiences in Consumer Judgment and Decision Making," *Journal of Consumer Psychology* 14 (2004): 332–348; and D. Kahneman and S. Frederick, "Representativeness Revisited: Attribute Substitution in Intuitive Judgment," in *Heuristics and Biases,* ed. T. Gilovich, D. Griffin, and D. Kahneman, 49–81 (Cambridge: Cambridge University Press, 2002).

3. The fast, automatic processes are often known as "System 1" and the slow, reflective processes as "System 2," a useful distinction first introduced by Steven A. Sloman, given these names by Keith E. Stanovich and Richard F. West, and advocated in an influential

paper by Daniel Kahneman and Shane Frederick. All of these papers are reprinted in Gilovich, Griffin, and Kahneman, *Heuristics and Biases*. For discussion of why the mind is designed this way, the following books all offer interesting perspectives: S. Pinker, *How the Mind Works* (New York: Norton, 1997); G. Marcus, *Kluge: The Haphazard Construction of the Human Mind* (New York: Houghton Mifflin, 2008); G. Gigerenzer, *Gut Feelings: The Intelligence of the Unconscious* (New York: Viking, 2007); and M. Piattelli-Palmarini, *Inevitable Illusions: How Mistakes of Reason Rule Our Minds* (New York: Wiley, 1994).

4. C. Kennedy, "ABB: Model Merger for the New Europe," *Long Range Planning* 23, no. 5 (1992): 10–17 (as cited by Rosenzweig, *The Halo Effect*). We are commenting on how Barnevik's management style was portrayed in the press, not on Barnevik himself.

5. Information on the Iridium project comes from Chapter 6 of P. B. Carroll and C. Mui, *Billion Dollar Lessons: What You Can Learn from the Most Inexcusable Business Failures of the Last 25 Years* (New York: Portfolio, 2008).

6. Harry Buxton-Forman, who had vouched for Wise's discovery, had expertise in the printing process and appeared to have collaborated on the scam with Wise.

7. Information on the Thomas J. Wise fraud comes from these sources: M. Jones, P. Craddock, and N. Barker, *Fake? The Art of Deception* (Berkeley: University of California Press, 1990); J. Carter and G. Pollard, *An Enquiry into the Nature of Certain XIXth Century Pamphlets* (London: Constable, 1934); and W. B. Todd, *Thomas J. Wise: Centenary Studies* (Austin: University of Texas Press, 1959).

8. M. Gladwell, *Blink: The Power of Thinking Without Thinking* (New York: Little, Brown, 2005), 3–8. Gladwell doesn't actually use the words *intuition* or *intuitive* much in *Blink*, but that is more a matter of word choice than of intended meaning. He argues that "there can be as much value in the blink of an eye as in months of rational analysis" (p. 17). Gladwell presents numerous examples of high-quality "snap" decisions made in the blink of an eye, without the benefit of deliberation—that is, decisions made intuitively.

9. Many readers of *Blink* take Gladwell's point about the power of rapid cognition to heart without fully appreciating the way he qualifies his claims. Gladwell notes that it is important to understand when intuitions will and will not be useful, and he provides examples in which intuitions fail: Warren Harding looked presidential, but turned out to be a bad president; musicians are selected more fairly when they are heard performing behind a screen than when the judges can see them play; New York City police officers rapidly fired forty-one bullets at Amadou Diallo on a cold Bronx night in 1999. *Blink* does give more weight to the successes of intuition than to its failures, often attributing the failures to other situational factors such as excessive stress or pressure. But it seems just as reasonable to think that rapid cognition should be most effective precisely when careful deliberation is impossible (due to stress or time pressure).

10. T. D. Wilson and J. W. Schooler, "Thinking Too Much: Introspection Can Reduce the Quality of Preferences and Decisions," *Journal of Personality and Social Psychology* 60 (1991): 181–192.

11. J. W. Schooler and T. Y. Engstler-Schooler, "Verbal Overshadowing of Visual Memories: Some Things Are Better Left Unsaid," *Cognitive Psychology* 22 (1990): 36–71. This article points out some earlier literature on the effect, going back to E. Belbin, "The Influence of Interpolated Recall Upon Recognition," *Quarterly Journal of Experimental Psychology* 2 (1950): 163–169.

12. In *Blink,* Malcolm Gladwell described a similar experiment and explained the verbal overshadowing effect this way: "Your brain has a part (the left hemisphere) that thinks in words, and a part (the right hemisphere) that thinks in pictures, and what happened as you described the face in words was that . . . your thinking was bumped from the right to the left hemisphere" (pp. 119–120). As we pointed out in Chapter 6, the idea that the two halves of our brain have radically distinct, nonoverlapping capabilities and modes of thought (words versus pictures) is part and parcel of the false belief that the pictorial and holistic right hemisphere is routinely suppressed by the verbal and analytical left, and that we can think much better by releasing its hidden potential.

13. Chabris and Hearst, "Visualization, Pattern Recognition, and Forward Search."

14. From Woody Allen's 1960s stand-up comedy, recorded on the album *Standup Comic,* released by Casablanca Records in 1979. The quote is from the final track, "Summing Up."